Spatial Econometrics Using Microdata

To the memory of Gilles Dubé.

For Mélanie, Karine, Philippe, Vincent and Mathieu.

Series Editor
Anne Ruas

Spatial Econometrics Using Microdata

Jean Dubé
Diègo Legros

WILEY

First published 2014 in Great Britain and the United States by ISTE Ltd and John Wiley & Sons, Inc.

ISTE Ltd
27-37 St George's Road
London SW19 4EU
UK

www.iste.co.uk

John Wiley & Sons, Inc.
111 River Street
Hoboken, NJ 07030
USA

www.wiley.com

Library of Congress Control Number: 2014945534

British Library Cataloguing-in-Publication Data
A CIP record for this book is available from the British Library
ISBN 978-1-84821-468-2

Contents

Acknowledgements

While producing a reference book does require a certain amount of time, it is also impossible without the support of partners. Without the help of the publisher, ISTE, it would have been impossible for us to share, on such a great scale, the fruit of our work and thoughts on spatial microdata.

Moreover, without the financial help of the Fonds de Recherche Québecois sur la Société et la Culture (FRQSC) and the Social Sciences and Humanities Research Council (SSHRC), the writing of this work would certainly not have been possible. Therefore, we thank these two financial partners.

The content of this work is largely the result of our thoughts and reflections on the processes that generate individual spatial data[1] and the application of the various tests and models from the data available.

We thank the individuals who helped, whether closely or from afar, in the writing of this work by providing comments on some or all of the chapters: Nicolas Devaux (student in regional development), Cédric Brunelle (Professor at Memorial University), Sotirios Thanos (Reseracher Associate at University College London) and

---

1 Our first works largely focus on the data of real estate transactions: a data collection process that is neither strictly spatial, nor strictly temporal (see Chapter 5).

Philippe Trempe (masters student in regional development). Without the invaluable help of these people, the writing of this book would certainly have taken much longer and would have been far more difficult. Their comments helped us orientate the book towards an approach that would be more understandable by an audience that did not necessarily have a lot of experience in statistics.

Preface

P.1. Introduction

Before even bringing up the main subject, it would seem important to define the breadth that we wish to give this book. The title itself is quite evocative: it is an introduction to spatial econometrics when data consist of individual spatial units. The stress is on microdata: observations that are points on a geographical projection rather than geometrical forms that describe the limits (whatever they may be) of a geographical zone. Therefore, we propose to cover the methods of detection and descriptive spatial analysis, and spatial and spatio-temporal modeling.

In no case do we wish this work to substitute important references in the domain such as Anselin [ANS 88], Anselin and Florax [ANS 95], LeSage [LES 99], or even the more recent reference in this domain: LeSage and Pace [LES 09]. We consider these references to be essential for anyone wishing to become invested in this domain.

The objective of the book is to make a link between existing quantitative approaches (correlation analysis, bivaried analysis and linear regression) and the manner in which we can generalize these approaches to cases where the available data for analysis have a spatial dimension. While equations are presented, our approach is largely based on the description of the intuition behind each of the equations. The mathematical language is vital in statistical and quantitative analyses. However, for many people, the acquisition of the knowledge necessary for a proper reading and understanding of the equations is often off-putting. For this reason, we try to establish the links between the intuition of the equations and the mathematical formalizations properly. In our opinion, too few introductory works place importance on this structure, which is nevertheless the cornerstone of quantitative analysis. After all, the goal of the quantitative approach is to provide a set of powerful tools that allow us to isolate some of the effects that we are looking to identify. However, the amplitude of these effects depends on the type of tool used to measure them.

The originality of the approach is, in our opinion, fourfold. First, the book presents simple fictional examples. These examples allow the readers to follow, for small samples, the detail of the calculations, for each of the steps of the construction of weighting matrices and descriptive statistics. The reader is also able to replicate the calculations in simple programs such as Excel, to make sure he/she understands all of the steps properly. In our opinion, this step allows non-specialist readers to integrate the particularities of the equations, the calculations and the spatial data.

Second, this book aims to make the link between summation writing (see double summation) of statistics (or models) and matrix writing. Many people will have difficulties matching the transition from one to the other. In this work, we present for some spatial indices the two writings, stressing the transition from one writing to the other. The understanding of matrix writing is important since it is more compact than summation writing and makes the mathematical expressions containing double summation, such as detection indices of spatial correlation patterns, easier to read; this is particularly useful in the construction of statistics used for spatial detection of local patterns. The use of matrix calculations and simple examples allow the reader to generalize the calculations to greater datasets, helping their understanding of spatial econometrics. The matrix form also makes the calculations directly transposable into specialized software (such as MatLab and Mata (Stata)) allowing us to carry out calculations without having to use previously written programs, at least for the construction of the spatial weighting matrices and for the calculation of spatial concentration indices. The presentation of matrix calculations step by step allows us to properly compute the calculation steps.

Third, in the appendix this work suggests programs that allow the simulation of spatial and spatio-temporal microdata. The programs then allow the transposing of the presentations of the chapters onto cases where the reality is known in advance. This approach, close to the Monte Carlo experiment, can be beneficial for some readers who would want to examine the behavior of test statistics as well as the behavior of estimators in some well-defined contexts. The advantages of this approach by simulation are numerous:

– it allows the intuitive establishment of the properties of statistical tools rather than a formal mathematical proof;

– it provides a better understanding of the data generating processes (DGP) and establishes links with the application of statistical models;

– it offers the possibility of testing the impact of omitting one dimension in particular (spatial or temporal) on the estimations and the results;

– it gives the reader the occasion to put into practice his/her own experiences, with some minor modifications.

Finally, the greatest particularity of this book is certainly the stress placed on the use of spatial microdata. Most of the works and applications in spatial econometrics rely on aggregate spatial data. This representation thus assumes that each observation takes the form of a polygon (a geometric shape) representing fixed limits of the geographical boundaries surrounding, for example, a country, a region, a town or a neighborhood. The data then represent an aggregate statistic of individual observations (average, median, proportion) rather than the detail of each of the individual observations. In our opinion, the applications relying on microdata are the future for not only putting into practice of spatial econometric methods, but also for a better understanding of several phenomena. Spatial microdata allow us to avoid the classical problem of the ecological error [2] [ROB 50] as well as directly replying to several critics saying that spatial aggregate data does not allow capturing some details that are only observable at a microscale. Moreover, while not exempt from the modifiable area unit problem (MAUP)[3] [ARB 01, OPE 79], they do at least present the advantage of explicitly allowing for the possibility of testing the effect of spatial aggregation on the results of the analyses.

Thus, this book acts as an intermediatiory for non-econometricians and non-statisticians to transition toward reference books in spatial econometrics. Therefore, the book is not a work of theoretical econometrics based on formal mathematical proofs[4], but is rather an introductory document for spatial econometrics applied to microdata.

P.2. Who is this work aimed at?

Nevertheless, reading this book assumes a minimal amount of knowledge in statistics and econometrics. It does not require any particular knowledge of geographical information systems (GIS). Even if the work presents programs that allow for the simulation of data in the appendixes, it requires no particular experience or particular aptitudes in programming.

More particularly, this booked is addressed especially to master's and PhD students in the domains linked to regional sciences and economic geography. As the domain of regional sciences is rather large and multidisciplinary, we want to provide some context to those who would like to get into spatial quantitative analysis and go a bit further

---

2 The ecological error problem comes from the transposition of conclusions made with aggregate spatial units to individual spatial units that make up the spatial aggregation.

3 The concept of MAUP was proposed by Openshaw and Taylor in 1979 to designate the influence of spatial cutting (scale and zonage effects) on the results of statistical processing or modeling.

4 Any reader interested in a more formal presentation of spatial econometrics is invited to consult the recent work by LeSage and Pace (2009) [LES 09] that is considered by some researchers as a reference that marks a "big step forward" in "for spatial econometrics" [ELH 10, p. 9].

on this adventure. In our opinion, the application of statistics and statistical models can no longer be done without understanding the spatial reality of the observations. The spatial aspect provides a wealth of information that needs to be considered during quantitative empirical analyses.

The books is also aimed at undergraduate and postgraduate students in economics who wish to introduce the spatial dimension into their analyses. We believe that this book provides excellent context before formally dealing with theoretical aspects of econometrics aiming to develop the estimators, show the proofs of convergence as well develop the detection tests according to the classical approaches (likelihood ratio (LR) test, Lagrange multiplier (LM) test and Wald tests).

We also aim to reach researchers who are not econometricians or statisticians, but wish to learn a bit about the logic and the methods that allow the detection of the presence of spatial autocorrelation as well as the methods for the correction of eventual problems occurring in the presence of autocorrelation.

P.3. Structure of the book

The books is split into six chapters that follow a precise logic. Chapter 1 proposes an introduction to spatial analysis related to disaggregated or individual data (spatial microdata). Particular attention is placed on the structure of spatial databases as well as their particularities. It shows why it is essential to take account of the spatial dimension in econometrics if the researcher has data that is geolocalized; it presents a brief history of the development of the branch of spatial econometrics since its formation.

Chapter 2 is definitely the central piece of the work and spatial econometrics. It serves as an opening for the other chapters, which use weights matrices in their calculations. Therefore, it is crucial and it is the reason for which particular emphasis is placed on it with many examples. A fictional example is developed and taken up again in Chapter 3 to demonstrate the calculation of the detection indices of the spatial autocorrelation patterns.

Chapter 3 presents the most commonly used measurements to detect the presence of spatial patterns in the distribution of a given variable. These measurements prove to be particularly crucial to verify the assumption of the absence of spatial correlation between the residuals or error terms of the regression model. The presence of a spatial autocorrelation violates one of the assumptions that ensures the consistency of the estimator of the ordinary least squares (OLS) and can modify the conclusions coming from the statistical model. The detection of such a spatial pattern requires the correction of the regression model and the use of spatial and spatio-temporal regression models. Obviously, the detection indices can also be used as descriptive tools and this chapter is largely based on this fact.

Chapters 4 and 5 present the autoregressive models used in spatial econometrics. The spatial autoregressive models (Chapter 4) can easily be transposed to spatio-temporal applications (Chapter 5) by developing an adapted weights matrix to the analyzed reality. A particular emphasis is put on the intuition behind the use of one type of model rather than another: this is the fundamental idea behind the DGP. In function of the postulated model, the consequences of the spatial relation detected between the residuals of the regression model can be more or less important, going from an imprecision in the calculation of the estimated variance, to a bias in the estimations of the parameters. The appendixes linked to Chapters 4 (spatial modeling) and 5 (spatio-temporal modeling) are based on the simulation of a given DGP and the estimation of autoregressive models from the weights matrices built previously (see Chapter 2).

Finally, the Conclusion is proposed, underlying the central role of the construction of the spatial weights matrix in spatial econometrics and the different possible paths allowing the transposition of existing techniques and methods to different definitions of the "distance".

We hope that this overview of the foundations of spatial econometrics will spike the interest of certain students and researchers, and encourage them to use spatial econometric modeling with the goal of getting as much as possible out of their databases and inspire some of them to propose new original approaches that will complete the current methods developed. After all, the development of spatial methods notably allows the integration of notions of spatial proximity (and others). This aspect is particularly crucial for certain theoretical schools of thought linked to regional science and new geographical economics (NGE), largely inspired by the works of Krugman [FUJ 04, KRU 91a, KRU 91b, KRU 98], recipient of the 2008 Nobel prize in economics [BEH 09].

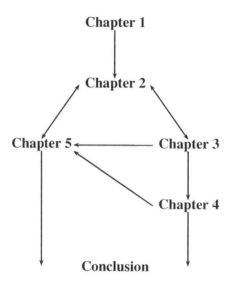

Figure P.1. *Links between the chapters*

Jean Dubé
and Diègo Legros
August 2014

1

Econometrics and Spatial Dimensions

1.1. Introduction

Does a region specializing in the extraction of natural resources register slower economic growth than other regions in the long term? Does industrial diversification affect the rhythm of growth in a region? Does the presence of a large company in an isolated region have a positive influence on the pay levels, compared to the presence of small- and medium-sized companies? Does the distance from highway access affect the value of a commercial/industrial/residential terrain? Does the presence of a public transport system affect the price of property? All these are interesting and relevant questions in regional science, but the answers to these are difficult to obtain without using appropriate tools. In any case, statistical modeling (econometric model) is inevitable in obtaining elements of these answers.

What is econometrics anyway? It is a domain of study that concerns the application of methods of statistical mathematics and statistical tools with the goal of inferring and testing theories using empirical measurements (data). Economic theory postulates hypotheses that allow the creation of propositions regarding the relations between various economic variables or indicators. However, these propositions are qualitative in nature and provide no information on the intensity of the links that they concern. The role of econometrics is to test these theories and provide numbered estimations of these relations. To summarize, econometrics, it is the statistical branch of economics: it seeks to quantify the relations between variables using statistical models.

For some, the creation of models is not satisfactory in that they do not take into account the entirety of the complex relations of reality. However, this is precisely one of the goals of models: to formulate in a simple manner the relations that we wish to formalize and analyze. Social phenomena are often complex and the human mind cannot process them in their totality. Thus, the model can then be used to create a summary of reality, allowing us to study it in part. This particular form obviously does not consider all the characteristics of reality, but only those that appear to be linked to the object of the study and that are particularly important for the researcher. A model that is adapted to a certain study often becomes inadequate when the object of the study changes, even if this study concerns the same phenomenon.

We refer to a model in the sense of the mathematical formulation, designed to approximately reproduce the reality of a phenomenon, with the goal of reproducing its function. This simplification aims to facilitate the understanding of complex phenomena, as well as to predict certain behaviors using statistical inference. Mathematical models are, generally, used as part of a hypothetico-deductive process. One class of model is particularly useful in econometrics: these are statistical models. In these models, the question mainly revolves around the variability of a given phenomenon, the origin of which we are trying to understand (dependent variable) by relating it to other variables that we assume to be explicative (or causal) of the phenomenon in question.

Therefore, an econometric model involves the development of a statistical model to evaluate and test theories and relations and guide the evaluation of public policies[1]. Simply put, an econometric model

---

1 Readers interested in an introduction to econometric models are invited to consult the introduction book to econometrics by Wooldridge [WOO 00], which is an excellent reference for researchers interested in econometrics and statistics.

formalizes the link between a variable of interest, written as y, as being dependent on a set of independent or explicative variables, written as $x_1, x_2, \ldots, x_K$, where K represents the total number of explicative variables (equation [1.1]). These explicative variables are then suspected as being at the origin of the variability of the dependent or endogenous variable:

$$y = f(x_1, x_2, \ldots, x_K) \hspace{4cm} [1.1]$$

We still need to be able to propose a form for the relation that links the variables, which means defining the form of the function $f(\cdot)$. We then talk of the choice of functional form. This choice must be made in accordance with the theoretical foundation of the phenomena that we are looking to explain. The researcher thus explicitly hypothesizes on the manner in which the variables are linked together. The researcher is said to be proposing a data generating process (DGP). He/she postulates a relation that links the selected variables without necessarily being sure that the postulated form is right. In fact, the validity of the statistical model relies largely on the DGP postulated. Thus, the estimated effects of the independent variables on the determination of the dependent variables arise largely from the postulated relation, which reinfirce the importance of the choice of the functional form. It is important to note that the functional form (or the type of relation) is not necessarily known with certitude during empirical analysis and that, as a result, the DGP is postulated: it is the researcher who defines the form of the relations as a function of the *a priori* theoretical forms and the subject of interest.

Obviously, since all of the variables, which influence the behavior during the study, and the form of the relation are not always known, it is a common practice to include, in the statistical model, a term that captures this omission. The error of specification is usually designated by the term ϵ. Some basic assumptions are made on the behavior of the "residual" term (or error term). Violating these basic assumptions can lead to a variety of consequences, starting from imprecision in the measurement of variance, to bias (bad measurement) of the searched for effect.

The simplest econometric statistical model is the one which linearly links a dependent variable to a set of interdependent variables equation [1.2]. This relation is usually referred to as multiple linear regression. In the case of a single explicative variable, we talk of simple linear regression. The simple linear regression can be likened to the study of correlation[2]. The linear regression model assumes that the dependent variable (y) is linked, linearly in the parameter, β_k, to the K ($k = 1, 2, ..., K$) number of independent variables (x_k):

$$y = \alpha + \beta_1 x_1 + \beta_2 x_2 + \cdots + \beta_K x_K + \epsilon \qquad [1.2]$$

The linear regression model allows us not only to know whether an explicative variable x_k is statistically linked to the dependent variable ($\beta_k \neq 0$), but also to check if the two variables vary in the same direction ($\beta_k > 0$) or in opposite directions ($\beta_k < 0$). It also allows us to answer the question: "by how much does the variable of interest (explained variable) change when the independent variable (dependent variable) is modified?". Herein also lies a large part of the goal of regression analysis: to study or simulate the effect of changes or movements of the independent variable on the behavior of the dependent variable (partial analysis). Therefore, the statistical model is a tool that allows us to empirically test certain hypotheses certain hypotheses as well as making inference from the results obtained.

The validity of the estimated parameters, and as a result, the validity of the statistical relation, as well as of the hypotheses tests from the model, rely on certain assumptions regarding the behavior of the error term. Thus, before going further into the analysis of the results of the econometric model it is strongly recommended to check if the following assumptions are respected:

---

2 In fact, the link between correlation and the analysis of simple linear regression comes from the fact that the determination coefficient of the regression (R^2) is simply the square of the correlation coefficient between the variable y and x ($R^2 = \rho^2$).

– the expectation of error terms is zero: the assumed model is "true" on average:

$$E(\epsilon) = 0; \tag{1.3}$$

– the variance of the disturbances is constant for each individual: disturbance homoskedasticity assumption:

$$E(\epsilon^2) = \sigma_\epsilon^2 \quad \forall\, i = 1, \ldots, N; \tag{1.4}$$

– the disturbances of the model are independent (non-correlated) among themselves: the variable of interest is not influenced, or structured, by any other variables than the ones retained:

$$E(\epsilon_i \epsilon_j) = 0 \quad \forall\, i \neq j. \tag{1.5}$$

The first assumption is, by definition, globally respected when the model is estimated by the method of ordinary least squares (OLS). However, nothing indicates that, locally, this property is applicable: the errors can be positive (negative) on average for high (low) values of the dependent variable. This behavior usually marks a form of nonlinearity in the relation[3]. Certain simple approaches allow us to take into account the nonlinearity of the relation: the transformation of variables (logarithm, square root, etc.), the introduction of quadratic forms (x, x^2, x^3, etc.), the introduction of dummy variables and so on and so forth.

The second assumption concerns the calculation of the variance of the disturbances and the influence of the variance of the estimator of parameter β. Indeed, the application of common statistical tests largely relies on the estimated variance and when this value is not minimal, the measurement of the variance of parameter β is not correct and the application of classical hypothesis tests is not appropriate. It is then necessary to correct the problem of heteroskedasticity of the variance of the disturbances. The procedures to correct for the presence of heteroskedasticity are relatively simple and well documented.

---

3 Or even a form of correlation between the errors.

The third assumption is more important: if it is violated, it can invalidate the results obtained. Depending on the form of the structure between the observations, it can have an influence on the estimation of the variance of parameters or even on the value of the estimated parameters. This latter consequence is heavier since it potentially invalidates all of the conclusions taken from the results obtained. Once again, to ensure an accurate interpretation of the results, the researcher must correct the problem of the correlation between the error terms. Here the procedures to correct for correlation among the error terms are more complex and largely depend on the type of data considered.

1.2. The types of data

The models used are largely linked to the structure and the characteristics of the data available for the analysis. However, the violation of one or several assumptions on the error terms is equally a function of the type of data used. Without a loss in generality, it is possible to identify three types of data: cross-sectional data, time series data and spatio-temporal data. The importance of the spatial dimension comes out particularly in the cross-sectional and spatio-temporal data.

The first essential step when working with a quantitative approach is to identify the type of data available to make the analyses. Not only do these data have particular characteristics in terms of violating the assumptions about the structure of the error terms, but they also influence the type of model that must be used. The type of model depends largely on the characterization of the dependent variables. Specific models are drawn for dummy variables (logit or probit models), for positive discrete (count) data (Poisson or negative binomial models), for truncated data (Heckman or Tobit models), etc. For the most part, the current demonstration will be focused on the models adapted to the case where the dependent variable is continuous (linear regression model).

1.2.1. *Cross-sectional data*

Cross-sectional data rely on a large number of observations (individuals, firms, countries, etc.) at a given time period. Database are usually defined as a file containing characteristic information from a set of observations: in a sense it is a picture giving the portrait of individuals at a fixed date. It is common practice to introduce some subindices to mark the individual observations. This subindex is written as i and the total number of observations is usually designated by N: $i = 1, 2, \ldots, N$.

For this type of data, the sources of the variation are interobservations, i.e. between the observations. It is then possible that the variation of the dependent variable is linked to some characteristics that are unique to the individuals. In the case where we cannot identify the majority of the factors that influence the variation of the dependent variable, we are faced with a problem of non-homogeneous variance, or heteroskedasticity problem. This behavior violates the second assumption of the behavior of the error terms. The linear regression model must then be corrected so that the estimated variance respects the base assumption so that the usual tests have the correct interpretation.

The tests for the detection of heteroskedasticity that are the best known are certainly those by Breusch and Pagan [BRE 79] and White [WHI 80]. The former suggests verifying if there is a significant statistical relation between the error terms squared (an estimation of the variance) and the independent variables of the model. In the case where this relation proves to be significant, we say that the variance is not homogeneous and depends on certain values of the independent variables. The second test is based on a similar approach. The White test suggests regressing the error terms squared for the whole set of the independent variables of the model as well as the crossed terms and quadratic terms of the variables. This addition of the quadratic and crossed terms allows us to consider a certain form of nonlinearity in the explanation of the variance. As for the previous case, the tests aim to verify the existence of a significant relation between the variance of the model and some independent variables or more complex terms, in which we must reject the homogeneity hypothesis of the variance.

This type of data is largely used in microeconomics and in all the related domains. The spatial data are cross-sectional data but incorporating another particularity: the error terms can be correlated among themselves in space since they share common localization characteristics. This behavior is then in violation of the third assumption, linked to the independence between the error terms. This is the heart and foundation of spatial econometrics (we will come back to it a bit later).

1.2.2. Time series

Time series rely on the accumulation of information, over time, of a given individual (a firm, an employee, a country, etc.). It is a continuous acquisition of information on the characteristics of an individual over time. Thus, it is quite common for the values of the observations to be dependent over time. As before, these series call upon the use of a subindex, marked t. The size of the database is given by the number of periods available to conduct the analysis, $T : t = 1, 2, \ldots, T$.

With this type of data the variation studied is intra-observation, i.e. over time, but for a unique observation. This type of data is likely to reveal a correlation between the error terms over time and thus be in violation of the third base assumption on the behavior of error terms. We then talk of temporal autocorrelation. In this case, the parameters obtained can be biased and the conclusions that we draw from the model can be wrong. The problems of temporal correlation between the error terms have been known for several centuries.

The most commonly used test to detect such a phenomenon is the Durbin and Watson statistic [DUR 50]. This test is inspired by a measurement of the correlation between the value of the residuals taken at a period, t, and one taken at the previous period, $t - 1$. It aims to verify that the correlation is statistically significant, in which case we are in the presence of temporal (or serial) autocorrelation. Another simple test consists of regressing the values of the residuals of the model at the period t for the value of the previous period, $t - 1$, and look to determine if the parameter associated with the time-lagged variable of the residuals is significant[4]. The correction methods are also largely documented and usually available in most software.

Time series can also bring additional complications such as a changing variance (increasing or decreasing) over time. The problem of non-homogeneous variance over time is in violation of the second assumption for the behavior of error terms and the modeling methods therefore become more complex.

This type of data is especially used in macroeconomics and related domains: the indicators of a spatial entity are followed for a certain number of periods. The data regarding the market indices of a company or of a bond also represent good examples of time series.

As we will see later on, the approach for the modeling of spatial data is largely inspired by models in time series. In fact, there exists an important parallel between the problems encountered in the analysis of time series (or temporal data) and the problems encountered in the analysis of spatial data. We will come back to this in Chapter 4.

1.2.3. Spatio-temporal data

There are also data that possess the two characteristics: individuals that are observed over time. We then talk of spatio-temporal data. Without loss of generality, there exist two types of spatio-temporal data: panel data (or longitudinal data) and the cross-section pooled over time. In the first case, these are the same individuals that are observed at each (or nearly) time period, while in the second case, these are different individuals that are observed in each of the periods. The distinction is small, but real and important (we will come back to it in Chapter 5). In both cases, the notation relies on the introduction of

---

4 This regression is usually estimated without a constant (or y-intercept).

two sub-indices: an index identifying the individual observation, i, and an index identifying the time period at which each of these observations are collected t. In the case of the panel, the subindices i are the same in each of the periods, while in the case of cross-sectional data pooled over time, these indices are different in each of the periods.

For this type of data, several problems are likely to arise: persistence of the behaviors over time, a non-homogeneous variance between the individuals and a correlation of the responses in space and time. The problems are potentially very important because the information contained in this data is a lot richer. This type of data is currently increasingly popular, notably because it enables not only the studying of variations between individuals and across time, but also the evolution of given individuals over time. This is certainly the data that provides the most information. Nevertheless, the introduction of the spatial dimension in this type of data is relatively new.

These types of data have recently captured a particular amount of attention and they are currently the object of numerous theoretical advances. Several pieces of software now allow the accurate modeling of this type of data. Spatio-temporal data is also likely to reveal several problems that invalidate the base postulations with regard to the behavior of error terms. There can exist not only a spatial correlation between the error terms but also a serial correlation. Moreover, the variance can depend on the relative situation in space, just like the behavior of the independent variable. Therefore, the richness of the source of the variation can result in several problems with the assumptions on the behavior of the residuals of the model, and that the use of appropriate models to take into account these phenomena is essential.

In summary, no matter what type of data considered, it is vital to verify that all three basic assumptions for the behavior of residuals are respected if we want to be sure of an accurate interpretation of the results. However, these postulations are largely linked to the type of data that the researcher is using.

1.3. Spatial econometrics

Why spatial econometrics? The simplest answer is that the spatial dimension of the mobilized data must be taken into account. As we saw previously, this type of data is susceptible to not respecting the assumptions relative to the disturbances of the linear regression model which, as a result, could invalidate the conclusions that could be made from the analysis. Thus, it is important to adopt a model that takes account of the correlation that could exist between the error terms. This correlation between the error terms can come from different sources (we will come back to this in Chapter 4). The use of statistical tools requires that the researcher be able to verify the assumptions formulated regarding the error terms of the models retained.

To summarize, we use spatial econometrics because we are working with data that possess information on the location of the observations and this location is an additional source of variation. Therefore, it is necessary to use quantitative tools that take into account the characteristics unique to each of the observations as well as their location. The location can hide several pieces of information: a grouped (or localized) heterogeneity, or even spilling or spillover effects, or the effects of externalities. Therefore, spatial econometric models aim to take into account these characteristics.

Ignoring the sources of variation can cause bias in the quantitative analyses since the basic assumptions concerning the behavior of the error terms are no longer respected. It is therefore essential, regardless of the type of data used, to use the appropriate modeling tool. This is the case when we are working with discrete or binary variables, with truncated data, counting data, etc. This is also the case for spatial data.

Obviously, there are several types of spatialized data. The most common case consists of geographical regions that describe towns, regions (states), countries, etc. For example, two neighboring regions, that share a common border, with a similar economic structure have high chances of sharing economic climates. Or even, a economic crash that is exogenous in the first region would influence the economic conditions in the second region. We then talk of spatial spillover effect (we will return to this in Chapter 4).

The spatial data can also rely on the observation of points. We then talk of spatial microdata: consumers, companies, residences, crimes, etc. This data is then defined by its precise geographical coordinates. We do not talk of the spatial relations based on a shared common boundary, but rather of the distance to be defined that separates the observations.

An example of a study that uses spatial microdata is the choice of location of companies. Since the companies export their production that can be used as input by another company and since they seek to minimize costs associated with shipping merchandise, it is highly likely that a company will locate close to the source of its main input or even the market that it serves. The localization decision of the company will in turn influence the localization decision of another firm that uses the production of the first firm as its principal input in its transformation process, and so on and so forth. The location decision can depend not only on the production process, but also on the location decisions of the other firms. Therefore, there exists a form of spatial dependence in the process of the localization of firms.

We can also cite the case of the price determination process of real estate as a typical example where space plays a crucial role. An old saying states that three factors influence real-estate price: the location, the location and the location. The view, local amenities and other spatial factors are likely to influence the price of a building. However, since these factors are fixed in space, it is possible that the spatial distribution of the values of the price of the real estate be very spatially structured: a panoramic view onto a lake or the proximity of a highly industrialized zone do not necessarily have the same effect on the value of the residences. Since these spatial amenities are shared between several residences, it is highly likely that the process of the creation of the value of real estate contains a non-negligible spatial component.

From these simple examples, it is possible to remark that spatial relations are potentially important in determining the processes that we wish to study. Therefore, it is essential, if space plays a role in the decisions/reactions of the variables under study, to take them into account in analyses. It is for all these reasons that it becomes essential to take an interest in spatial econometrics.

The main particularity of spatial data is that the source of variation is richer. Not only does a spatial database contain information on the heterogeneity (the characteristics) of behavior of the individuals, but it also provides information on the relative location of observations in space. This relative localization usually enables the identification of the fact that two relatively close (spatially or even socially) individuals are likely to have behaviors that resemble each other's than if we were comparing with the case where individuals that are relatively far from each other. Therefore, spatial analysis aims to include this other source of variation in the quantitative analyses and is largely caused not only by the progress made in the domain of quantitative geography, but also by recent developments in econometrics.

Space introduces a relatively complex form of the influences that can occur between the realizations of a random variable. This characteristic is fundamental and differentiates the spatial data from non-spatial (aspatial) data, usually labeled as a cross-sectional data base. Spatial data is, in a sense, a natural extension of the cross-section data since they include additional information that is likely to bring another explanation regarding the source of the variation of the data.

1.3.1. *A picture is worth a thousand words*

To properly visualize the presentation of the previous examples, we will complete these cases with an image allowing a better understanding of the importance and the form of the spatial links between the observations.

By taking a simple example based on a variable y, for four observations (points) 1, 2, 3 and 4, whose realizations are given as y_1, y_2, y_3 and y_4 (Figure 1.1), respectively, the spatiality implies that the variables are potentially all linked together. In other words, the value of

y_1 can depend in part on the values taken by the other observations of the variable y (y_2, y_3 and y_4). In the same manner, the values taken by y_2 can depend on the other values taken by the other observations of variable y, and so on and so forth.

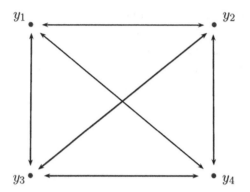

Figure 1.1. *Representation of the spatial relations between variables for four observations*

In this case, the variation of the variable for observation 1, y_1, in turn influences the response of the other observation which, in turn, influences the response of observation 1 and so on and so forth. LeSage and Pace [LES 09] qualify these effects of retroaction as indirect effects, while Abreu *et al.* [ABR 04] speak of induced effects. The decomposition of the marginal effects then takes on a much different form from the classical way. The responses all being linked to each other, the movement of a variable for a given observation indubitably causes a movement in the same variable for the other observations.

This particularity also marks the complexity of the spatial relations in the quantitative analysis that must be taken into account when the observations are spatialized. This type of relation must be integrated in the statistical models since it influences the DGP. Therefore, the challenge is to mathematically incorporate this effect.

It goes without saying that one of the central elements in spatial analysis and in spatial econometrics is the specification and the structuring of the spatial links between the variables. This formalization of the possible spatial links is usually done through the construction of a spatial weights matrix (Chapter 2). As we will see throughout all the chapters, the spatial weights matrix plays a fundamental role in spatial econometrics. Therefore, it is essential to properly define the construction of this matrix before going any further into the presentation of spatial descriptive statistics (Chapter 3) or even in statistical modeling (Chapters 4 and 5).

1.3.2. *The structure of the databases of spatial microdata*

The structure of file of spatial data is not different from the structure of a conventional file of non-geolocalized data: a flat file in which a line represents an observation for which the detail of its description relies on a set of columns, each describing observable characteristics (variables).

An observation can be, for example, an individual characterized by age, academic degree level, income level, etc. In the same manner, a line can represent a real estate transaction whose characteristics, given by the detail of the columns, would enable the identification of the number of pieces, the area of the terrain (or the lot), the age of the building, etc.

If the structure of the database in table format is more or less the same, the possibility of locating the observations, in relative terms, makes all the difference. By resorting to the exact geographical coordinates (longitude, latitude or Cartesian coordinates) of the observation, it is possible to relativize its position in relation to the other observations. This particularity gives the researcher the possibility of taking into account possible relations that could intervene between a given observation (an individual or a region) and its neighbors.

The role of localization is twofold. First, the location gives rise, for an observation, to the construction of new characteristics linked to the description of the surroundings, notably the proximity to particular infrastructures or services. Second, localization identifies the neighboring observations of a given observation. In both cases, geolocalization allows us to incorporate a set of relations relying on spatial distances. We will return to this in Chapter 2.

This book only briefly covers the possibilities of generating new variables that express the relative distancing of an observation from centers of interest. This domain is of great interest to users of geographical information systems (GISs), as well as geographers. In such a context, geographical information allows us to make the links between that which appears at one location and the characterization of this location. GISs contextualize events as a function of the spatial description of the surroundings, as well as visually processing the data by notably producing a set of maps that can describe a given situation. While they do play an important role in the processing of spatialized information and are increasingly used, we do not go into detail on the function of these tools. Any readers interested in becoming more familiar with this tool can consult the work by Longley *et al.* [LON 01].

1.4. History of spatial econometrics

Spatial econometrics is a relatively new branch and its influence has only really been felt in the last two decades. Two reasons explain the attraction for this new branch of statistical analysis in economics.

The first reason is the increasing development of statistical models and estimators that integrate the spatial dimensions as well as the establishment of their theoretical properties. The second reason is linked to the importance of technological progress: the appearance of high-performance computers and the variety of specialized software helping with the processing of geolocalized data. Like several domains in which calculation capacities are used extensively, the popularity of the field has not truly been able to take off since the accessibility of various numerical techniques has become public.

In a recent article, Griffith [GRI 13] retraces the history of the developments of spatial analysis and spatial econometrics. He notably stresses the importance of the first works that highlighted the hypothesis according to which spatialized data behaves in a particular way. Among these authors are famous statisticians such as Student, Yule, Stephan, Fischer and Yates. All have noted a certain tendency toward the grouping of the values measured in space. The notion of spatial dependence was then slowly starting to appear. However, it was only later that particular attention began being paid to the consideration of spatial effects in data modeling.

In fact, spatial phenomena have long captured attention without being explicitly considered in quantitative analysis. The example that stands out the most is certainly the case in London, in 1854, where John Snow, a doctor, identified the source of a cholera epidemic: by mapping all of the reported cases, the doctor managed to identify the well from which the people were getting their water as the source of the propagation. Thus, it was possible to stop the progression of the epidemic by blocking the well. However, this story remains controversial.

Formally, the first statistic test developed to detect the presence of spatial links between a given variable goes back to the works by Moran, 60 years ago [MOR 48, MOR 50]. Following this, Geary [GEA 54] proposed another one with a detection measurement of the spatial schema based on a different similarity index. Thus, the term of spatial autocorrelation makes an appearance[5].

Despite these developments from the 1950s, the possible link between spatialized variables was only formally defined in 1970 by Tobler who pronounced the first law of geography. This stipulates that all phenomena are spatially linked together, but that the phenomena that are the closest are the most strongly linked [TOB 70].

Thus, the importance of the spatial dimension reveals the "problem" of spatial correlation of variables [CLI 69]. This concept is formally defined by Anselin and Bera [ANS 98] as the coincidence of value similarity with locational similarity.

---

5 The term of autocorrelation refers to an existing correlation between a given variable and the value of the same variable for a given neighboring space. We talk of spatial autocorrelation when the notion of neighboring is applied to spatial demarcation and temporal autocorrelation when the dimension of the neighboring is applied to time periods.

It was only a decade later that the term of spatial econometrics appears following works by Paelinck and Klassen [PAE 79]. Anselin retraces the timeline of 30 years of spatial econometrics in an article published in *Papers in Regional Science* [ANS 10]. Several articles propose a census of the main fields of application in spatial econometrics [ARB 08, ARB 10], a presentation of the new developments [ARB 10, ELH 10] or even an opening toward future perspectives [ANS 07, ANS 09, PIN 10].

Formally, it is only during the 1990s that spatial autocorrelation became a subject that is really considered in the literature [ANS 98, GRI 92, HEP 00]. Getis [GET 09, p. 299] is of the opinion that the concept of spatial autocorrelation is now a unavoidable: "no other concept in empirical spatial research is as central as spatial autocorrelation". Currently, the ramifications of this subject are such that it is impossible to ignore this problem when working with geolocalized data [ANS 07].

In the last few years, the development of estimation routines and specialized software has largely facilitated the use of spatial econometrics methods [ANS 92b, ANS 06, BIV 06, LES 99]. The appearance of two pieces of software freely available for download on the internet (GeoDa and R) has also favored a certain democratization of the methods of spatial analysis. Reference works are now increasingly common [ANS 00, ANS 04, CRE 93, CRE 10, LES 09, MUR 04, PAE 09] while the techniques and the models are increasingly diverse.

Moreover, the creation of the Spatial Econometric Association (SEA) in 2007 can be seen as a sign of the increasing popularity of spatial econometrics, in particular, and spatial analysis, in general. In a text retracing the history of the evolution of works in spatial econometrics since the creation of the SEA, Arbia [ARB 11] suggests that the main developments in the field relied on the appearance of the notion of spatial autocorrelation following the works by Cliff and Ord [CLI 69] (see also [CLI 73]). The 40 years since the appearance of this notion are underlined in a special publication of the review *Geographical Analysis* in 2009[6].

The field's popularity can be noted, notably by the number of articles published in relation to spatial econometrics. Judging by the strong increase in the number of works on the subject from the research conducted on the search engine *Scopus*, the fields of spatial analysis and spatial econometrics truly took off around the end of the 1990s and the beginning of the 2000s (Figure 1.2). In fact, in the five years alone covering the period of 2007–2012, more that 60% of all the publications with articles containing the key words "spatial analysis" and more than 75% of all the publications containing the key words "spatial econometrics" were listed. In the same period, a particular emphasis was placed on the development of models using spatial panel data (Figure 1.3).

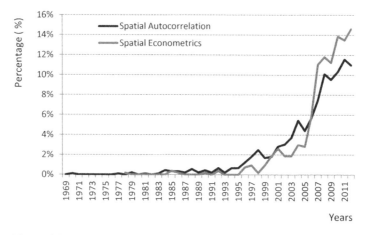

Figure 1.2. *Percentage of articles published in the most important journals, key words: spatial econometrics, spatial autocorrelation 1969–2011*

Currently, several reviews and scientific journals have been focused on several applications and developments of spatial econometrics and spatial statistics. Articles on the applications and theoretical

---

6 A set of articles is the object of the special publication in volume 41 (4).

developments are published in reviews of regional science (Tables 1.1, 1.2 and 1.3), of which most active are: *Geographical Analysis, Regional Science and Urban Economics, Papers in Regional Science, Journal of Regional Science, Spatial Economic Analysis, Economic Letters* and *Annals of Regional Science.* A particularly active journal in the domain of spatial econometrics since 2007, has been, without a doubt, the *Journal of Econometrics.* The review *Journal of Applied Econometrics* has also published a number of studies linking theoretical developments to empirical applications.

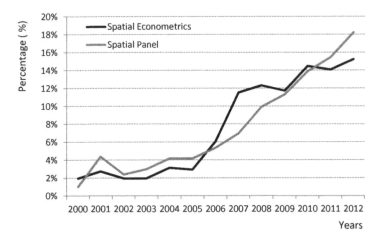

Figure 1.3. *Percentage of articles published in the most important journals, key words: spatial econometrics, spatial panel 2000–2012*

The most prolific authors in the domain are Griffith, previous editor of the review *Geographical Analysis*, Fingleton, editor of the review *Spatial Economic Analysis*, Anselin, one of the first to further spatial econometric analysis and conceiver of the GeoDa software, and also Baltagi, LeSage, Lee, Florax, Nijkamp, Kelejian, Elhorst, Getis and LeGallo (Tables 1.4, 1.5 and 1.6).

The classical way to approach the modeling of spatial autocorrelation relies on methods that attempt to control, for a certain form of spatial heterogeneity via, notably, the geographically weighted regression (GWR) – [FOT 98, FOT 02]), the locally weighted regression (LWR) – [CLE 88, MCM 96]), and expansion of the coefficients from a previously established spatial segment [CAS 72, CAS 97], or even by an autoregressive specification of the error terms [LES 09]. We will return shortly, in slightly more detail, to the spatial autoregressive model in Chapters 4 and 5. Other models propose the isolation of the phenomenon of spatial autocorrelation generated by the omission of an important explicative variable or even from an autoregressive process on the dependent variable or on the independent variables (or explicative) [LES 09].

Rank	Review	# article	%	IF*
1	Regional Science and Urban Economics	38	7.1	1.008
2	Papers in Regional Science	32	6.0	1.430
3	Journal of Regional Science	22	4.1	2.000
4	Journal of Geographical Systems	18	3.4	1.171
5	American Journal of Agricultural Economics	15	2.8	1.169
6	Spatial Economic Analysis	14	2.6	1.200
7	Geographical Analysis	12	2.2	1.054
8	Economics Letters	11	2.1	0.447
9	Annals of Regional Science	11	2.1	1.026
10	Journal of Econometrics	11	2.1	1.349
11	Review of Regional Studies	10	1.9	0.696
12	Journal of Economic Geography	9	1.7	3.261
13	Regional Studies	7	1.3	1.187
* : *Impact factor* in 2012				

Table 1.1. *List of the most active reviews in spatial econometrics*

While there are certain geostatic approaches that allow us to consider latent variations, by developing explicative variables [DUB 12, KRI 66, TRI 67, WID 60], we will not formally deal with these models.

1.5. Conclusion

The particularity of the data requires the use of tools adapted to each of the cases: after all, quantitative analysis is only a tool that allows dealing with research questions using a hypothetico-deductive approach. To ensure that we answer these questions properly, it is essential to use the right tools. The addition of a spatial dimension to the data in cross-sectional data makes it possible to exploit an additional source of variation. It means that relations between the observations (the points) can be made explicit, which is not possible with data in cross-sections that are not localized.

Rank	Reviews	# article	%	IF*
1	Geographical Analysis	43	4.9	1.054
2	Landscape Ecology	32	3.6	2.897
3	Journal of Biogeography	31	3.5	4.863
4	Journal of Geographical Systems	27	3.1	1.366
5	Acta Geographica Sinica	22	2.5	n.d.
6	Regional Science and Urban Economics	22	2.5	1.228
7	International Journal of Health Geographics	21	2.4	2.200
8	International Journal of Geographical Information Science	19	2.2	1.613
9	Social Science and Medicine	18	2.0	2.733
10	Proceedings of the National Academy of Sciences of the USA	16	1.8	9.737
11	Papers in Regional Science	12	1.4	1.541
12	American Journal of Physical Anthropology	12	1.4	2.481
13	Annals of the Association of American Geographers	12	1.4	2.110
* : *Impact factor* in 2012				

Table 1.2. *List of the most active reviews in spatial autocorrelation*

This book seeks to present the tools developed in spatial econometrics so as to cover the quantitative analysis of spatial data pooled over time. The second chapter looks to go even further to formalize the possible links between spatial observations through the construction, in an exogenous way, of the spatial weights matrix, an essential input in spatial econometrics. This matrix allows the formalization of the relations of spatial proximity between the observations, but can be easily transposed to other types of distances. This makes spatial econometrics more attractive for the formalization, for example, of the effect of social, organizational, economic and other proximities on the various economical behaviors.

Rank	Reviews	# article	%	IF*
1	Regional Science and Urban Economics	20	4.0	1.228
2	Spatial Economic Analysis	18	3.6	1.375
3	Journal of Econometrics	14	2.8	1.710
4	Papers in Regional Science	11	2.2	1.541
5	Journal of Regional Science	11	2.2	2.279
6	Economics Letters	11	2.2	0.509
7	Journal of Urban Economics	10	2.0	1.910
8	Journal of Geographical Systems	9	1.8	1.366
9	Journal of Economic Geography	8	1.6	2.600
10	Economic Modeling	7	1.4	0.557
11	Proceedings of the National Academy of Sciences of the USA	7	1.4	n.d.
12	Annals of Regional Science	6	1.2	0.901
13	Empirical Economics	6	1.2	0.614
14	China Economic Review	6	1.2	1.390
15	Review of Regional Studies	6	1.2	0.785
* : *Impact factor* in 2012				

Table 1.3. *List of the most active reviews in spatial panels*

The third chapter is dedicated to the presentation of the main statistical tests that enable the detections of dependence patterns or patterns of spatial heterogeneity of the quantitative variables. We present, in a detailed manner, the indices of global and local detection of spatial autocorrelation at the base of a descriptive analysis of the spatial data, a step that often precedes a more advanced quantitative analysis.

The fourth chapter aims to present the different autoregressive models used in spatial econometrics to capture the spatial effects, either of dependence or of heterogeneity from the generalization of the standard model of linear regression. We establish the link that exists between the methods related to spatial data and those related to temporal data. The econometric models developed, *a priori* in line with theories of the researchers, are presented, as are several statistical tests that allow us to select one spatial autoregressive model over another.

Rank	Authors	# article	%
1	Griffith, D.A.	30	3.4
2	Sokal, R.R.	9	1.0
3	Thomas, I.	8	0.9
4	Tiefelsdorf, M.	7	0.8
5	Le Gallo, J.	6	0.7
6	Getis, A.	6	0.7
7	Kelejian, H.H.	6	0.7
8	Anselin, L.	6	0.7
9	Oden, N.L.	6	0.7
10	Thomson, B.A.	5	0.6
11	Baltagi, B.H.	5	0.6
12	Khamis, F.G.	5	0.6
13	Elhorst, J.P.	5	0.6
14	Paez, A.	5	0.6
15	Novak, R.J.	5	0.6
16	Jacob, B.G.	5	0.6
17	Netrdova, P.	5	0.6
18	Martellosio, F.	5	0.6
19	Kockelman, K.M	4	0.5
20	Lu, Y.	4	0.5
Total		137	15.5
For the period 1978–2012			

Table 1.4. *List of the most active authors in spatial autocorrelation*

The fifth chapter deals with some applications of spatial models in the case where spatial microdata are gathered in a continuous manner over time without the individual observations necessarily being repeated (pooled cross-section data). Several case figures resemble this type of data collection, although currently few theoretical developments have been made in relation to this type of data. Most of the developments relate to data in cross-sectional, or even spatial panel data. A presentation on the construction of spatio-temporal weights matrices enables the use of the outlines developed in Chapter 4, while taking into account the two dimensions of the data: spatial and temporal.

Rank	Authors	# article	%
1	Fingleton, B.	16	3.0
2	Anselin, L.	13	2.4
3	Pfaffermayr, M.	8	1.5
4	Egger, P.	7	1.3
5	LeSage, J.P.	7	1.3
6	Florax, R.J.G.M.	7	1.3
7	Griffith, D.A.	6	1.1
8	Lacombe, D.J.	6	1.1
9	Kosfeld, R.	6	1.1
10	Nijkamp, P.	6	1.1
11	Le Gallo, J.	5	0.9
12	Mur, J.	5	0.9
13	Piras, G.	5	0.9
14	Eckey, H.F.	5	0.9
15	Angulo, A.	5	0.9
16	Baltagi, B.H.	5	0.9
17	Pace, R.K.	5	0.9
18	Elhorst, J.P.	5	0.9
19	Turck, M.	3	0.6
20	Lewis, D.J.	3	0.6
Total		128	24.0
For the period 1978–2012			

Table 1.5. *List of the most active authors in spatial econometrics*

One of the main objectives of this book is especially to present a way in which to spatially link the observations among themselves and thus verify and test the presence of (spatial) links or spatial correlation (or autocorrelation) between the variables as suggested by the first law of geography. This particularity of spatial relations can modify the statistical approaches normally used. The geographical coordinates of the observations allow us, in this context, to take into account the possible links that can exist between the observations, which is impossible with databases that do not contain any information on the geographical location. The particularity of spatial links relies on these links. The multidirectionality of the links stipulates that a given variable can influence the behavior of another neighboring variable, and that this very neighboring variable in turn influences the behavior (or the realization) of the variable considered.

Rank	Authors	# article	%
1	Baltagi, B.H.	14	2.8
2	Lee, L.F.	9	1.8
3	Yu, J.	9	1.8
4	Pfaffermayr, M.	8	1.6
5	Fingleton, B.	7	1.4
6	Crowder, K.	7	1.4
7	South, S.J.	7	1.4
8	Tosetti, E.	6	1.2
9	Moscone, F.	6	1.2
10	Laurisden, J.	5	1.0
11	Griffith, D.A.	4	0.8
12	Papalia, R.B.	4	0.8
13	Kelejian, H.H.	4	0.8
14	Egger, P.	4	0.8
15	Nijkamp, P.	4	0.8
16	Pirotte, A.	4	0.8
17	Rodriguez-Pose, A.	4	0.8
18	Tselios, V.	4	0.8
19	Kockelman, K.M.	4	0.8
20	Millimet, D.L.	4	0.8
Total		117	23.2
For the period 2000–2012			

Table 1.6. *List of the most active authors in panel spatial econometrics*

A second objective of the book is to provide an introduction to applied spatial econometric models. For this reason, we have deliberately decided to not go into detail in the calculations of the estimators and the mathematical proofs of the various properties of the estimators and statistical tests. We propose, instead, an approach based on the intuitive presentation of the main tools and models as well as a presentation where the behavior of the various statistical tools is numerically studied using programs, presented in the appendix. These programs can simulate spatial data according to the process that the reader is willing to provide them.

2

Structuring Spatial Relations

2.1. Introduction

The particularity of spatial data relies, as we have seen, on the links that it is possible to establish between the observations. Spatial relations, dictated by proximity, therefore have a possible role in the realization of the values of the variables. However, this idea of spatial proximity needs to be formalized before going any further. The question that is focused upon in this chapter is determining how to express spatial proximity in a simple manner.

The structure of spatial links is usually described using a spatial weights matrix. This matrix formalizes the relative proximity between the observations and relies on the first law of geography defined by Tobler [TOB 70] that stipulates that all the phenomena are linked together, but that those which are closer are linked more strongly. In spatial econometrics, the notion of proximity therefore relies on a measurement of the distance which acknowledges the relative separation among the observations in space. In this sense, it is primordial to take time on these notions of measurements before even looking to present the base tools of spatial analysis and spatial econometrics.

This chapter aims specifically to present certain measurements of distance separating the observations to then go on to define the relations of spatial proximity that are essential for the construction of the spatial weights matrix. Following this introductory section, the chapter is divided into seven further sections. Section 2.2 is dedicated to the spatial representation of microdata with the ultimate intention of calculating a distance that separates two observations. Section 2.3 covers the construction of distance matrices and presents the different distances that can be retained to measure the distances between the observations. Section 2.4 goes back to the distance matrix so as to reflect the intensity of the spatial relations between the observations. We talk then of the construction of the spatial weights. A set of alternatives is then presented in detail, stressing the best known and most used relations. In section 2.5, we present the standardization of the spatial weights matrices. While this step is not strictly required, it offers several advantages. Section 2.6 exposes examples built on fictitious data[1]. Section 2.7 presents the advantages and the disadvantages of spatial micro-data. Finally, Section 2.8 ends the chapter.

2.2. The spatial representation of data

The spatial particularity of microdata means that it is possible to locate the observations in a two-dimensional space: one-dimension based on the north–south relation and another based on the east–west relation. This spatial relation can, for example, be expressed in a Cartesian plane. Thus, each of the observations possesses a location that is its own and that is described by a couple of points (X, Y), that synthesizes its geographical coordinates. In a conventional manner, the X axis appears horizontally (marking the east–west axis), while the Y axis appears vertically (marking the north–south axis) (Figure 2.1).

The representation of points in the Cartesian plane can then be used to determine the distances between each of the points. These distances can then be used to determine the distances between each of the points,

---

1 Readers seeking to extend the exercise to a greater number of observations can take inspiration from the Monte Carlo program in the Appendix, section A3.4. This program enables the simulation of a number of spatial observations whose coordinates are *a priori* established but that can vary from one program to another.

in other words expressing a measurement of the intensity of the relations between the observations: each of the points represents a particular observation and each of the observations possesses its own characteristics. For the moment, we will leave aside the individual characteristics of the points, which will be exploited to verify the presence of spatial patterns in the distribution of the variables (Chapter 3) and in econometric modeling (Chapters 4 and 5). We are looking to use the information on the location of the points to express the spatial relations from the relative locations between each point.

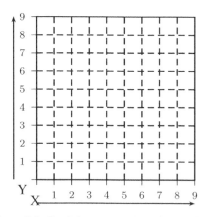

Figure 2.1. *Spatial representation of a regular grid*

Since the spatial relations are based on the idea of proximity or of spatial distance, it is necessary to determine, when working with microdata, the distance that separates each point. The first law of geography means that a stronger relation is taken by observations that are closer spatially. Nevertheless, two questions remain: (1) how do we calculate the distance between the points (and which distance to choose)?; and (2) how do we establish the weights that express the spatial relations between the observations?

The calculation of the distance can be based on several metrics. Two main distances are mainly mobilized in the spatial econometric applications: (1) the Euclidian distance; and (2) the Manhattan distance. By linking two observations, written as p_i and p_j, with their respective geographical coordinates being (X_i, Y_i) and (X_j, Y_j), it is possible to calculated the two metrics from relations established in a right-angle triangle (Figure 2.2)[2].

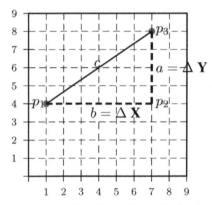

Figure 2.2. *Spatial representation of a regular grid with three observations*

The Euclidian distance corresponds to the length of the segment separating the two points (solid line – c). This is the length of the hypotenuse, which is obtained using Pythagorus' theorem (equation [2.1]). The theorem stipulates that the square of the hypotenuse (the side opposite to the right angle of the triangle) is equal to the sum of the squares of the two other sides (the two sides opposite the right angle a and b):

$$c^2 = a^2 + b^2 \tag{2.1}$$

From the equation [2.1], it is possible to express the measurement of segment c as being equal to the square root of the sum of the squares of the lengths of the sides of the triangle (equation [2.2]):

$$c = \sqrt{a^2 + b^2} \tag{2.2}$$

---

2 The reader can consider a set of more or less complex possibilities from the general measurement of the distance: $d_{ij} = \{|X_i - X_j|^q + |Y_i - Y_j|^q\}^{\frac{1}{q}}$ where q is a constant that belongs to the natural number system. The case of $q = 1$ corresponds to the Manhattan distance, while $q = 2$ belongs to the Euclidian distance.

This distance corresponds to what geographers call the distance as the crow flies.

It does not take into account geographical constraints and natural obstacles that are present, and corresponds to the smallest distance separating the two points.

However, the Manhattan distance, corresponds to the sum of the lengths of the sides forming a right angle (a and b) (Figure 2.2). It is therefore defined by the length of the segment d representing the length of the two added segments (equation [2.3]).

$$d = a + b \qquad\qquad [2.3]$$

The principle of the Manhattan distance is simple: it corresponds to the consideration of certain physical constraints related to an urban setting. If an individual wishes to travel from one address to another, he/she will have to get around buildings. The path that will need to be followed (on foot or by car) goes along roads or sidewalks, which are often laid out, especially in American cities, in a grid system. The name of the distance is taken from the geographical particularity of the town of Manhattan which is built following a checker layout of the buildings and roads.

The two distances therefore rely in part on the length of sides a and b. Thus, going from the metric defining the unit of the Y axis and of the X axis, it is simple to determine the length of the two respective sides and thus to define the length of the other sides c and d. By assuming that the units of the axes are in meters or kilometers, the calculation of the distance of the sides is given, respectively, by equations [2.5] and [2.4], where X_i and Y_i respectively correspond to the value of X and of Y for point p_i and X_j and Y_j correspond to the value of X and Y for point p_j:

$$a = \Delta Y = |Y_i - Y_j| \qquad\qquad [2.4]$$

$$b = \Delta X = |X_i - X_j| \qquad\qquad [2.5]$$

The distance allows us to judge the relative relation between a set of points. We say that the two points are spatially close if the distance that separates them is small. On the contrary, two points are said to be far if the distance that separates them is great. However, this distance is effectively relative, and not absolute. A distance of 10 km constitutes considerable effort, in terms of time and energy, if this distance is covered on foot, rather than on a bicycle or in a car. In the same way, 10 km can appear a considerable distance, if we are considering a plane of 10 km × 10 km, or even a small distance if we are considering a plane of 1,000 km × 1000 km. In other words, the calculation of the distance is a useful notion, but does not represent a finality.

After having calculated the distance between each of the observations, it is necessary to measure the intensity of the relations between each of these observations. This step of passing the distances in spatial relations is the key in all spatial analysis since, as we will see in the other chapters, the measurements, the statistics and the tests in spatial econometrics rely systematically on the spatial weights matrix. Hereafter, all of the intensities of the relations between each of the observations will be presented in the form of a spatial weights matrix. Thus, before going in to the presentation of these tools, it is essential to take the time to precisely cover the steps of the construction of the spatial weights matrix.

2.3. The distance matrix

By generalizing the calculation of the distance among N observations, the measurements of the Euclidian (d_{ij}) and Manhattan ($d_{ij}^{\star}$) distances are obtained with the equations [2.6] and [2.7]:

$$d_{ij} = \sqrt{(Y_i - Y_j)^2 + (X_i - X_j)^2} \quad \forall\, i,j = 1, \ldots, N \qquad [2.6]$$

$$d_{ij}^{\star} = |Y_i - Y_j| + |X_i - X_j| \quad \forall\, i,j = 1, \ldots, N \qquad [2.7]$$

The calculated distances (Euclidian or Manhattan) can be classed in a square table (a matrix) in which each line and column number corresponds to the considered observation. In this manner, it is possible to synthesize all of the distances that separate the observations from the distance matrix (equations [2.12] and [2.13]) where each particular element of the matrix, d_{ij} or $d_{ij}^{\star}$ establishes the distance separating an observation i from another observation j.

The calculations can be produced in a sequential manner by calculating the individual values. However, when the number of observations, N, is high, the matrix notation must be privileged (instead of using loop operators) as they speed up the calculations greatly.

By noting $\mathbf{X}$ the vector of the geographical coordinates X_i of dimension $(N \times 1)$, $\mathbf{Y}$ the vector of the geographical coordinates Y_i of dimension $(N \times 1)$ and ι a vector composed of elements all equal to 1, also of dimension $(N \times 1)$, we can calculate the distance matrix between all of the observations by applying the following matrix operations:

$$\mathbf{D}_X = |\mathbf{X} \times \iota' - \iota \times \mathbf{X}'| \tag{2.8}$$

$$\mathbf{D}_Y = |\mathbf{Y} \times \iota' - \iota \times \mathbf{Y}'| \tag{2.9}$$

$$\mathbf{D} = \sqrt{(\mathbf{D}_X \odot \mathbf{D}_X) + (\mathbf{D}_Y \odot \mathbf{D}_Y)} \tag{2.10}$$

$$\mathbf{D}^{\star} = \mathbf{D}_X + \mathbf{D}_Y \tag{2.11}$$

where the matrix $\mathbf{D}_X$, of dimension $(N \times N)$, gives the distance between the coordinates X_i for all of the N points, the matrix $\mathbf{D}_Y$, of dimension $(N \times N)$, provides the distance between each of the coordinates Y_i.

Matrix $\mathbf{D}$, of dimension $(N \times N)$, expresses the Euclidian distance between each of the observations (equation [2.12]), while matrix $\mathbf{D}^{\star}$, of dimension $(N \times N)$, provides the Manhattan distance between the observations (equation [2.13]). The operator $\odot$ represents the Hadamard product: a matrix operation carrying out the product term by term of two matrices of identical dimension[3]:

$$
\mathbf{D} = \begin{pmatrix}
0 & d_{12} & \cdots & d_{1j} & \cdots & d_{1N} \\
d_{21} & 0 & \cdots & d_{2j} & \cdots & d_{2N} \\
\vdots & \vdots & \vdots & \vdots & \vdots & \vdots \\
d_{i1} & d_{i2} & \cdots & d_{ij} & \cdots & d_{iN} \\
\vdots & \vdots & \vdots & \vdots & \vdots & \vdots \\
d_{N1} & d_{N2} & \cdots & d_{Nj} & \cdots & 0
\end{pmatrix}
\qquad [2.12]
$$

$$
\mathbf{D}^{\star} = \begin{pmatrix}
0 & d_{12}^{\star} & \cdots & d_{1j}^{\star} & \cdots & d_{1N}^{\star} \\
d_{21}^{\star} & 0 & \cdots & d_{2j}^{\star} & \cdots & d_{2N}^{\star} \\
\vdots & \vdots & \vdots & \vdots & \vdots & \vdots \\
d_{i1}^{\star} & d_{i2}^{\star} & \cdots & d_{ij}^{\star} & \cdots & d_{iN}^{\star} \\
\vdots & \vdots & \vdots & \vdots & \vdots & \vdots \\
d_{N1}^{\star} & d_{N2}^{\star} & \cdots & d_{Nj}^{\star} & \cdots & 0
\end{pmatrix}
\qquad [2.13]
$$

It is important to note that the main diagonal of the distance matrices are all equal to 0. This situation is explained by the fact that distance separating one point from itself is, by definition, zero. Moreover, since the distance is symmetrical[4], the values below the main diagonal are only replicas of the values that appear above the main diagonal.

The distance matrix is composed of $(N \times N)$ elements. Each of the lines contains N elements and provide the distance between all of the point in relation to a given point. Since the matrix contains as many lines as points, we then have N lines, each containing N elements, which explains the dimension of the matrix.

Since the distance is symmetrical, it is only theoretically necessary to calculate half of the distances to express the exhaustivity of the

---

3 This matrix operator will be used again in the construction of the spatio-temporal weights matrix (Chapter 5).

4 The distance separating points p_1 and p_2 is the same as the distance that separates points p_2 and p_1.

measurements. It is therefore necessary only to calculate $(N \times N)/2$ elements. Moreover, since the distance separating a point from itself is equal to zero, it is therefore only necessary to calculate $(N - 1)$ distances for each of the points. In the end, to obtain the complete portrait of the distances between the points, it is only necessary to calculate $N \times (N - 1)/2$ distances.

However, the calculation of the distance between the observations is only a step leading to construction of a general matrix allowing the expression of the intensity of the spatial links between the observations (or the points). The distances are then transformed to express the relations of spatial proximity.

Obviously, the notion of distance cannot be limited to geographic distance (whether it is Euclidian or Manhattan) separating the observations (or variables) p_i and p_j. We could, for example, construct a social distance by comparing the social strata in which the individuals live [DUB 14]. The spatial (or geographic) distance is usually retained in spatial econometrics, but some recent applications suggest that these distances can be extended to other metrics [CON 99, CON 03]. The new metrics can then reflect networks as well as the connectivity of these networks and the tools of spatial econometrics can be used to express other realities and test other hypotheses[5]. In other words, spatial econometrics may be revealed as a highly powerful analytical tool for social science empirical studies and is easily adopted for network analysis.

2.4. Spatial weights matrices

Up to here, the discussion has been focused on the calculation of the distance separating observations. However, the distance alone does not permit the expression of the spatial relations as described by the first law of geography. In fact, the use of the distance even expresses

---

[5] While the possibilities are great in several fields of research, we leave it up to the reader to discover these applications. The goal of this book is especially to present the functioning of the tools of spatial econometrics.

the opposite message: the distance is greater as the observations are further. It is therefore necessary to carry out a transformation (inverse) on the distance to get a spatial weight that explicitly takes into account the proximity structure. The calculation of the distance between the observations is therefore only a first step toward the formalization of the spatial proximity relations as these must decrease in function of the distance. The weights matrix is the essence of the transformation of the distance matrix so as to express the spatial proximities between observations.

The debate over the very structure of the spatial weights matrix as well as the on the type of relations that identify the spatial proximity are numerous. The optimal form is not clearly defined in the literature [FIN 09, GET 09, GET 04, GRI 96, GRI 81]. Nevertheless, the general principles on the way to construct the spatial weights matrices are largely recognized [UPT 85]. In nearly every case, the formalization of the relations between variables is usually established exogenously, based notably on measurements of the distances separating the variables at a given time period [CHA 08].

Some authors [HAI 09, LEG 93] have identified the dangers linked to a mechanical specification of the spatial weights matrix: a specification that does not take into consideration the context in which the data are collected. In their opinion the detection of a spatial autocorrelation schema between variables can simply come from a wrong specification of the statistical model and, as a result of the bad choice of data generating process (DGP) postulated by the researcher (Chapter 4). Obviously, the spatial autocorrelation schema can also come from a lack of information that generates a latent (or unobservable) residual that possesses a particular spatial structure [DUB 12]. The possibility of a wrong specification of the functional form leading to the detection of spatial autocorrelation is also proposed by McMillen [MCM 10]. The latter goes further by suggesting that the geographical coordinates of the variables can influence the studied behavior and therefore can be included in the list of explicative variables, an idea inspired from the geographical statistics.

Thus, one of the major challenges in spatial econometrics is being able to effectively express the possible structure of the spatial links between the variables. This formalization is then used to systematically detect the presence of spatial autocorrelation (Chapter 3) and to model the effects of spatial spillover or externalities effects via the use of an appropriate statistical model (Chapters 4 and 5).

The spatial weights matrix is traditionally designated by $\mathbf{W}$. A particular element of this matrix, w_{ij}, represents the intensity of the spatial proximity between two observations i and j. Just like the distance matrices, the spatial weights matrix is of dimension $(N \times N)$. For a set of N localized observations, the spatial weights matrix expresses, in an exogenous specification, the relations of spatial proximity between each of the observations.

The general elements of the matrix $\mathbf{W}$, $w_{ij} \ \forall \ i, j = 1, \ldots, N$, are said to be non-stochastic [6], non-negative and finite. Each of these elements coming from the individual elements of the distance matrix (equation [2.14]):

$$\mathbf{W} = \begin{pmatrix} 0 & w_{12} & \cdots & w_{1j} & \cdots & w_{1N} \\ w_{21} & 0 & \cdots & w_{2j} & \cdots & w_{2N} \\ \vdots & \vdots & \vdots & \vdots & \ddots & \vdots \\ w_{i1} & w_{i2} & \cdots & w_{ij} & \cdots & w_{iN} \\ \vdots & \vdots & \vdots & \vdots & \ddots & \vdots \\ w_{N1} & w_{N2} & \cdots & w_{Nj} & \cdots & 0 \end{pmatrix} \qquad [2.14]$$

There are several ways to transform the distances so as to express the spatial relations, or even the weights: w_{ij}. Without claiming to be fully exhaustive, here we present four categories in detail:

– relations based on connectivity;

– relations based on the inverse of the distance;

– relations based on the inverse exponential;

– Gaussian relations.

---

6 Meaning non-random.

2.4.1. *Connectivity relations*

A connectivity relation is defined by a dichotomization of the distance elements. For observation i, a particular element of the weights matrix, w_{ij} acquires a value of 1 when observation j is located at a distance equal or smaller than $\overline{d}$. If this not the case, the assigned value is then zero (equation [2.15]):[7]

$$w_{ij} = \begin{cases} 1 \text{ if } d_{ij} \leq \overline{d} \; \forall \, i, j = 1, \ldots, N \; ; \; i \neq j \\ 0 \text{ otherwise} \end{cases} \tag{2.15}$$

The connectivity relations thus identifies the observations that are within a given radius (Figure 2.3). The practical challenge is to identify the optimal length of the radius, which means determining the spatial relation that enables the capturing or expression of the spatial pattern in the best possible manner. It is important to mention that during the construction of the spatial weights, the researcher must be aware that all the observations must be connected to at least one other observation (see Figure 2.5)[8].

A variant of connectivity involves considering a radius that varies for each of the observations, $\overline{d}_{i(k)}$. This particular case corresponds to what is referred to in the literature as the nearest neighbors criterion. Thus, the distance for each of the observations can be adjusted so that each of the observations is connected to a given number of observations, and to k (equation [2.16]):

$$w_{ij} = \begin{cases} 1 \text{ if } d_{ij} \leq \overline{d}_{i(k)} \; \forall \, i, j = 1, \ldots, N \; ; \; i \neq j \\ 0 \text{ otherwise} \end{cases} \tag{2.16}$$

---

7 From hereon, we will no longer distinguish between d_{ij} and $d_{ij}^{\star}$. We will conserve the notation of d_{ij} to mark the distance between the observations (points).

8 This constraint is essential if we want to use the spatial weights matrix to estimate an autoregressive model from the method of maximum likelihood. However, it is not strictly necessary in the case where we are looking to calculate the spatial autocorrelation (global or local) of a given variable. We will return to the constraint of the rank of the matrix $\mathbf{W}$ in Chapter 4.

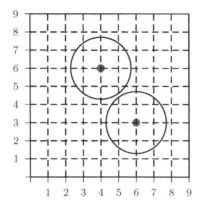

Figure 2.3. *Connectivity relation for two observations from a previously defined radius*

The nearest neighbors relations is therefore a variation on the connectivity relation previously represented schematically (Figure 2.4).

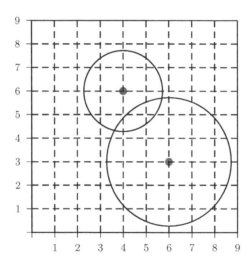

Figure 2.4. *Nearest-neighbors relations for two observations*

The main advantage of this approach lies without a doubt in the simplicity of the interpretation of the spatial relations. It is notably for this reason that the connectivity relation of the k nearest neighbors is often encountered in practice. It also facilitates the interpretation of the marginal effects since the products of the weights matrices then represents relations of neighbors, or of a higher order neighborhood. Moreover, this approach is largely the one retained in the analysis based on individuals represented by a geographical aggregation.

However, its main disadvantage is that it does not necessarily respect the intensity of the relations in function of the distance. By assuming that the radius of influences is fixed at 1 km, an observation j located 10 m from observation i receives an identical weight as another observation located at a kilometer from observation i. Limiting the connectivity relation to more restrained number, and constant number, of observations (k neighbors) makes this disadvantage less pronounced. Nevertheless, it is common practice to decrease the effect of a given observation in function of its relative distance. The other categories of spatial weights use this more explicitly. In this sense, the relation of nearest neighbors can also be twinned with the relations of inverse distance.

2.4.2. *Relations of inverse distance*

A simple transformation of the distance to express the proximity consists of taking the inverse, or even the inverse squared of the distance separating the observations. This transformation enables the construction of weights matrix that respects Tobler's law: the weights are greater (smaller) as the observations are spatially closer (further apart) (equation [2.17]):

$$w_{ij} = \begin{cases} 1/d_{ij}^{\gamma} = d_{ij}^{-\gamma} \ \forall \, i,j = 1,\dots,N \\ 0 \qquad\qquad\qquad \forall \, i = j \end{cases} \qquad [2.17]$$

It must be noted that the distance can be Euclidian, d_{ij}, or even Manhattan, $d_{ij}^{\star}$ (or any other more general metric).

Parameter γ allows us to penalize, more or less strongly, the spatial proximity in function of the distance. Two cases are usually encountered in practice: (1) the inverse of the distance ($\gamma = 1$); and (2) the inverse of the distance squared ($\gamma = 2$). Obviously the choice of penalty parameter has a direct influence on the weight, w_{ij}, given to the observations in function of their distance[9]. The inverse of the distance ($\gamma = 1$) places more weight on variables that are spatially closer (smaller distance) so as to leave less weight for variables that are further apart, while the inverse of the distance squared ($\gamma = 2$) places an even greater weight on close observations and leaves a marginal role for observations located further away (Figure 2.5).

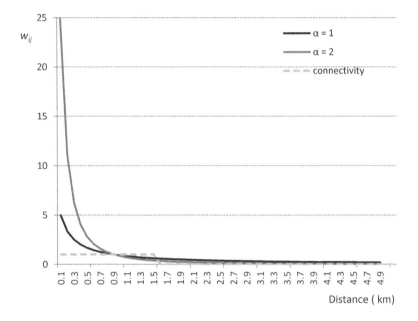

Figure 2.5. *Spatial representation for a set of observations*

9 Recent works suggest optimizing this parameter in the process of simultaneous iterations aiming to determine the optimal value of the γ parameter according to some statistical criteria such as Akaike information criteria or the Schwartz (Bayesian) information criteria. In such a case, the value of parameter γ is then continuous and non-discrete. We do not consider this extension in the book.

These relation are particularly interesting when the observations consist of unique space (or possess geographical coordinates that are different) and when the observations are sufficiently far apart so that there is problem of overly strong weights for the observations located at small distances.

It is also possible to limit the influence that certain observations can have on other observations. This limiting effect is usually introduced, as previously, by a threshold distance, $\overline{d}$, for which the observations located at a greater distance are assumed to have no spatial relations with a given observation. As a result, the proximity relation for the observations separated by a distance greater than the threshold $\overline{d}$ are equal to zero (equation [2.18]).

$$
w_{ij} = \begin{cases} d_{ij}^{-\gamma} & \text{if } d_{ij} \leq \overline{d} \; \forall \, i,j = 1, \ldots, N \\ 0 & \forall \, d_{ij} > \overline{d} \\ 0 & \forall \, i = j \end{cases} \qquad [2.18]
$$

This form of weight is particularly interesting when the number of observations is great. It avoids falling into the trap of the over-connectivity of the weights matrix [SMI 09]. Once again, the challenge consists of finding the optimal measurement of the critical distance, $\overline{d}$. A certain number of variations are proposed: maximize the value of the likelihood function, minimize the average of the errors squared, minimize the information criterion (Akaike or Schwartz) or even maximize the value of the autocorrelation calculated from Moran's I statistic (Chapter 3). In the latter case, it is possible to build a variogram of the statistic of spatial autocorrelation as a function of the critical distance chosen[10].

------

10 We will return to this more formally in Chapter 3.

2.4.3. *Relations based on the inverse (or negative) exponential*

Another possible transformation of the distance is the inverse of the exponential or the negative exponential of the distance (equation [2.19]).

$$w_{ij} = \frac{1}{e^{d_{ij}}} = e^{-d_{ij}} \quad \forall\, i \neq j \,;\, i,j = 1,\ldots,N \qquad [2.19]$$

As for the inverse distance transformation, this transformation puts more importance on spatially close observations and less importance on observations that are further apart. The advantage of this approach is that the weight converges quickly toward zero when the distance between the observations increases. When compared with relations based on the inverse of the distance (and the inverse of the distance squared), the transformation of the inverse of the exponential of the distance places less importance on very close observations. This transformation have the advantage of limiting the effect to the observations that are spatially close without introducing a threshold distance cut-off value that limit the relation to a small radius of influence (Figure 2.6).

Another advantage of measuring the inverse of the exponential of the distance relies on the fact that observations that share the same location (the same geographical coordinates) are considered as being part of the spatial relations. A distance of zero leads to a weight equal to 1 since the exponential of zero is 1. This transformation is therefore favored over the transformations that use the inverse of the distance (and the inverse of the distance squared) if some locations are repeated while consisting of different observations.

Finally, let us note that it is also possible to introduce a certain threshold distance, $\overline{d}$ for spatial relations based on the inverse exponential of the distance. In this case, the spatial relations over a distance more than $\overline{d}$ are assumed to be equal to zero (equation [2.20]):

$$w_{ij} = \begin{cases} e^{-d_{ij}} \,\forall\, d_{ij} \leq \overline{d} \,;\, i \neq j \,;\, i,j = 1,\ldots,N \\ 0 \qquad \forall\, d_{ij} > \overline{d} \\ 0 \qquad \forall\, i = j \end{cases} \qquad [2.20]$$

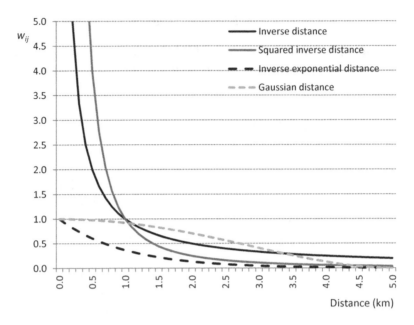

Figure 2.6. *Decrease in the distance relation according to the selected penalty parameter (γ)*

Once again, this transformation introduces a limit to the spatial connections. This constraint relate to the definition of a cut-off distance value can have a beneficial effect when the sample size is large since it fix many relations to zero. The transformation limit the ptoential problem of over-connectivity of the spatial weights matrix [SMI 09]. However, this problem is less pronounced than in the case of spatial relations based on the inverse of the distance or even the inverse of the distance squared since the weights converge rapidly and naturally toward zero for large distances.[11]

---

11 Readers can find in the Appendix, the Stata code for the simulation of geographical coordinates and the construction of the different weights matrices. The same procedure will also be used to generate data that will be used in the calculation of spatial autocorrelation indices (Chapter 3), in the estimation of autoregressive spatial models (Chapter 4) or even to estimate autoregressive spatio-temporal models (Chapter 5).

2.4.4. *Relations based on Gaussian transformation*

It is possible to consider an alternative to the transformations based only on the distance between observations. It is the Gaussian transformation, which is based on a threshold distance, usually written as $\bar{d}$ (equation [2.21]) [LES 03]:

$$
w_{ij} = \begin{cases} [1 - (d_{ij}/\bar{d})^2]^2 \; \forall \, d_{ij} \leq \bar{d} \; ; \; i \neq j \; ; \; i,j = 1, \ldots, N \\ 0 \qquad\qquad\qquad \forall \, d_{ij} > \bar{d} \\ 0 \qquad\qquad\qquad \forall \, i = j \end{cases} \qquad [2.21]
$$

This transformation has the advantage of explicitly taking into account a threshold distance, above which the spatial relation is assumed to be zero. This threshold distance can be the average distance, or even the maximal distance, meaning that all the observations are taken into consideration in the establishment of the spatial relations.

One of the disadvantages of this approach is that the proximity relation is not very sensitive to the starting distance, thus placing a near-identical weight on observations located in a larger radius. Nevertheless, the idea of the first law of geography is still followed: the observations that are closest together receive a greater weight than observations that are further apart (Figure 2.6).

Another disadvantage of this approach lies in the necessity of finding the optimal value of the threshold distance, $\bar{d}$ in a context where the decision processes accumulate as the analyses evolve. Therefore there exists a certain implication in the application of the usual hypotheses tests. We will come back to these in the section on local indices (Chapter 3). However, this disadvantage is also present for the other transformations that consider a critical (or limit) distance.

2.4.5. *The other spatial relation*

In an article on the construction of spatial weights matrices, Getis and Aldstadt [GET 10, GET 04] provide a list of the transformations possible for the construction of spatial relations between the entities. On top of the previous transformations, they suggest to consider the spatial relations based on tri-cube type decreasing functions [MCM 04] as well as recent developments linked to models of geographical weighted regressions (GWR) [FOR 02, FOR 98]. GWR, which is mainly dedicated to studying the spatial heterogeneity of the behaviors, is currently the object of a certain number of criticisms [JET 05, WHE 05], however, the transformations of the distance elements are still interesting.

2.4.6. *One choice in particular?*

Obviously, it would be possible to envisage a multitude of transformations of distances between the observations so as to capture, as best as possible, the spatial dependence relation between the observations, while ensuring that the first law of geography is respected. Griffith [GRI 96] suggests four empirical rules that should be respected in the development of weights matrices. Some of these rules are mainly applicable to geographical data bases where individual units are defined by geometrical shapes. Nevertheless, some rules are general enough to be applicable to the cases of individual spatial data. These rules are the following:

– it is always preferable to use a random specification rather than to ignore the possibility of spatial links between the observations (spatial independence);

– it is preferable to use a sample made up of a minimal number of observations, which is, in practice, set to 60;

– the simplest model is preferable to a more complex model (notably for that which deals with autoregressive orders), for parsimonious reasons;

– it is preferable to use a spatial weights matrix that is under-specified (with a threshold distance that is less than the optimal threshold distance) than a spatial weights matrix that is over-specified (with a threshold distance that is greater than the optimal threshold distance).

Once again, let us remind ourselves that there is no clear way in the literature to identify the optimal form of the weights matrix. Some research tries to find a way to estimate the weight of the matrix at the same time as the parameters of the autoregressive models [BHA 11] or even to estimate the penalty parameters imposed on the inverse distance relations. While the techniques do no evolve, it is important to remember that the specification retained must be able to capture the process of spatial dependence that we suspect to be behind the set of available data.

Recently, an article by Chen [CHE 13] suggests certain rules with regards to the choice of form of the spatial relations that dictate the construction of the weights. These rules can be summarized as the following:

– the relation based on the inverse of the distance is preferable if the scale of the geographical system being studied is large (*large scale complex*);

– the relation based on the inverse of the exponential of the distance is preferable if the scale of the geographical system being studied is small (*small scale* or *quasi-local correlation*);

– the relation based on connectivity should be retained if the suspected relations are local (*local action*).

In this sense, there is still a lot that is not clearly defined in the choice of matrices, despite the existence of simple rules.

2.4.7. *To start*

Finally, the elements w_{ij} that define the spatial weights matrix offer many possibilities on how to determine an intensity on the possible spatial relations seen in Chapter 1 and based on the distance relations. However, as previously mentioned, it is important to note that all of the observations must have at least one spatial relation with another observation, otherwise a line of the spatial weights matrix must only contain elements equal to 0 and, in this particular case, the estimation of spatial econometric models (Chapter 4) and spatio-temporal models (Chapter 5) becomes difficult, or even impossible.

Before going any further and formally presenting the statistical measurements of spatial autocorrelation (Chapter 3) as well as the autoregressive models (Chapters 4 and 5), it is important to present an extra step: the step of standardization of the weights matrix. This step is usually used before even carrying out the tests of detection of spatial autocorrelation, as well as the estimation of autoregressive spatial effects. In fact, standardization, as we will see, has certain positive effects despite the fact that its use causes a modification of the form of the spatial relations.

2.5. Standardization of the spatial weights matrix

The row-standardization of the spatial weights matrix consists of ensuring that the sum of the elements on a given line, expressing the spatial proximity between an observation i and the other observations, are equal to 1, or 100% (equations [2.22] and [2.23]). The relative spatial relations between observations are given by the proportions presented in line i of the row-standardized spatial weights matrix:

$$w_{ij}^{\star} = \frac{w_{ij}}{\sum_{j=1}^{N} w_{ij}} \qquad\qquad [2.22]$$

$$\sum_{j=1}^{N} w_{ij}^{\star} = 1 \qquad\qquad [2.23]$$

As mentioned, row-standardization is not a strictly necessary step. However, it does bring two interesting advantages. On the one hand, the calculation of spatially lagged variables (Chapters 3, 4 and 5) gives, in this case, for each observation i, the average values of a variable y in function of its neighborhood (we will come back to this later). On the other hand, row-standardized matrices help in the interpretation of the calculations of statistic tests, the interpretation of the coefficients and enables the comparison of the results obtained with different weight matrices. For these reasons, it is current practice to standardize the weights of the matrix.

From this construction results the creation of the row-standardized spatial weights matrix (equation [2.24]). The new resulting matrix is written $\mathbf{W}^\star$ as:

$$\mathbf{W}^\star = \begin{pmatrix} 0 & w_{12}^\star & w_{13}^\star & \cdots & w_{1N}^\star \\ w_{21}^\star & 0 & w_{23}^\star & \cdots & w_{2N}^\star \\ w_{31}^\star & w_{32}^\star & 0 & \cdots & w_{3N}^\star \\ \vdots & \vdots & \vdots & \ddots & \vdots \\ w_{N1}^\star & w_{N2}^\star & w_{N3}^\star & \cdots & 0 \end{pmatrix} \qquad [2.24]$$

Finally, using the standardized spatial weights matrices allow us to calculate spatial autocorrelation statistics (Chapter 3) as well as the estimation of spatial and spatio-temporal autoregressive models (Chapters 4 and 5).

However, before going any further, let us take a few lines to illustrate the theory put forward in this chapter.

2.6. Some examples

A small and simple example based on the spatial distribution of nine fictitious observations (Figure 2.7) illustrates the construction of spatial weights from the distances that separate all of the observations $i, j = 1, 2, 3, \ldots, 9$ (or of the points) and then allows us to carry out the standardization of this spatial weights matrix.

The location of the points is given by the geographical coordinates: (X_i, Y_i). This information is usually listed in a rectangular table, or a flat file. These files contain at least two different columns that allow us to characterize the east–west and north–south situations of the different observations. For the moment, we do not know the other characteristics of the points. Let us focus on the geographical coordinates of each observations, as listed in table on top of knowing the other characteristics unique to the different observations (Table 2.1).

From the different formulae used to calculate the distances (equation [2.6]) it is possible to calculate the distance matrices separating all of the observations, both for the Euclidian distance (Table 2.2) as for the Manhattan distance (Table 2.3). As an example, the distance that separates observation 1 ($i = 1$) from observation 2 ($j = 2$), assuming that each of the metrics represents one kilometer, is $\sqrt{(4-8)^2 + (1-7)^2} = \sqrt{4^2 + (-6)^2} = \sqrt{16+36} = 7,21$ kilometers in Euclidian distance and $|4-8| + |1-7| = 4+6 = 10$ kilometers using the Manhattan distance.

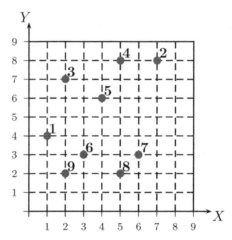

Figure 2.7. *Spatial representation of a regular grid with nine observations (fictitious case)*

Identification	Coordinate X	Coordinate Y
1	1	4
2	7	8
3	2	7
4	5	8
5	4	6
6	3	3
7	6	3
8	5	2
9	2	2

Table 2.1. *List of the observations and geographical coordinate of each*

Points	1	2	3	4	5	6	7	8	9
1	0	7.21	3.16	5.66	3.61	2.24	5.10	4.47	2.24
2	7.21	0	5.10	2.00	3.61	6.40	5.10	6.32	7.81
3	3.16	5.10	0	3.16	2.24	4.12	5.66	5.83	5.00
4	5.66	2.00	3.16	0	2.24	5.39	5.10	6.00	6.71
5	3.61	3.61	2.24	2.24	0	3.16	3.61	4.12	4.47
6	2.24	6.40	4.12	5.39	3.16	0	3.00	2.24	1.41
7	5.10	5.10	5.66	5.10	3.61	3.00	0	1.41	4.12
8	4.47	6.32	5.83	6.00	4.12	2.24	1.41	0	3.00
9	2.24	7.81	5.00	6.71	4.47	1.41	4.12	3.00	0

Table 2.2. *Matrix of Euclidian distances between the observations*

Points	1	2	3	4	5	6	7	8	9
1	0	10.0	4.0	8.0	5.0	3.0	6.0	6.0	3.0
2	10.0	0	6.0	2.0	5.0	9.0	6.0	8.0	11.0
3	4.0	6.0	0	4.0	3.0	5.0	8.0	8.0	5.0
4	8.0	2.0	4.0	0	3.0	7.0	6.0	6.0	9.0
5	5.0	5.0	3.0	3.0	0	4.0	5.0	5.0	6.0
6	3.0	9.0	5.0	7.0	4.0	0	3.0	3.0	2.0
7	6.0	6.0	8.0	6.0	5.0	3.0	0	2.0	5.0
8	6.0	8.0	8.0	6.0	5.0	3.0	2.0	0	3.0
9	3.0	11.0	5.0	9.0	6.0	2.0	5.0	3.0	0

Table 2.3. *Matrix of the Manhattan distances between the observations*

Since the distances are symmetrical $(d_{ij} = d_{ji})$, the transformations of the spatial relations between the observations are therefore the same $(w_{ij} = w_{ji})$.

Once the distances are established, it is possible to perform the transformations desired so as to obtain the spatial weights. For the present case, let us consider the inverse of the distance (equation [2.17]). The spatial weights matrix is therefore a simple transformation, term by term, of the distance matrix. For example, for the weight linking observation 1 ($i = 1$) to observation 2 ($j = 2$), the general element, w_{ij}, is set to $1/7.21 = 0.14$ (Table 2.4).

Points	1	2	3	4	5	6	7	8	9
1	0	0.139	0.316	0.177	0.277	0.447	0.196	0.224	0.447
2	0.139	0	0.196	0.500	0.277	0.156	0.196	0.158	0.128
3	0.316	0.196	0	0.316	0.447	0.243	0.177	0.171	0.200
4	0.177	0.500	0.316	0	0.447	0.186	0.196	0.167	0.149
5	0.277	0.277	0.447	0.447	0	0.316	0.277	0.243	0.224
6	0.447	0.156	0.243	0.186	0.316	0	0.333	0.447	0.707
7	0.196	0.196	0.177	0.196	0.277	0.333	0	0.707	0.243
8	0.224	0.158	0.171	0.167	0.243	0.447	0.707	0	0.333
9	0.447	0.128	0.200	0.149	0.224	0.707	0.243	0.333	0

Inverse of the Euclidian distance

Table 2.4. *Spatial weights matrix*

The final step is then to take each of the individual weights and to standardize them in line, which means dividing each of the elements of a line by the sum of the elements on the same line. For example, the standardized spatial relation between observation 1 and observation 2 is equal to $01.14/2.22 = 0.06$, while the standardized spatial relation between observation 2 and observation 1 is equal to $0.14/1.75 = 0.08$ (Table 2.5). As can be seen, the symmetry property no longer holds after this transformation ($w_{ij}^\star \neq w_{ji}^\star$).

Readers can easily repeat the calculations for all of the elements that have served in the construction of the previous tables. Another interesting exercise is to look back at the example for the two types of distance seen as well as for all of the transformations suggested[12].

---

12 A code allowing the simulation of one's own observation a grid of a previously determined size is provided in the Appendix 1, section A.1.

Points	1	2	3	4	5	6	7	8	9
1	0	0.062	0.142	0.080	0.125	0.201	0.088	0.101	0.201
2	0.079	0	0.112	0.286	0.158	0.089	0.112	0.090	0.073
3	0.153	0.095	0	0.153	0.216	0.117	0.086	0.083	0.097
4	0.083	0.234	0.148	0	0.209	0.087	0.092	0.078	0.070
5	0.111	0.111	0.178	0.178	0	0.126	0.111	0.097	0.089
6	0.158	0.055	0.086	0.065	0.112	0	0.118	0.158	0.249
7	0.084	0.084	0.076	0.084	0.119	0.143	0	0.304	0.104
8	0.091	0.065	0.070	0.068	0.099	0.183	0.289	0	0.136
9	0.184	0.053	0.082	0.061	0.092	0.291	0.100	0.137	0

Inverse of the Euclidian distance

Table 2.5. *Standardized spatial weights matrix*

2.7. Advantages/disadvantages of micro-data

The advantage of working with spatial microdata is that certain difficulties linked to data based on using aggregate spatial units to form geometrical figures are avoided. The use of the distance to define the spatial relations eliminates the problem of the absence of neighbors for some given units. This is usually the case when the geometrical figures, describing countries or regions, end up isolated, like islands[13]. An example of this is Japan considering data aggregated at the country's level.

The second advantage comes from the fact that spatial relation is based on a common and unique measurement: distance. It does not depend on the shape of a geometrical entity. Since the distances between the spatial units described by geometrical entities are usually defined from the center of the geometrical shape (the centroid), the distances can vary depending on the shape of the polygon considered. Thus the problem of topological invariance, raised by Cliff and Ord [CLI 81, CLI 73], cannot be applied in the case of spatial microdata.

---

13 In technical terms, a spatial weights matrix that is not of full rank can lead to several problems during the estimation of the parameters of autoregressive models (see notably [ANS 88] and [LES 09] on this subject).

Obviously, there are not only advantages associated with using spatial microdata. One of the disadvantages comes from the fact that certain observations can share a common location, and as a result, have the same geographical coordinates. We can think of businesses located in the same building. In this case, the use of the inverse of the distance (or the inverse of the distance squared) return a spatial relation set to 0. In this sense, for such data, it is necessary to introduce an additional constraint to the definition of the spatial relations (equation [2.25]):

$$
w_{ij} = \begin{cases} d_{ij}^{-\alpha} & \text{if } d_{ij} \leq \overline{d} \,\forall\, i,j = 1,\ldots,N \\ \kappa & \text{if } d_{ij} = 0 \,\forall\, i \neq j \\ 0 & \forall\, d_{ij} > \overline{d} \\ 0 & \forall\, i = j \end{cases} \qquad [2.25]
$$

where κ is a constant term (a scalar) that can, for example, be equal to the greatest value taken by the transformation of the distance (inverse).

As mentioned previously, this problem is not present when using the inverse of the exponential of the distance or even the Gaussian specification.

A second potential problem comes from the possible over-connectivity problem of the spatial weights matrix [SMI 09]. This problem is also linked to the fourth rule laid down by Griffith [GRI 96] and is particularly important when the database is voluminous in terms of the number of observations. This problem can lead to bias in the evaluation of the spatial autoregressive coefficients of the spatial models as well as leading to other substantial problems. The use of threshold distances helps eliminates this problem.

2.8. Conclusion

This chapter has taken time to formalize the spatial proximity relations that can exist between a set of spatialized observations and measured from coordinates their geographical coordinates, as defined by X and Y for each observation. The spatial proximity relations must reflect the premise of the first law of geography: all elements are linked between themselves in space, but the closest ones are more so. This postulation of the relations between the localized observations is the cornerstone of spatial econometrics.

The formalization of spatial proximity relations relies, in a first step, on the calculation of the distance separating the points. Obviously, there are several notions of distance: Euclidian, Manhattan, commuting time, social, organizational, etc. In the cases of Euclidian and Manhattan distances, the use of the properties of right-angle triangles has proved to be particularly interesting in this exercise of the determination of distances.

It is, in a second step, necessary to carry out a transformation on the distances if we wish to obtain spatial proximity relations that respect the first law of geography. Some mathematical transformations are applied to the distances. The resulting weights are then gathered in a table, of dimension $(N \times N)$, which constitutes the spatial weights matrix. We have also seen how certain constraints on the spatial proximity relations, notably through the introduction of threshold distances, or even the limitation of connectivity relations to some number of observations that are spatially close can limit the number of spatial relations connecting the observations. These constraints have the advantage of eliminating possible over-connectivity in the spatial weights matrices [SMI 09]. The condition of this limitation is that it then requires a justification to fix the critical distance or the number of nearest neighbors. This identification can then be carried out from a graphical analysis based on the variogram or be based on any other statistical criteria. In a sense, it is a practice similar to the one aiming to maximize likelihood or minimize the Akaike or Schwartz information criteria.

Once the spatial weights matrix built, we have shown how the weights could be transformed and standardized so as to facilitate interpretation of the statistics and the autoregressive coefficients. Standardization notably enables the comparison of the amplitude of the statistics that allow the detection of spatial autocorrelation (Chapter 3) as well as the comparison of the coefficients obtained in the autoregressive econometric models (Chapters 4 and 5).

Standardization of the spatial weights matrix causes a change in the spatial weights matrix so that the spatial variables calculated on this basis provide an average estimation of the variable in function of the defined neighborhood (when calculating a spatial lagged variable). This approach results in the elimination of the symmetry property of the spatial weights matrix, property that is nevertheless present for the non-standardized matrix, but not necessary in the calculation of the statistics and in the estimation of the models (Chapters 3, 4 and 5).

In the end, the reader will notice that it is essential to be transparent in the construction of the spatial weights matrix and to test different specifications and possibilities. Since spatial econometrics is based largely on the (exogenous) conception of this matrix, it is imperative to carry out some test verifying the robustness of the result in function of the type of matrix retained. A conclusion should not depend on the form of the matrix retained, but should be robust enough to be invariant (or vary little) in the face of specification changes of the matrix.

3

Spatial Autocorrelation

3.1. Introduction

After having defined how the observations can be linked between themselves in space, it becomes possible to propose a measurement that allows us to judge the form of the relation as well as the intensity of this relation for a given variable. This measurement of the spatial relation for a given variable is called spatial autocorrelation. It measures the direction of the linear association between the variables and the degree of intensity of the spatial pattern of a given variable with the same variable, but for a defined neighborhood.

The first statistical measurement proposed is still the most used today. It is Moran's I statistic [MOR 50, MOR 48]. Another measurement is the c statistic from Geary [GEA 54]. While both statistics measure more or less the same thing, they are based on different measurements of association between variables: Moran's I is based on the measurement of covariance, while the Geary's c is based on the gap between two measurements of the same variable.

The measurement of Moran's I can be seen as a spatial adaptation of the correlation coefficient: it measures the linear association between the value of a given variable, y_i, and the value of this same variable in the neighborhood, y_j. This is the main idea of the Moran diagram (we will return to this later).

In opposition to correlation, which measures the degree of linear association between two different variables, the term autocorrelation rather refers to the correlation of a variable with itself. Therefore, this concept considers the possibility of measuring the value of the variable considered for an established neighborhood. It is here that role of the spatial weights matrix is felt. An average value of the variable considered is defined in a given space: we then talk of a spatial lagged variable.

Moran's I statistic is robust in detecting the presence of a spatial pattern amongst a variable [ANS 95, GRI 12]. Moreover, its calculation is similar to the correlation coefficient. For these reasons, it is the most widely used statistic to detect the presence of a spatial pattern in the distribution of a variable.

According to Legendre [LEG 93], "spatial autocorrelation describes the average resemblance of the values of a series in relation to the values located" in the neighborhood. In other words, the value of a variable, in a given location, may be related to the values taken by this same variable in nearby areas. The phenomena located in a same area influence other phenomena located nearby, which in turn interact with other spatially close phenomena. All these interdependencies reveal a certain level of organization of the values of a variable in space.

The notion of spatial autocorrelation has its roots in the notion of homogeneity. Homogeneity refers to particular state of a geographical distribution for which the values of the variables resemble each other, present common characteristics, similarities of structure, function or distribution. This resemblance usually results from the process of construction or generation of data, themselves sculpted by historical events or modes that influence the realizations over a greater or smaller amount of time. The measurement of autocorrelation seeks to determine if there exists (or not) a form of (spatial) dependence between the realizations of a given variable in space.

Spatial autocorrelation can be identified when the values taken by a given variable is (linearly) relate, in part or totally, to the value taken by the same variable located nearby[1]. Obviously, the search for spatial association structures requires the definition of a reference situation in relation to which there can be an absence of spatial structure. This reference situation is there is an absence of spatial autocorrelation. It corresponds to the null hypothesis, H_0, and proposes an independence between the values of the statistical variable studied y_i and all other values of the variable expressed by the average value defined in the established neighborhood, y_j.

The null hypothesis of the absence of spatial correlation of a variable corresponds to a random spatial distribution of the values of the variable of interest. This distribution is largely comparable to a dispersion diagram in the bivariate case (Figure 3.1). It corresponds to the case where the values of the statistical variable studied, y, are drawn randomly in space. In this case, the probability of drawing a particular value is then independent of the value taken by the same variable nearby. This property can also be expressed in terms of randomization: the localization of the values of variable y can be modified[2] without changing the informational content of the data. In other words, randomly changing the values on the geographical coordinates does not have any influence or does not change the explicative power of a model[3]. Thus, in the absence of spatial autocorrelation, the data generating process (DGP) is completely independent of the location of the variables. This interpretation of the null hypothesis is the basic idea for the statistical tests based on permutation in spatial statistics (we will return to this later).

Obviously, a hypothesis test requires the specification of an alternative hypothesis allowing the comparison of two relative situations between themselves, so as to lean more toward one hypothesis or another. Two distinct situations are, in general, retained

---

1 There also exists a form of multivariate autocorrelation that measures the spatial interaction between two variables. We will not present this formally in this book.

2 By randomly modifying the geographical coordinates of the variables (or observations).

3 In other words, the data generating process (DGP), formally reviewed in Chapter 4, has no link to space location.

as the alternative hypothesis in the case of spatial autocorrelation. The two situations serve to determine the possible behavior hypotheses of the spatial distribution of the values of a variable in function of similar localization. Similar localization being defined by the relative distance separating two individual observations (points) in a two-dimensional schematic representation. This spatial relation is formally described by the spatial weights matrix (see Chapter 2).

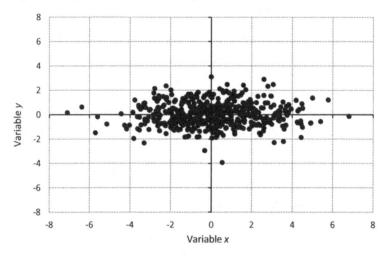

Figure 3.1. *Absence of correlation*

The first alternative is positive spatial autocorrelation. It corresponds to the case where low values of a given variable are statistically associated with other low values within a similar localization (and vice versa). In other words, a given variable y_i which presents a value under the mean is surrounded by other variables, y_j, that are also under the mean value. As we will see a little later, in this precise case, the Moran diagram is equivalent to a dispersion diagram between two variables for which the global linear trend is positive (Figure 3.2).

The second situation is where the spatial autocorrelation is negative. This situation corresponds to the case where the differences between the values of a given variable, y, namely y_i and y_j for two similar locations are significantly greater than the differences registered between two variables of random localization. In this situation, given variable, y_i, presents values under the mean value of y, while the values that surround it, y_j, present values that are over the mean value. Thus, high values are surrounded by low values and vice versa. Graphically, this situation is comparable to the case where the dispersion diagram for two given variables, x and y, shows a negative linear trend (Figure 3.3). In the spatial case, the dispersion diagram is constructed using the original variable, y_i, and its spatially lagged counterpart, y_j.

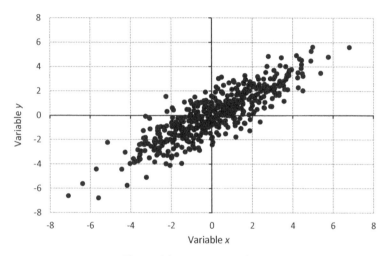

Figure 3.2. *Positive correlation*

The detection of spatial autocorrelation for a given variable is not necessarily a problem. After all, the only information that the statistics provide, is that a given variable is spatially structured. Why then place so much emphasis on this notion? The answer is simple and is linked to the three basic assumptions on the behavior of error terms of a regression model. Spatial autocorrelation is actually problematic when it is detected among residuals of a multiple linear model.

The violation of the assumption of independence among error terms may have two consequences: (1) it can introduce a bias into the estimated variance of parameters and, as a result, invalidate the interpretation of the common statistical tests (including F test and t

test); and/or (2) it introduces a bias into the estimation of the coefficients in (simple or multiple) linear regression [BIV 80, CLI 81]. Therefore, spatial autocorrelation statistics is not so much so as to measure the presence or the absence of geographical structures between the variables located in space. It is especially crucial in detecting autocorrelation between the error terms of a statistical model.

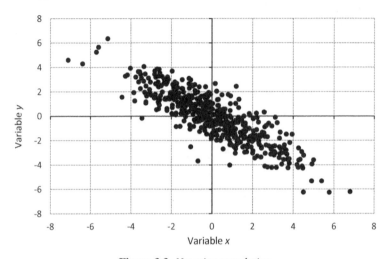

Figure 3.3. *Negative correlation*

LeGallo [LEG 02] explains that presence of spatial autocorrelation can come from two sources. The first source is related to the fact that spatial data is generated from processes that imply a relation between the location. The DGP is thus at the origin of a particular spatial pattern of interactions between the variables (we will return to this in Chapter 4). Thus, the absence of the consideration of this structure in the model means that this structure is found in the error term of the model: this explains the detection of the spatial pattern among the residuals. An eloquent example is certainly the development of the new residential neighborhoods. These often have similar architecture, share common infrastructure and uniform rules and so on.

The second source is, as already proposed by several researchers, linked to a wrong specification of the functional form or a wrong transformation of the analyzed variable (dependent and independent).

This wrong specification would lead to the generation of a form of spatial autocorrelation. This source of spatial autocorrelation is usually underlined in econometric analyses where a certain spatial structure is noted between the error terms of the estimated model[4]. Therefore, this latent spatial structure can be generated because some important spatial variables are not integrated into the model (omission of variables) or even because the operational form chosen by the researcher is not appropriate [MCM 10].

We must mention the fact that not noting any particular global pattern between the values of a given variable (global spatial autocorrelation) does not mean, in any case, that particular patterns cannot be found locally. We then talk of local spatial correlation.

In this chapter we will cover first of all Moran's I statistic, a statistic of global spatial autocorrelation associated with the quantitative variables. Section 3.3 introduces a local version of Moran's I index (I_i) that allows us to measure local spatial autocorrelation, a spatial descriptive approach that allows us to identify, *a priori*, certain particular patterns of the distribution of a spatially structured variable.

3.2. Statistics of global spatial autocorrelation

The statistics that measure spatial dependence come mainly from geography [CLI 73, CLI 81]. All of the measurements of spatial autocorrelation use the same process of construction. Each statistic of autocorrelation is constructed on the basis of a crossed product between a similarity index, generally written as c_{ij}, of the values taken by a variable of interest y and the values (on average) taken by the observations of the neighborhood. The neighborhood is, as seen

---

4 This behavior violates one of the assumptions on the behavior of the error terms which ensures that the estimators obtained by the ordinary least squares are still the best estimators that could be obtained under this linear specification. We discussed this briefly in Chapter 1, but we will come back to this a bit later, in Chapter 4.

previously, defined by the form of the spatial weights (or connectivity) matrix $\mathbf{W}$ defined exogenously by the researcher (Chapter 2)[5].

Formally, the statistics that allows the expression of the value of a variable taken in the neighborhood is defined by the product of a measurement allowing the establishment of the similarity, or dissimilarity, c_{ij}, between the values of y, and the indicator of the spatial connectivity between the variables, w_{ij} (equation [3.1]):

$$\Gamma = \sum_{i=1}^{N} \sum_{j=1}^{N} w_{ij} \times c_{ij} \qquad [3.1]$$

where w_{ij} is the element located on line i and column j of the spatial weights matrix $\mathbf{W}$. The measurement of similarity or dissimilarity, c_{ij}, usually allows us to gauge the gap between the values taken in the neighborhood, y_j and the value of the variable considered, y_i. The statistics of the products is then normalized by various multiplicative constants. Obviously, there are different measurements of similarity/dissimilarity between the values of variable y. The different measurements of detection are based on these differences of specification of the measurements used.

The Geary index [GEA 54] is built using the measurement of association (or aggregation). The similarity of the values of variable y is measured by the difference between two values at different locations, y_i and y_j, which are then elevated to the square, to avoid compensation between the comparable positive and negative values of amplitude (equation [3.2])[6]:

$$c_{ij} = (y_i - y_j)^2 \qquad [3.2]$$

---

5 It must be noted that the matrix can also represent a proximity that reflects something other than the geometrical distance [GET 91, HUB 76, MAN 67, UPT 85].

6 Geary's c index is presented in the Appendix, section A2.1, but is not discussed in depth.

Other measurements of similarity/dissimilarity are possible when generalizing the previous equation to introduce a value of power, p, rather than the square[7].

Moran's I statistic is based on a measurement of covariance type. The similarity between the values of variable y is defined as the product of the differences between each value of the variable for a given observation y_i and the average value taken by the same variable in the neighborhood y_j (equation [3.3]):

$$c_{ij} = (y_i - \overline{y})(y_j - \overline{y}) \hspace{3cm} [3.3]$$

In both cases, variable y_j is an expression allowing for the synthesis of the behavior of variable y for the neighborhood of observation i. This term is usually obtained through the multiplication of the spatial weights linking observation i to the other observations j to the values taken by variable y for observations j (equation [3.4]):

$$\underset{(N \times 1)}{[y_j]} = \sum_{j=1}^{N} w_{ij} \times y_j \hspace{3cm} [3.4]$$

We can simplify this expression by using the matrix notation. All of the spatial weights are gathered in the spatial weights matrix $\mathbf{W}$ of dimension $(N \times N)$ while the values of variable y appear in the vector y of dimension $(N \times 1)$. The result of the matrix product (equation [3.5]), $\mathbf{W}$y, is then of dimension $(N \times 1)$ and provides the average value taken by y in the neighborhood of i (y_j):

$$y_j = \mathbf{W}\mathbf{y} = \mathbf{W} \times \mathbf{y} \hspace{3cm} [3.5]$$

The Moran or Geary statistics give similar results with regard to the detection of the presence or absence of autocorrelation of a variable. The main difference between the two statistics relies on the definition of the

---

7 The general function of similarity is written as: $(y_i - y_j)^p$.

similarity index. On the one hand, the Geary index measures to see if the variability of the variable considered is significantly smaller than the one expected theoretically of a random spatial distribution. On the other hand, the Moran index looks to establish whether the resemblance of localized variable is significantly greater than the one observed in a random spatial distribution of the variable. In the next section, we present Moran's I index more formally.

3.2.1. *Moran's I statistic*

As previously mentioned, Moran's I statistic is the statistic of spatial autocorrelation that is the most well known and most often used in practice [CLI 81, UPT 85]. It can be applied to all the variables measuring continuous phenomena. Moran's I statistic of spatial autocorrelation takes the form described in equation [3.6]:

$$I = \frac{N}{\sum_{i=1}^{N} \sum_{j=1}^{N} w_{ij}} \frac{\sum_{i=1}^{N} \sum_{j=1}^{N} w_{ij}(y_i - \overline{y})(y_j - \overline{y})}{\sum_{i=1}^{N}(y_i - \overline{y})^2} \qquad [3.6]$$

where N represents the total number of observations, $\overline{y}$ is the arithmetic average of the values taken by the variable y over all of the observations (equation [3.7])[8] and w_{ij} is a particular element of the spatial weights matrix allowing us to link observation i with other observations j defining the neighborhood j:

$$\overline{y} = \frac{\sum_{i=1}^{N} y_i}{N} \qquad [3.7]$$

The sum of the spatial weights, $(\sum_{i=1}^{N} \sum_{j=1}^{N} w_{ij})$, is usually referred to with the term S_0. It expresses a scale factor[9] that allows us to compare the different statistics between them, and this no matter whether the

---

8 In matrix notation, the calculation of the arithmetic average is written: $\overline{y} = \frac{1}{N}\iota'\mathbf{y}$, where $\mathbf{y}$ is the vector of the variable of interest, of dimension $(N \times 1)$ and the vector ι is a vector of 1 dimension $(N \times 1)$.

9 In other words, any constant.

weights matrix is row-standardized or not. When the spatial weights matrix is row-standardized, this element is then simply equal to the size of the sample ($S_0 = N$) since the sum of the elements on each line is equal to 1, and that the sum of the elements over all the lines is, therefore, equal to N ($N \times 1 = N$). Thus, the use of a row-standardized spatial weights matrix implies that the first term on the right of equation [3.6] is equal to the unit, and that the calculation is simplified slightly.

It is also possible to rewrite Moran's I index in a more compact form. The use of matrix algebra allows us to greatly simplify the calculation, at least in its conception. By writing $\mathbf{y}^\star$ the vector of the demeaning variable y_i of dimension ($N \times 1$), meaning that $y_i^\star = y_i - \overline{y}$, and we can then write Moran's I index as the result of the matrix operation (see also [CHE 13]) (equation [3.8]):

$$I = \frac{N}{S_0} \frac{\mathbf{y}^{\star'} \mathbf{W} \mathbf{y}^\star}{\mathbf{y}^{\star'} \mathbf{y}^\star} \tag{3.8}$$

As previously seen, when the spatial weights matrix $\mathbf{W}$ is row-standardized, then the expression is simplified, since $N = S_0$. The calculation then becomes the essence of a simple matrix product (equation [3.9]):

$$I = \frac{\mathbf{y}^{\star'} \mathbf{W} \mathbf{y}^\star}{\mathbf{y}^{\star'} \mathbf{y}^\star} \tag{3.9}$$

The expectation and the variance of Moran's I statistic are calculated under two distinct assumptions [CLI 81]. The first assumption suggests that the values of the random variable y taken by observations i, y_i, come from the n independent draws of a normal population. The second hypothesis presumes that values y_i are the realizations of a random variable y whose distribution is unknown.

Under the normality assumption of the random variable y, the expectation and the variance of Moran's I statistic[10] are given, respectively, by the expressions [3.10] and [3.11]:

$$E(I) = -\frac{1}{N-1} \qquad [3.10]$$

$$Var(I) = \frac{N^2 S_1 - N S_2 + 3 S_0^2}{S_0^2 (N^2 - 1)} - \left(E(I)\right)^2 \qquad [3.11]$$

where N is the total number of observations and where the terms S_0, S_1, S_2, $w_{i\cdot}$, $w_{\cdot i}$ are defined, respectively, by the following identities (equations [3.12], [3.13], [3.14], [3.15] and [3.16]):

$$S_0 = \sum_{i=1}^{N} \sum_{j=1}^{N} w_{ij} \qquad [3.12]$$

$$S_1 = \frac{1}{2} \sum_{i=1}^{N} \sum_{j=1}^{N} \left(w_{ij} + w_{ji}\right)^2 \qquad [3.13]$$

$$S_2 = \sum_{i=1}^{N} \left(w_{i\cdot} + w_{\cdot i}\right)^2 \qquad [3.14]$$

$$w_{i\cdot} = \sum_{j=1}^{N} w_{ij} \qquad [3.15]$$

$$w_{\cdot i} = \sum_{j=1}^{N} w_{ji} \qquad [3.16]$$

---

10 Readers can note that the values of I depend in part on the spatial structure linking the observations, i.e. on the form of the spatial weights matrix $\mathbf{W}$ [BOO 00]. This is why it is important to be able to test different forms of spatial weights matrix to make sure that the calculation obtained does not depend on the choice of the spatial weights matrix.

It is also possible to simplify these calculations and express them in the form of a matrix calculation[11]. The expressions of the expectation and the variance remain the same (equations [3.10] and [3.11]), but the detail of the components that make up the variance is written more compactly (equations [3.17], [3.18] and [3.19]):

$$S_0 = \iota' \mathbf{W} \iota \qquad\qquad [3.17]$$

$$S_1 = \frac{1}{2} \iota' \big((\mathbf{W} + \mathbf{W}') \odot (\mathbf{W} + \mathbf{W}') \big) \iota \qquad\qquad [3.18]$$

$$S_2 = \iota \big((\mathbf{W} + \mathbf{W}') \odot (\mathbf{W} + \mathbf{W}') \big) \qquad\qquad [3.19]$$

The calculations can also be established from a linear regression model where the only explicative variable used is a constant. They can be extended to the case where several independent variables are also considered, which is the same as verifying the assumption of the spatial autocorrelation among the residuals (see [LEG 02]).

Since the Moran's I statistic is a statistic of spatial autocovariance, the expected values, in large samples, vary between -1 and +1[12]. Moreover, the domain of the values of the Moran's I statistic is identical to the domain of the classical correlation coefficient and its interpretation is similar.

In the absence of autocorrelation, the Moran's I statistic tends toward zero. A positive spatial autocorrelation corresponds to a value of the I statistic that is greater than zero and, inversely, a negative autocorrelation is represented by a value less than zero.

We must bear in mind that this test only has an asymptotic value. Its application requires a large number of observations. Once centered and reduced, Moran's I statistic follows (asymptotically) a standard normal

---

11 The details of the poofs are left and are not present here.

12 This is one of the advantages in comparison to the Geary's c statistic for which there is no domain of the bounded values.

distribution [CLI 73, SEN 76] and the I statistical test adopts the usual form (equation [3.20]):

$$t = \frac{I - E(I)}{\sqrt{Var(I)}} \qquad\qquad [3.20]$$

where $\sqrt{Var(I)}$ is the square root of the variance of I, and therefore its standard deviation.

The t statistic aiming to verify the null hypothesis of the absence of spatial autocorrelation of the variable y is distributed normally. The decision rule suggests rejecting the null hypothesis if the t statistic, as an absolute value, is greater than the critical value at a previously define threshold α[13]. The decision rules, as a function of the alternative hypothesis, suggest rejecting the null hypothesis in favor of the presence of negative spatial autocorrelation if the value of t is negative and far enough from zero (or lower than the critical value), while the spatial autocorrelation is positive if the value of t is positive and far enough from zero (or greater than the critical value).

Obviously, the validity of the test relies on the normality assumption under the null hypothesis of the absence of spatial autocorrelation [CLI 81]. It is possible for this normality assumption not to be respected. In this case, it is preferable to change the approach of the statistical test to opt for an approach by permutations.

3.2.2. Another way of testing significance

The significance test by permutations is based on a Monte Carlo type approach that consists of creating several samples (hundreds, even thousands) by randomly changing the values of the variable y over each of the points. In this case, the greater the number of permutations, the more the standard deviation of Moran's I statistic tends toward its

---

13 These values correspond to a value of 1.96 (for a significance threshold of 95% and a bilateral test), or even a value of 1.64 (for a significance threshold of 90% and a bilateral test).

theoretical value. In practice, it would seem that 1,000 permutations generate a reliable value for the evaluation of the standard deviation[14].

The approach by permutations relies on the null hypothesis, H_0, of the absence of spatial autocorrelation in the distribution of the variable of interest y for a given sample $\Theta = \{y_1, y_2, \ldots, y_N\}$. Under the null hypothesis, the order of the distribution of the values of the sample Θ is changeable, meaning that it has no importance. Thus, if the null hypothesis is true, then all the $N!$ possible permutations of the sample have an equal probability of appearing[15].

This intuition guides the elaboration of a hypothesis test based on the permutation of the realization in the sample on the locations. The permutation relies on the choice of a test statistic t (equation [3.20]), for which we start by calculating the observed values, written as t_{obs}, on the original non-permuted sample. Statistic t_{obs} is considered to be the reference value.

The idea is then to calculate the test statistic on the permuted samples, Y_π, obtained through a permutation π of the values of variable y on the geographical coordinates (or the points) inside the sample Θ. These values are written as t_π.

By considering the distribution of the values obtained t_π, for the test statistic t on these $N!$ possible permutations, we can construct the permutational distribution of t. The proportion of the values of t_π that are greater than or equal to t_{obs} in the permutational distribution is called the permutational p-value of the test statistic t written as p_π. The decision rule then consists of rejecting the null hypothesis of the absence of spatial autocorrelation when p_π is smaller or equal to the nominal level α *a priori* retained for this test.

The permutation test can be carried out for small sample sizes ($N \leq 10$). For bigger sizes, the numbering of all of the permutations

---

14 This rule is proposed in the user manual for the GeoDA software.

15 $N!$ is N factorial. This is the following product: $N \times (N - 1) \times (N - 2) \times (N - 3) \times \ldots \times 2 \times 1$.

becomes difficult. It is then preferable to opt for a randomization test [EDG 87]. This test consists of randomly carrying out a limited number of permutations instead of exhaustively carrying out the possible permutations. A high number of random permutations is nevertheless necessary to obtain a precise number of the value of the probability (the pseudo p-value). The decision rule in relation to the form of the null hypothesis remains comparable to the case presented for the tests of permutations.

The point of the tests of permutations and randomization is to avoid calling upon a particular hypothesis over the distribution of the statistic being tested. Thus, this situation avoids having to analytically develop the moments of the statistic under the assumption of the absence of autocorrelation.

3.2.3. *Advantages of Moran's I statistic in modeling*

Moran's I statistic allows us to detect spatial autocorrelation patterns for a given variable. As mentioned previously, the detection of a spatial pattern in the distribution of a variable is not necessarily a "problem". In fact, through simplification, only the assumption of the absence of any particular spatial schema in the error terms is of vital importance for the researcher carrying out a statistical analysis. The presence of a pattern of spatial autocorrelation in a variable y can easily be explained by a similar pattern in an independent (or explicative) variable x_k. In this case, the error term has no particular spatial structure. This is one of the three fundamental assumptions on the behavior of the error term, enabling optimal effectiveness of the estimators obtained by the method of ordinary least squares (OLS).

Thus, one of the utilities of the detection test of Moran's I over the residuals of the model is to ensure that the error terms are not autocorrelated spatially among themselves. When there is no significant correlation, it is not necessary to assume that the estimated variance is homogeneous and that the results obtained by the regression model, estimated by the OLS, are optimal. Thus, there must be an issue with the heteroskedasticity variance even if the error terms are not spatially correlated.

However, in the case where the statistical test allows us to detect the presence of a significant spatial pattern among the residuals of the model, this situation must then be corrected. The first option, which is the simplest, consists of introducing a new explanatory independent variable that contains a spatial dimension "comparable" to that of the information expressed through the error term. In other words, this spatial correlation can be caused by the omission of a significant variable in the model. Adding this variable should allow us to capture the residual spatial pattern. Once the variable is added to the model, it is enough to carry out the detection test of Moran's I to verify whether a significant spatial pattern persists in the error terms of the model. If the statistic is not significant, then the problem is resolved.

The problem often comes from the fact that the addition of such variables, with a "comparable" spatial dimension, is often difficult, or even impossible. Since the structure can be the result of an unobservable structure (or latent structure), the addition of this variable is not always possible. Thus, it is possible that the inclusion of all the independent (or explicative) variables available cause a resurgence of a spatial structure between the residuals of the model. In this case, it is then necessary to pass by an explicit model of the phenomenon of spatial autocorrelation. This is dealt with directly in the next chapter with the presentation of the different intuitions behind the choice of the autoregressive spatial models.

3.2.4. *Moran's I for determining the optimal form of* W

As mentioned in Chapter 2, part of the challenge of spatial analysis is the identification of the optimal form of the spatial weights matrix, W, that is likely to identify the spatial autocorrelation pattern detected among the residuals and present in the data. Boots and Dufournaud [BOO 94] suggest, in this case, testing a set of specifications and use the specification that maximizes the value of the spatial autocorrelation calculated.

A version of this proposition consists of introducing a threshold distance for the different cutoff distances considered (see Chapter 2) and opt for the spatial weights matrix that has the threshold distance meaning that the spatial autocorrelation calculated is maximal. This criterion is often known as the criterion based on the variogram.

The variogram consists of constructing a graph in two dimensions whose y-axis expresses Moran's I index calculated, while the x-axis expresses the selected threshold distances. It is then common practice to opt for the threshold distance that results in the highest value of the statistic. Visually, the variogram (Figure 3.4) allows us to easily identify this point, which corresponds to the summit of the distribution of the values of I calculated.

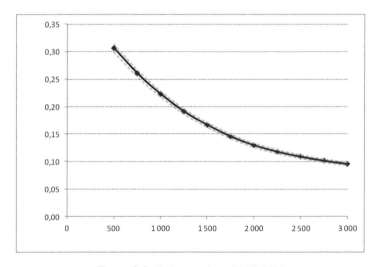

Figure 3.4. *Variogram from [DUB 13b]*

Let us note that despite the statistical criterion identified, nothing guarantees the researcher that the selected matrix is indeed the one that allows the best identification of the form of the spatial dependence. In fact, this criterion allows us to identify, from all of the previously selected options, the matrix that most intensely captures the relations of spatial dependence for the variable considered. This criterion assumes that to begin with the transformation retained for the distance is the one that is effectively the best, and the distance retained is also the appropriated metric. However, nothing ensure that the spatial autocorrelation pattern is not generated by something else than local specification. It could well be generated by something that does not rule out geographical logic. Moreover, it is not because a given variable exhibits a certain pattern that the error terms of a relation will display exactly the same pattern. Therefore, this exercise is interesting, but the researcher's judgment in the construction of the spatial weights matrix remains essential, as previously mentioned.

Finally, let us note that another way of determining the optimal form of the spatial weights matrix consists of selecting the matrix that maximizes other statistical criteria (Schwartz or Akaike information criteria) once the statistical model is estimated.

3.3. Local spatial autocorrelation

Moran's I index lets us get an idea of the intensity of the "average" spatial autocorrelation in a given sample for a given variable. When the global statistics indicated the presence of positive spatial autocorrelation, the measurement is assumed to be identical (on average) at every point of the space considered. These statistics do not allow us to evaluate the local structure of the spatial autocorrelation.

The advantages of global spatial autocorrelation are real when the spatial units (observations) being studied are homogeneous (or relatively homogeneous), which is rarely the case. Therefore, it is legitimate to ask whether there are local clusters of low or high values. These local concentrations can indicate particular behaviors or isolated spatial particularities.

Local spatial autocorrelation also allows us to identify the individual contributions to the global spatial autocorrelation. The objective of the statistics of local spatial autocorrelation is to verify whether, for a given observation i it is surrounded by similar values to its own value, y_i or if, on the contrary, it is surrounded by values of the variable y_j that are far from its own value. In other words, it is the value observed at i positively (similarity) or negatively associated (dissemblance) with the neighboring observations. If the global measurement masks atypical localizations or pockets of local non-stationarity, the local measurement allows us to clearly identify them.

Its main advantage is: local spatial autocorrelation is a descriptive method. It provides the identification of the patterns of concentration of high or low values. We talk of hot spots (high values) or cold spots low values).

Formally, the calculation of the indices of local spatial autocorrelation founded on the local statistic I_i relies on the decomposition of the index of global spatial autocorrelation allowing us to obtain the contribution of each of the pairs of observations in the calculation of the global Moran's I. Another version of the measurement of local spatial autocorrelation relies on the statistics $G_i(d)$ [GET 92, ORD 95]. These measurements are often used to study the significance of the spatial clusters around individual locations[16].

The advantage of the I_i statistic compared to the $G_i(d)$ statistic is that it also enables the identification of opposite local behavior, meaning locations that present high variables of the variable, while the value of the neighborhood for the same values is low. For this reason, and notably due to its tight link with the I statistic, the I_i statistic is the most often used.

All of the local statistics I_i are visually represented by the pairs of observations allowing the generation of the value of the statistic I. This is the representation of the Moran scatter plot [ANS 96, ANS 95]. It expresses in a two-dimensional Cartesian plane, the value of the centered-reduced variable $y_i^\star$ on the x-axis as a function of the value taken by the same variable in the neighborhood $y_j^\star$, or $\mathbf{W}y^\star$, on the y-axis. This representation in two dimensions enables the visualization

---

16 We will not formally present this index, but interested readers can consult the articles by Anselin [ANS 95], Ord and Getis [ORD 95] and Getis and Ord [GET 92].

of local spatial instability and the identification of the couples of the points whose values are judged to be extreme.

The construction of statistics of local autocorrelation follows the same process as the global autocorrelation statistic, taking inspiration in the crossed products statistics. We present, in the following few lines, the local indicators of spatial association of Moran's I. Unsurprisingly, the calculation of local indicators relies largely on the specification of the spatial weights matrix.

3.3.1. *The LISA indices*

Local indicators of spatial association (or autocorrelation) named after Anselin's proposition [ANS 95] and usually referred to by the acronym LISA are used to not only test the hypothesis of a random distribution of the y variable in space, but also verify the individual contribution of the couples of points (y_i, y_j) in the calculation of the global Moran's I statistic of spatial autocorrelation.

These measurements decompose the global index of spatial autocorrelation so as to identify the individual contribution of each observation (or location); they successively measure the spatial dependence/association between the value of the variable taken at this location and the values taken by the observations in its neighborhood. The local indices allow us to detect local patterns of spatial autocorrelation.

The two main properties that the local indices must have to be considered, according to Anselin [ANS 95], as LISA are:

– for a given spatial observation, LISA determines the area of a cluster formed by neighboring units, which possess values close to its own;

– the sum of the LISA provides an index proportional to the global indicator, or $\sum I_i = \gamma I$ with γ as the proportionality factor.

The next few lines are dedicated to the transposition of the calculation of Moran's I global indicator into local individual contributions (local indices and statistics) that allow us to formally deal with the null hypothesis of the absence of local spatial autocorrelation for a given variable y.

3.3.1.1. *The local version of Moran's I*

There are as many local indices as there are observations. The local Moran indices, written as I_i are defined by equation [3.21]:

$$I_i = (y_i - \overline{y}) \sum_{j=1}^{N} w_{ij}(y_j - \overline{y}) \quad \text{for } i \neq j \tag{3.21}$$

The formula corresponds to the product of the demeaning variable y of observation i and the value of the demeaning variable y taken in the neighborhood j. The demeaning is done by subtracting, for each of the observations, the arithmetic average calculated over the total number of observations (equation [3.7]).

It is also possible to summarize the formula of the LISA index in its matrix formulation. As previously seen, by writing $\mathbf{y}^\star$ as the vector of the demeaning variable y[17] of dimension $(N \times 1)$, we can write the local index of Moran's I, I_i as the following matrix expression (equation [3.22]):

$$I_i = \mathbf{y}^\star \odot \mathbf{W}\mathbf{y}^\star \tag{3.22}$$

where $\odot$ is the Hadamard product, and as previously seen, $\mathbf{W}$ is the row-standardized spatial weights matrix[18].

Under the null hypothesis, H_0, the expectation and the variance of the local Moran's I_i are defined, respectively, by equations [3.23] and [3.24]:

$$E(I_i) = \frac{-w_i}{(N-1)} \tag{3.23}$$

---

17 $y_i^\star = y_i - \overline{y}$.

18 For simplicity's sake, we use the notation $\mathbf{W}$ as if it were the row-standardized spatial weights matrix $\mathbf{W}^\star$ (see Chapter 2).

$$Var(I_i) = \frac{w_{i(2)}(N - b_2)}{(N - 1)} + \frac{2w_{i(kh)}(2b_2 - N)}{(N - 1)(N - 2)} - \frac{w_i^2}{(N - 1)^2} \qquad [3.24]$$

where the term w_i is defined by the sum of the elements w_{ij} for all of the j columns on line i (equation [3.25]):

$$w_i = \sum_{j=1}^{N} w_{ij} \qquad [3.25]$$

and where the quantities b_2, m_4, $w_{i(2)}$ and $w_{i(hk)}$ are, respectively, defined by equations [3.26], [3.27], [3.28], [3.29] and [3.30]:

$$b_2 = m_4/m_2^2 \qquad [3.26]$$

$$m_4 = \sum_{i=1}^{N} y_i^{\star 4}/N \qquad [3.27]$$

$$m_2 = \sum_{i=1}^{N} y_i^{\star 2}/N \qquad [3.28]$$

$$w_{i(2)} = \sum_{j=1,j\neq i}^{N} w_{ij}^2 \qquad [3.29]$$

$$w_{i(hk)} = \sum_{k\neq i}\sum_{h\neq i} w_{ik}w_{ih} \qquad [3.30]$$

Let us note that in the case where the spatial weights matrix is row-standardized, the term w_i takes a value of one and the expectation of all the local indices is equal to the expectation of the global index I (equations [3.6] or [3.8]).

As previously seen, these calculations can be written in matrix notation. In this case, the expectation vector of the local indices is given by equation [3.31], while the components that enable the calculation of the variances of the indices are given by equations [3.32], [3.33], [3.34] and [3.35]:

$$E(I_i) = \frac{-\mathbf{W}\iota}{N-1} \tag{3.31}$$

$$m_4 = \frac{1}{N}(\mathbf{y}^\star \odot \mathbf{y}^\star \odot \mathbf{y}^\star \odot \mathbf{y}^\star)\iota \tag{3.32}$$

$$m_2 = \frac{1}{N}(\mathbf{y}^\star \odot \mathbf{y}^\star)\iota \tag{3.33}$$

$$w_{i(2)} = (\mathbf{W} \odot \mathbf{W})\iota \tag{3.34}$$

$$w_{i(hk)} = \frac{1}{2}(\mathbf{W}\iota \odot \mathbf{W}\iota) - (\mathbf{W} \odot \mathbf{W})\iota \tag{3.35}$$

This matrix approach allows us to proceed, in a compact manner, with many calculations[19].

The expectation and the variance of the local indices can be used to obtain a test of significance for each of the local indices. However, seeing as it is very likely for the LISA statistics to be correlated among themselves, since they have neighboring observations in common, Anselin [ANS 95] proposes the approximation of the level of significance using a Bonferroni correction[20] which consists of penalizing the significance threshold as a function of the size of the sample. Thus, the significance threshold is no longer α, but rather α/N. Another way of simplifying the significance levels is to use the Sidak correction which defines the significance threshold as $1 - (1 - \alpha)^{1/N}$.

---

19 The detail of the calculations is available in the Appendix, section A2.3. Therefore, the reader can reuse the lines of code to apply them to any variable.

20 The Bonferroni method allows the correction of the significance threshold for multiple comparisons.

The calculation of these individual statistical tests must be interpreted with caution. Contrarily to the case of the global Moran's I, the distribution of the standardized statistic (equation [3.20]) is unknown[21]. Boots and Tiefelsdorf [BOO 00] notably demonstrate that the distribution of the centered statistic does not have normal distribution. Nevertheless, it can be interesting to carry out normal calculations of statistical tests, all the while remaining critical with regard to the use of these statistics.

Therefore, statistical inference requires the use of the permutations approach [ANS 95]. The critical probabilities are then based on pseudo-level of significance. These levels can be applied to all of the local spatial autocorrelation indices of Moran's I, I_i. The permutations process consists of generating a reference distribution from the data gathered, reflecting the null hypothesis of the absence of spatial autocorrelation or even a random distribution in space. For a given observation, the value of the variable, y_i, is considered stable and constant, while the values of the other observations, y_j, $j \neq i$ are permuted randomly over the total number of observations, and with the same probability. In the calculation algorithm, each of the values is drawn randomly and without replacement.

The significance test can be obtained by calculating the proportion p of the results of the permutations that provide values of I_i that are greater than, lesser than or equal to the observed value of I_i.

With regard to the interpretation of Moran's local index of spatial autocorrelation, a low value of p ($p < 0.10$) indicates that a given variable y_i is associated with relatively high values of variable y_j in the neighborhood. An overly high value of p ($p > 0.90$) indicates that y_i is associated with neighboring values, y_j that are relatively low. Therefore, the local Moran statistic, I_i, allows the identification of the zones for which the spatial clustering of values of the variable of interest y is significant, while adding that it is a cluster of similar values (LISA > 0) or dissimilar (LISA < 0).

---

21 Contrarily to the Getis and Ord statistics.

3.3.1.2. *The Moran scatter plot*

It is possible to graphically analyze local and global spatial association. The graphical analysis of the local indices relies on the Moran scatter plot [ANS 95], which represents the spatially lagged variable $\mathbf{W}\mathbf{y}^\star$ (or $y_j^\star$) on the y-axis as a function of the value of the original variable, $\mathbf{y}^\star$ (or $y_i^\star$), on the x-axis.

The scatter plot divides the space into four quadrants and the points belonging exclusively to one of these quadrants (Figure 3.5). Each of the quadrants corresponds to a type of particular local spatial association.

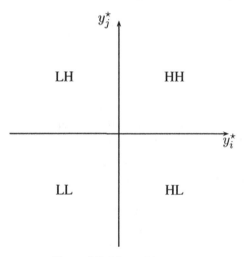

Figure 3.5. *Moran Diagram*

The *High-High* (HH) quadrant corresponds to the case where the value of the demeaning variable, $y^\star$, which is high[22], is surrounded by observations that also present a high value of variable $y_i^\star$. The *Low-Low* (LL) quadrant corresponds to the inverse of the case where low value of $y^\star$ is associated with low values of the same variable for the neighboring observations. When the majority of the points are within these two quadrants, we then say that there is global positive

---

22 High (respectively, low) means above (or below) the arithmetic average.

spatial autocorrelation, meaning that we note a spatial clustering of similar values ($y_i^\star$ and $y_j^\star$ are similar).

The *High-Low* (HL) quadrant corresponds to the case where a high value of the variable $y^\star$ is associated with low values of the neighboring variables, while the *Low-High* (LH) quadrant corresponds to the inverse situation: a low value of the variable $y^\star$ is associated with a high value of the neigboring values. When the majority of the points pass through the HL or LH quadrants, we note a global negative spatial autocorrelation schema.

In the case of positive spatial autocorrelation, the observations present in the HL and LH quadrants mark atypical localizations. The observations located in the HL quadrant are usually designated as *diamonds in the rough*. Inversely, the observations located in the LH quadrant are usually designated as *black sheep*.

3.3.1.3. *Local I_i and global Moran's I*

There is a tight relation between the I_i indices and the I index. Formally, the estimation of the parameter of the slope from the points in the Moran diagram allows us to directly obtain the value of the I statistic when the spatial weights matrix is standardized in lines.

The relations between the global and local Moran statistics can be obtained by carrying out the sum of the local indices (equation [3.36]). The global index is proportional to the sum of the local Moran indices (equation [3.36]):

$$I = \frac{\sum\limits_{i=1}^{N} I_i}{\gamma} \qquad [3.36]$$

where the sum of the local indices and the proportionality factor γ are given, respectively, by the equations [3.37] and [3.38]:

$$\sum_{i=1}^{N} I_i = \sum_{i=1}^{N} (y_i - \overline{y}) \sum_{j=1}^{N} w_{ij}(y_j - \overline{y}) \qquad [3.37]$$

$$\gamma = S_0 \frac{\sum_{i=1}^{N} (y_i - \bar{y})^2}{N} \qquad [3.38]$$

where, once again, S_0 is equal to N when the spatial weights matrix is row-standardized.

It is also possible to transpose these equivalences into matrix products (equations [3.40] and [3.41]):

$$I = \iota'[\mathbf{y}^* \odot \mathbf{W}\mathbf{y}^*]/\gamma \qquad [3.39]$$

$$I = \frac{\iota I_i}{\gamma} = \frac{\mathbf{y}^{\star'}\mathbf{W}\mathbf{y}^{\star}}{\gamma} \qquad [3.40]$$

$$\gamma = \frac{S_0}{N}(\mathbf{y}^{\star'}\mathbf{y}^{\star}) \qquad [3.41]$$

The reader will note that the sum of the local indicators corresponds to the numerator of the global Moran's I index (equation [3.6] and [3.8]). Thus, the sum of the local indicators is proportional to the global indicator. This proportion is given by the numerator of the global index (equation [3.38]). Therefore, in other words, there is the following mathematical relation between the global Moran's I index and the local Moran's I_i index (equation [3.42]):

$$I = \frac{\iota' I_i}{\gamma} \qquad [3.42]$$

Therefore, exposed differently, the global Moran's I index corresponds to the weighted average of the local Moran's I_i indices.

3.4. Some numerical examples of the detection tests

Once the statistics are formally presented theoretically, it is interesting to see how, definitively, these calculations can be applied. In this section, we present a numerical example in line with the presentation based on the fictive points taken from Chapter 2. The

Moran's I statistics and the statistics of the LISA I_i are formally presented from the fictitious example presented in the previous chapter.

On going back to the spatial distribution of the observations of Figure 2.7 and assuming that we observe the values of a random variable y_i (Table 3.1), for example the number of crimes per location, the number of employees in a firm, or even the price of property per square meter (in hundreds of dollars), we can then formalize the calculation of the statistics presented in the chapter.

Observation	Coordinate X	Coordinate Y	Value of y
1	1	4	7
2	7	8	15
3	2	7	11
4	5	8	13
5	4	6	12
6	3	3	8
7	6	3	10
8	5	2	9
9	2	2	7

Table 3.1. *List of the observations, geographical coordinates of each and observed values of y_i*

From the spatial weights matrices calculated previously (Chapter 2), we can calculate the I_i indices and global I index. Before even starting with the calculations, it is important to create the new standardized variable, written as $y_i^\star$, which is obtained by subtracting the demeaned $\bar{y}$ from the original variable y_i. The average of y is provided simply by adding all of the values and dividing by the number of observations:

$$\bar{y} = \frac{\sum\limits_{i=1}^{9} y_i}{9} = \frac{(7+15+11+13+12+8+10+9+7)}{9} = 10.22$$

With the arithmetical average in hand, it is now easy to create the new demeaned variable (first column of Table 3.2).

From the specification based on the inverse of the distance and the standardized spatial weights matrix (see the example of Chapter 2), it is possible to calculate the value of the neighborhood variable, $y_j^\star$, for each of the observations. The calculation simply corresponds to the product of the elements of the standardized spatial weights matrix, $w_{ij}^\star$ to the values taken by variable y in the neighborhood. For example, for the first observation, the value of $y_j^\star$ is given by:

$$\sum_{i=1}^{N} w_{1j} y_j^\star = (15 \times 0.06) + (11 \times 0.14) + (13 \times 0.08) + (12 \times 0.12)$$

$$+(8 \times 0.20) + (10 \times 0.09) + (9 \times 0.10) + (7 \times 0.20) = 9.836$$

Therefore, we can obtain all of the values for variable y_j (column two of Table 3.2).

Next, it is necessary to demean these variables by subtracting the average, $y_j^\star = y_j - \overline{y}$. Therefore, in the case of the first observation, the value of the new variable is given by:

$$y_1^\star = (9.836 - 10.222) = -0.386$$

and so on and so forth for all of the other observations (column three of Table 3.2).

Finally, the product of the elements of the first column with the elements of the third column allows us to directly obtain the local indices of spatial autocorrelation I_i (column four of Table 3.2). The points can also be carried onto a Cartesian plane in two dimensions in which the values of column three are carried onto the y-axis and the values of column one are carried onto the x-axis. This figure corresponds exactly to the Moran scatter plot (Figure 3.6).

The global I index of spatial autocorrelation can then be obtained from relation [3.42] or even by calculating the coefficient of the slope corresponding to the regression of the values of the variables in the neighborhood $y_j^\star$ on the values of the original variables $y_i^\star$. The results are identical[23].

$y_i^\star$	y_j	$y_j^\star$	I_i
-3.222	9.836	-0.386	1.2451
4.778	10.560	0.338	1.6135
0.778	10.299	0.077	0.0599
2.778	11.027	0.805	2.2349
1.778	10.318	0.096	0.1702
-2.222	9.401	-0.821	1.8240
-0.222	9.833	-0.390	0.0866
-1.222	9.748	-0.475	0.5799
-3.222	9.443	-0.779	2.5116

Note: $y_i^\star = y_i - \overline{y}$

$$y_j = \sum_{j=1}^{N} w_{ij} y_j$$

$$y_j^\star = y_j - \overline{y}$$

Table 3.2. *Synthesis of the calculations carried out*

3.5. Conclusion

In summary, the third chapter presents the methods of exploratory spatial data analysis (ESDA). This step of the description of data is usually the first step when a researcher decides to conduct an analysis of spatialized data. Once again, the reader will notice the dominating role of the spatial weights matrix in the calculations to be carried out. It goes without saying that a different structure of the matrix can lead to different results. This is why it is important to carry out several tests and calculations by varying the definition of the spatial weights matrix

---

23 The reader is encouraged to do the proof of the calculation by determining beforehand the value of $\sum_{i=1}^{N} (y_i - \overline{y})^2$. Moreover, the reader can redo this exercise for the other forms of the matrix and determine the value of the local indices of spatial autocorrelation and thus verify the variations in the calculations in function of the specification retained.

so that the results obtained are not simply linked to the chance of the choice of matrix, but rather a robust conclusion.

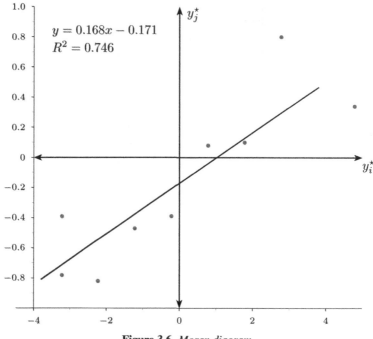

Figure 3.6. *Moran diagram*

Moreover, we have seen how the descriptive spatial statistics can be useful to find and determine an optimal form of the spatial weights matrix starting from the analysis based on the creation of a variogram. These analyses can also be used in the case where the data are not strictly spatial, but also include a temporal dimension (Chapter 5).

Descriptive spatial analysis also has another interesting use: to reveal certain information on behaviors linked to a variable of interest. Notably, it allows us to identify spatial variables that are likely to be linked together by their spatial behavior. Thus, the tests for the detection of spatial autocorrelation among residuals of a regression model can lead to the identification of a spatial variable that is likely to capture the spatial pattern not otherwise explained. The identification of this variable (assuming that it is measurable and available) could thus allow us to deal with the problem of spatial autocorrelation among residuals and avoid using spatial autoregressive models.

Therefore, this step is a precursor in the estimation of statistical models, strictly speaking, which we will see soon in Chapter 4. Autoregressive spatial models are of particular interest in testing certain theories, but equally in making sure that the behaviors of the error terms of the regression model respect the basic assumptions made previously (Chapter 1). Thus, descriptive spatial analysis not only serves in identifying spatial patterns in certain variables, it also serves in identifying the presence of such patterns among residuals of a given statistical (linear) model. This step proves to be crucial before calling upon particular spatial autoregressive models.

The construction of indices is relatively simple: a previously established recipe needs to be followed. There is no need to use any type of software, or make any estimation. In fact, the reader can easily conduct the exercise from any software that is able to carry out basic mathematical operations, such as Excel[24]. We leave it up to the reader to redo the calculations presented as well as pushing the exercise further by carrying out the calculations for other forms of matrices developed in the previous chapter.

Finally, we have taken the liberty of not presenting certain local spatial autocorrelation indices so as to stay with the most commonly used measurement, and probably the most flexible[25]. Readers interested in taking the use of descriptive spatial statistics further to other metrics can easily make the transition from the material presented in this chapter. The pieces of software behind the construction and the calculation of an index are relatively similar: once the mechanics of an index are mastered, it becomes relatively easy to transpose this approach to other existing measurements of statistics.

---

24 We propose, in the Appendix, section A2.3, the implementation of the matrix calculation from the Stata software to generate the local and global statistics of spatial autocorrelation.

25 Interested readers can find in the Appendix, section A2.1 the detail of the calculations Geary's c index.

4

Spatial Econometric Models

4.1. Introduction

In the previous chapters we discussed the construction of spatial weights matrices that allow us to express the spatial relations between the observations with respect to the first law of geography (Chapter 2). These matrices were then mobilized in order to calculate the statistics for detecting the presence of spatial association patterns and for measuring the level of spatial association for a given variable (Chapter 3).

We also found that the overall spatial autocorrelation can be separated into components for expressing the contribution of each observation in the composition (Chapter 3). Finally, we have shown the relationship between the global and local spatial autocorrelation statistics.

As mentioned, the spatial autocorrelation is not itself a problem [LEG 93]. It only underlines a spatial pattern in the distribution of a variable. A spatial pattern indicates that a distribution of a variable is not random but rather spatially structured. Spatial autocorrelation is a real problem for a researcher if detected among residuals (or error terms) in a regression model. In this case the assumption of independence among the error terms no longer holds and the impact on the estimators of the parameters β and the variance of the parameters β

can be various: imprecision of the estimated variances, which invalidate significance tests[1] and introduction of a bias on the estimated coefficients [LEG 02]. It is here that the spatial econometric models are used to correct for such problems. They allow spatial autocorrelation integration and thus ensure the validity of the obtained estimators (β and σ).

In the recent years, spatial econometric methods have been developed and are now mobilized in many areas [ARB 11]. The spatial econometric models take into consideration the spatial dimension of the data generating process (DGP) by incorporating them into the functional form. Spatial models give the possibility to model the spatial interaction phenomena in different ways. Models are now being developed to take into account the nature of spatial data, such as panel data or qualitative data[2]. In this chapter we focus on spatial econometric models related to cross-sectional data for continuous dependent variables.

This chapter provides an introduction to the consideration of the phenomenon of spatial autocorrelation among residuals of linear statistical models. The focus is on the intuition of the DGP behind each type of spatial autoregressive specification. It is essential to correct the problem of spatial autocorrelation among residuals; it is also very important to examine the advantages and disadvantages of each DGP in order to solve the problem. The models do not necessarily give the same results and may affect the calculation of the marginal, meaning how much and how the dependent variable changes according to a change in the independent, or explanatory variables. In this sense the researcher should not just opt for a simple model to correct for the presence of a correlation among the error terms but should also take into consideration the DGP in line with the assumptions we wish to test and its possible impact on the interpretation of the results.

---

1 Since the tests are based on variance estimation.

2 There is also a set of models developing these possibilities for models with dummy variables (discrete choice) or models with count data. However, we do not formally discuss these models in this book.

The chapter is divided into six sections. Section 4.2 presents the usual multiple linear statistical model in matrix notations. This enables a more compact presentation and simplifies the presentation of the spatial DGP. The linear model is then extended to autoregressive models (temporal and spatial). We think that it may be intuitive to address the spatial autoregressive modeling by drawing parallels with the temporal approaches since they are relatively well documented and long recognized, compared to the spatial approach (Chapter 1). Particular attention is paid to the intuition behind the autoregressive model choices. We do not formally present the construction of maximum likelihood (ML) estimators[3]; we choose an intuitive approach for explaining why the researcher should opt for a particular model type rather than an other. Afterward we present a series of formal statistical tests that allows us to discriminate between the different autoregressive specifications. The researcher should then be able to make an informed choice when using spatially selected autoregressive models in empirical analysis.

4.2. Linear regression models

As we mentioned in the introduction to Chapter 1 (section 1.1), a multiple linear regression model allows us to evaluate the effect of an independent variable x_k on the behavior of the dependent variable y considering an absence of variation of the other independent variables (*cetris paribus*). This analysis (equation [4.1]) is similar to partial correlation analysis and allows us to isolate the effect of certain variables of interest at given circumstances:

$$y = \alpha + \beta_1 x_1 + \beta_2 x_2 + \cdots + \beta_K x_K + \epsilon \qquad [4.1]$$

We talk about linear regression when the equation is linear in its parameters, this means in the coefficients β_k. In general, a change in a given independent variable k, denoted by x_k allows to retrieve its

---

3 More information can be found in the Appendix, section A3.3, including the details related to the likelihood function and its maximization.

marginal effect on the behavior of the dependent variable. This marginal effect is simply equal to the parameter β_k (equation [4.2]).

$$\frac{\partial y}{\partial x_k} = \beta_k \qquad [4.2]$$

This parameter is also used in calculating the elasticity of the variable y compared to variable x_k (equation [4.3]).

$$\varepsilon = \lim_{\Delta x \to 0} \frac{\Delta y}{\Delta x} \frac{x}{y} = \frac{\partial y}{\partial x} \frac{x}{y} \qquad [4.3]$$

Of course, nothing prevents the researcher from introducing some effects of nonlinearity by carrying out transformations over the variables y and x_k, such as quadratic transformation or some cross-product of the independent variables. Logarithmic transformations also allow for the introduction of some form of nonlinearity in the relationship between the variables.

The transformation of both dependent and independent variables affects the functional form of the relationship. There are several functional forms; all based on relation specification that remains linear in the parameters [BOX 64, HAL 81]. Of course, the functional form is not necessarily known with certainty in empirical analysis. The functional form must be based on theoretical considerations and a set of statistical tests identifying the possible omission of quadratic and nonlinear effects.

In addition to allowing consideration of a form of nonlinearity in the relationship, the functional form is a source of reflection related to the data generating process. The postulated relation (equation [4.1]) expresses how the researcher conceives the shape of the link between the independent variables and the dependent variable. This vision affects the calculations related to the effect on the dependent variable, arising from changes in one of the independent variables. For example, for a linear relationship in the parameters, we consider two types of relations: a first relation in which variable x is related to variable y

(equation [4.4]) and a second relation in which the logarithm of variable x is related to variable y (equation [4.5]):

$$y = \alpha + \beta x + \epsilon \qquad\qquad [4.4]$$

$$y = \alpha + \beta \log(x) + \epsilon \qquad\qquad [4.5]$$

By applying in both cases $\alpha = 1$ and $\beta = 1$, it is easy to see that the value of y predicted by both models is different for the same x value. If $x = 1$, then we have $y = 2$ for [4.4] and $y = 1$ for equation [4.5][4]. Thus, although the relation pattern is always linear in the parameters, the transformations of some variables may induce different effects on the dependent variables. In other words, the effect of the independent variables on the dependent variable is largely dependent on the chosen relation. Hence, the importance of identifying the best possible functional relation pattern [DUB 11]. The choice of the functional form largely affects the conclusions that can be obtained using statistical modeling.

In practice, the most used functional forms are the log-log or semi-log models. In the first case, both the independent and dependent variables are expressed using a logarithmic transformation. In the second case, only the dependent variable is expressed using logarithmic transformation[5].

There exist other approaches for testing the linearity assumption of a relationship and for reducing the importance of the functional form. These other approaches, termed non-parametric and/or semi-parametric, are more flexible in the study of behavior. However,

---

4 The reader can construct a scatter plot using the different x values (on the x axis) and reconstruct y values (on the y axis) depending on the model (equations [4.4] and [4.5]) for visualizing the difference in the relation pattern between the two variables.

5 In this particular case, the dependent variable distribution is referred to as a log-normal, which means that the logarithm of the dependent variable follows a normal distribution. This is the case for several variables, including the wages or the sales price of a property.

the interpretation of these models is more difficult, which explains why the linear regression approach largely dominates in empirical analysis.

Ultimately the goal of a multiple linear regressions model is to quantify the relationships between the independent variables to the dependent variables. To do this, it is necessary to find estimators of the coefficients[6] $\alpha, \beta_1, \ldots, \beta_K$. The coefficient estimation is carried out based on the observed values of a set of variables $(y_i, x_{i1}, x_{i2}, \ldots, x_{iK})$ for each statistical unit[7] $i = 1, \ldots, N$. The researcher thus has a table of data showing the different variable values for each observation. The characterization of a statistical unit (or observation) is given in detail in line i of the table.

y	x_1	x_2	$\cdots$	x_K
y_1	x_{11}	x_{12}	$\cdots$	x_{1K}
y_2	x_{21}	x_{22}	$\cdots$	x_{2K}
$\vdots$	$\vdots$	$\vdots$	$\vdots$	$\vdots$
y_i	x_{i1}	x_{i2}	$\cdots$	x_{iK}
$\vdots$	$\vdots$	$\vdots$	$\vdots$	$\vdots$
y_N	x_{N1}	x_{N2}	$\cdots$	x_{NK}

Table 4.1. *Data table*

The available data are usually derived from a representative sample group assumed to represent the population of interest[8]. This population is governed by a law that will be best understood using the sample at our disposal.

---

6 Also referred to as parameters.

7 Usually the observations are: individuals, households, firms, countries, regions, etc.

8 It can obviously be a sub-sample of the total population that is different from the general population, e.g. cancer patients. However, in this particular case, it must be noted that the results obtained using statistical analysis cannot be generalized for the general population. The findings may apply, if the population subset is still representative, like of the cancer population.

4.2.1. *The different multiple linear regression model types*

For observation i, the researcher assumes that the relationship between variable y and variables $x_1, x_2, \ldots, x_K$ is linear (equation [4.6]) and it is this relation that has to be verified for each member of the sample population. The multiple linear model assumes that it is possible to identify critical behavior of the dependent variable y_i based on the set of characteristics of the independent variable, x_{ik}:

$$y_i = \alpha + \beta_1 x_{i1} + \beta_2 x_{i2} + \cdots + \beta_K x_{iK} + \epsilon_i \quad \forall\, i = 1, \ldots, N \quad [4.6]$$

The last equation is the representation of the DGP: we assume a particular relation among the x_k variables and the y variable.

It is conventional to write the linear regression in the form of a matrix for simplicity and to show the expression of the statistical model in more compact form. The matrix form expresses the individual linear relations (equation [4.6]) for all the set of observations. The system of equations used for the all observations then provides the expression of the linear regression model (equation [4.7]):

$$\begin{cases} y_1 = \alpha + \beta_1 x_{11} + \beta_2 x_{12} + \cdots + \beta_K x_{1K} + \epsilon_1 \\[4pt] y_2 = \alpha + \beta_1 x_{21} + \beta_2 x_{22} + \cdots + \beta_K x_{2K} + \epsilon_2 \\[4pt] \quad\vdots \\[4pt] y_i = \alpha + \beta_1 x_{i1} + \beta_2 x_{i2} + \cdots + \beta_K x_{iK} + \epsilon_i \\[4pt] \quad\vdots \\[4pt] y_N = \alpha + \beta_1 x_{N1} + \beta_2 x_{N2} + \cdots + \beta_K x_{NK} + \epsilon_N \end{cases} \quad [4.7]$$

Pooling the individual equations, we have a system of N equations with $(K + 1)$ unknown parameters (to be estimated). Obviously writing this takes up quite a lot of space, even more space than simply the number of observations, N. For this reason, the matrix notation is used. It allows to simplify how the used system of equations is written by integrating into the vectors and matrices each variable of the model and distinguishing parameters that are assumed to be identical for all observations (equation [4.8])[9]:

$$\begin{pmatrix} y_1 \\ y_2 \\ \vdots \\ y_i \\ \vdots \\ y_N \end{pmatrix} = \alpha \begin{pmatrix} 1 \\ 1 \\ \vdots \\ 1 \\ \vdots \\ 1 \end{pmatrix} + \beta_1 \begin{pmatrix} x_{11} \\ x_{21} \\ \vdots \\ x_{i1} \\ \vdots \\ x_{N1} \end{pmatrix} + \cdots + \beta_K \begin{pmatrix} x_{1K} \\ x_{2K} \\ \vdots \\ x_{iK} \\ \vdots \\ x_{NK} \end{pmatrix} + \begin{pmatrix} \epsilon_1 \\ \epsilon_2 \\ \vdots \\ \epsilon_i \\ \vdots \\ \epsilon_N \end{pmatrix} \quad [4.8]$$

Thus, the linear regression model can be written as a combination of all individual relations (equation [4.9]):

$$\mathbf{y} = \alpha \iota + \beta_1 \mathbf{x_1} + \cdots + \beta_K \mathbf{x_K} + \epsilon \quad [4.9]$$

where $\mathbf{y}$ is a vector of dimension $(N \times 1)$ that contains N observations of the dependent variable and ι is a vector of 1 of dimension $(N \times 1)$. The K vectors $\mathbf{x_1}, \mathbf{x_2}, \ldots, \mathbf{x_K}$ of dimension $(N \times 1)$ represent the stacked explanatory variables. Each variable, x_k, takes different values between the observations. The observation heterogeneity characterization thus comes from the variation of values of x_k between the N observations. The (average) influence of each explanatory variable is measured by each of the K coefficients $\beta_1, \beta_2, \ldots, \beta_K$. Finally, ϵ is a vector dimension $(N \times 1)$, representing random perturbations assumed to be independent with a mean of zero and a constant variance for all observations.

To further simplify the presentation, it is customary to gather the set of K vectors related to explanatory variables in a single matrix named $\mathbf{X}$ and composed of the unit vector ι located in the first column, followed by the K explanatory variables. Finally, the matrix $\mathbf{X}$ is of

---

9 The reader will have noted that the solution of the system of equations is possible only when the number of observations in the sample is greater of the number of parameters to be estimated, meaning $N > K + 1$.

dimension $(N \times (K + 1))$ (equation [4.10]). Similarly, it is possible to include all the parameters $(\alpha, \beta_1, \ldots, \beta_K)$, in vector β containing the parameters (unknowns) to be estimated, including the constant term (equation [4.11]):

$$\underset{(N \times (K+1))}{\mathbf{X}} = \begin{pmatrix} 1 & x_{11} & \cdots & x_{1,K} \\ \vdots & \vdots & \vdots & \vdots \\ 1 & x_{i,1} & \cdots & x_{iK} \\ \vdots & \vdots & \vdots & \vdots \\ 1 & x_{N,1} & \cdots & x_{N,K} \end{pmatrix} \qquad [4.10]$$

$$\underset{((K+1)\times 1)}{\beta} = \begin{pmatrix} \alpha \\ \beta_1 \\ \vdots \\ \beta_k \\ \vdots \\ \beta_K \end{pmatrix} \qquad [4.11]$$

Using this simplified presentation, the multiple linear regression model is expressed in matrix form using the equation [4.12]:

$$\mathbf{y} = \mathbf{X}\beta + \epsilon \qquad [4.12]$$

Again, the validity of the result interpretation and estimation precision depends largely on the three assumptions made about the error term ϵ behavior in the model (see Chapter 1). The parameters of the linear regression model are usually estimated using the ordinary least squares (OLSs) method. The idea is to minimize the sum of squared errors. The minimization program solution allows us to determine the estimators with the lowest square values for the vector of parameters β. When the assumptions of the linear regression model are met, these estimators prove to be the best linear unbiased estimators possible[10].

The usual assumptions regarding the disturbance behavior are essential for ensuring the quality of the obtained results. In practice, these assumptions are rarely checked and their non-compliance often depends on the type of data used by the researcher. The cross-sectional data are often affected by the disturbance variance heterogeneity. The time series often show a temporal autocorrelation of the error terms. Spatial data can give rise to spatial correlation between the error terms. There is therefore a link among the temporal and spatial approaches: both show a possible correlation between the error terms, thus violating the assumption of regression error term independence. There are also other types of data including panels and pooled cross-sections data over time that consider two dimensions (spatial and temporal) at a time. These data are therefore susceptible to two types of error term correlations, which complicates the analysis[11].

4.3. Link between spatial and temporal models

The time series analysis is well-documented nowadays, especially the relationship (correlation) between the observation value occurring at time $t - 1$ and at time t. Temporal or serial autocorrelation occurs when a variable correlates with its own temporally lagged observations. This situation is similar for spatial data: an observation located at a particular coordinate has a chance to be correlated with a nearby observation. The spatial autoregressive models can be seen , as we will se, as a transposition of temporal autoregressive models to the spatial case.

Corrado and Fingleton [COR 11] formally presented the similarities between the econometric time series models and those developed with

---

10 A formula for estimating the parameters of interest using OLS is presented in the Appendix, section A3.2. The reader who is not interested in this demonstration can easily go on to section 4.3.

11 Chapter 5 explicitly deals with the individual cross-sectional data pooled over time.

spatial econometrics. Temporal (or spatial) correlation can be modeled using an autoregressive specification over the dependent variable, over the independent variables or over the error terms. From a technical point of view, the easiest case to deal is when the autoregressive process is imposed on the independent variables, as it ignores the possible endogeneity related issues. Therefore, before presenting spatial autoregressive models, we will present temporal autoregressive models. This is designed to simplify the understanding of spatial autoregressive specification models.

4.3.1. *Temporal autoregressive models*

For a time series, the definition of proximity is relatively simple: it is the value of the variable in the previous period. This is called a temporal lagged variable. In this case, the temporal autocorrelation occurs between the value taken by the variable at period t, and the value taken by the same variable at period $t - 1$ (Figure 4.1).

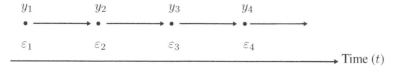

Figure 4.1. *Mapping temporal effects (dependent variable and/or error term)*

The first characteristic of the temporal dimension is its unidirectional link: the temporal logic implies that it is impossible to go back. The value of the variable at the time period $t - 1$ influences the value of the same variable at the time period t which in turn influences the value of the same variable at the time period $t + 1$, and so on. Thus, for a dependent variable, y, independent variables, x_k or the error term, ϵ, the definition of proximity is relatively simple. This unidirectional link behavior is not valid in spatial cases, however, it needs to be taken into consideration when spatial data are collected over time (Chapter 5).

Temporal autoregressive models are constructed by introducing a lagged variable in the list of explanatory variables. As previously mentioned, the lagged specification can be on the independent variables, on the dependent variable or on the error term (respectively, equations [4.13], [4.14] and [4.15]):

$$\mathbf{y} = \mathbf{X}\beta + L.\mathbf{X}\theta + \epsilon \qquad\qquad [4.13]$$

$$\mathbf{y} = L.\mathbf{y}\rho + \mathbf{X}\beta + \epsilon \qquad\qquad [4.14]$$

$$\mathbf{y} = \mathbf{X}\beta + \eta$$
$$\eta = L.\eta\lambda + \epsilon \qquad\qquad [4.15]$$

where $\mathbf{y}$ is a vector of dimension $(T \times 1)$, where T is the total number of periods during which the variables are observed, $\mathbf{X}$ is a matrix of independent variables of dimension $(T \times (K + 1))$, with K the number of total independent variables, ϵ and η are vectors of error terms of dimension $(T \times 1)$.

The vector η, also of dimension $(T \times 1)$ is assumed to be correlated over time and thus depends on past values, whereas the vector ϵ is independent and identically distributed.

The operator $L.$ marks the time lagged, indicating that $L.\mathbf{X} = \mathbf{X}_{t-1}$ where $\mathbf{X}_{t-1}$ is the value of the independent variables x in the previous period. Finally, β, θ, ρ and λ are parameters to be estimated. The vector of dependent variable, $\mathbf{y}$, and its temporal lagged value, $L.\mathbf{y}$, are thus "closely" related (equations [4.16] and [4.17]):

$$\underset{(T\times 1)}{\mathbf{y}} = \begin{pmatrix} y_1 \\ y_2 \\ \vdots \\ y_t \\ \vdots \\ y_T \end{pmatrix} \qquad\qquad [4.16]$$

$$L.\mathbf{y}_{(T\times 1)} = \begin{pmatrix} y_0 \\ y_1 \\ \vdots \\ y_{t-1} \\ \vdots \\ y_{T-1} \end{pmatrix} \qquad\qquad [4.17]$$

The expression for a given variable with a temporal lag $(L.\mathbf{y})$ is therefore based on past values of y: it is therefore a vector of dimension $(T \times 1)$ where the value on the first line is set to zero (we do not observe the value of the variable y before the first period, $y_0 = 0$, but only in period 1), the second line gives the value of the variable at period 1, and so on. The last line of the vector $L.y$ is then the value of the variable at period $T - 1$. For this reason, most estimation methods for temporal autoregressive process estimation only use $T - 1$ observations instead of the ful sample T. Another way of expressing variable $L.\mathbf{y}$ is by using a lagged matrix that can isolate the past values of y (equation [4.18]):

$$L.\mathbf{y} = \mathbf{W}\mathbf{y} \qquad\qquad [4.18]$$

where:

$$\mathbf{W}_{(T\times T)} = \begin{pmatrix} 0 & 0 & 0 & 0 & \cdots & 0 \\ 1 & 0 & 0 & 0 & \cdots & 0 \\ 0 & 1 & 0 & 0 & \cdots & 0 \\ 0 & 0 & 1 & 0 & \cdots & 0 \\ \vdots & \vdots & \vdots & \vdots & \ddots & \vdots \\ 0 & 0 & 0 & 0 & \cdots & 0 \end{pmatrix} \qquad\qquad [4.19]$$

There also exists a very close link between the temporal lag variable and the spatial lag variable: both are expressed using a weight matrix. In the temporal case the weight matrix $\mathbf{W}$, of dimension $(T \times T)$ allows to isolate the value of the variable in the previous period by positioning the 1 under the principal diagonal (equation [4.19]). The same procedure can be adopted in the case of independent variables or error terms. In all cases, the form of the **W** matrix remains unchanged.

Temporal autoregressive models of equations [4.13], [4.14] and [4.15] are well-known in time series econometrics. The first model (equation [4.13]) corresponds to what is traditionally referred to as the *finite distributed lag* (FDL). The second model (equation [4.14]) corresponds to a model with dynamic effects: the dependent variable depends on its value in the previous period. Finally, the third (equation [4.15]) corresponds to a model of moving averages.

From temporal autoregressive model specifications, we can see that the omission of a lagged variable implies that the error term is correlated over time. This behavior violates the assumption that there is no temporal autocorrelation among the error term.

The temporal autoregressive behavior can be detected through a graphical representation based on the model residuals. The positive autoregressive process implies that the disturbance values at time t undergo a similar effect as the disturbance values at the previous period, $t - 1$ (Figures 4.2, 4.3 and 4.4). In the case of a negative autoregressive process, the disturbance values at period t vary in the opposite direction as compared to the disturbance values taken at the period $t - 1$ (Figures 4.5, 4.6 and 4.7).

Common practice is to estimate the multiple linear regression model and then check, based on the statistics of Durbin and Watson [DUR 51, DUR 50] or other appropriate statistics, to see if the linear model residuals are temporally autocorrelated. If the temporal correlation is significantly deviates from zero, it is necessary to opt for a autoregressive specification to correct the issue. The consequences of the results obtained using OLS vary depending on the type of model used: for models with dynamic effects and/or a finite delay, the parameters obtained using OLS are biased, whereas in the moving average model, only the estimator variance is affeted [HAM 94].

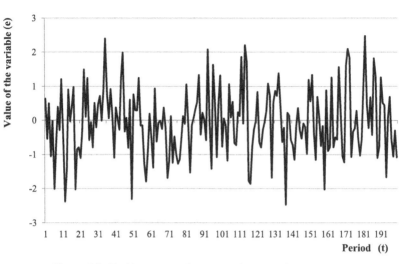

Figure 4.2. *Positive temporal autocorrelation evolution pattern*
Process AR(1) ($\rho = 0.1$)

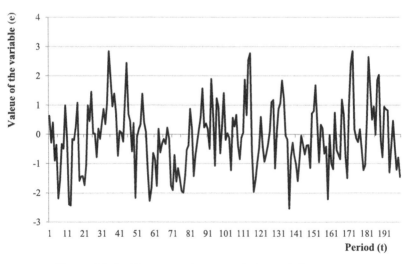

Figure 4.3. *Positive temporal autocorrelation evolution pattern*
Process AR(1) ($\rho = 0.5$)

Figure 4.4. *Positive temporal autocorrelation evolution pattern*
Process AR(1) ($\rho = 0.9$)

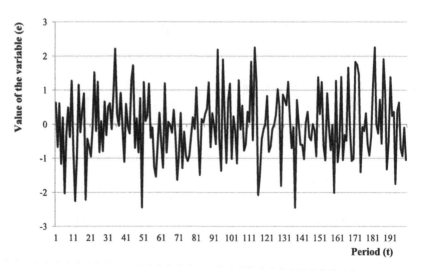

Figure 4.5. *Negative temporal autocorrelation evolution pattern*
Process AR(1) ($\rho = -0.1$)

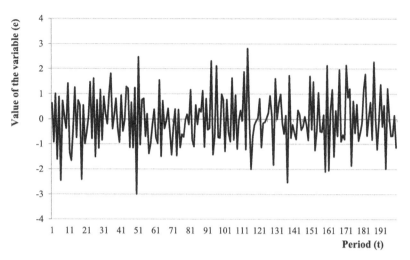

Figure 4.6. *Negative temporal autocorrelation evolution pattern Process AR(1) ($\rho = -0.5$)*

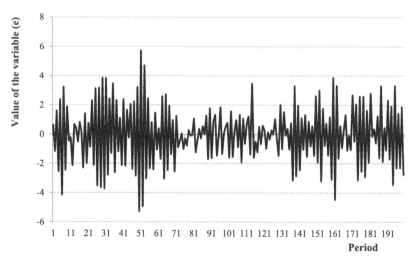

Figure 4.7. *Negative temporal autocorrelation evolution pattern Process AR(1) ($\rho = -0.9$)*

The spatial approach is substantially similar; however, it is based on a different definition of "lagged", which differs due to the specific nature of the spatial data. In this sense, there exist certain similarities between the Durbin-Watson and the I Moran statistics.

4.3.2. *Spatial autoregressive models*

In contrast to models developed in time series analysis, in which the notion of lag or even lagged variables is unambiguous, the concept of spatial lag in spatial econometrics is slightly more complex. Not only is the definition of spatial lag is relatively arbitrary (based on the exogenous spatial weights matrix)[12], but also the extension of this concept to higher lag order is not immediate and requires some adjustments (see [DUB 13]). The definition of the concept of proximity is complicated by the multidirectional nature of the spatial relations: a given unit can influence a nearby unit, which in turn can influence the examined unit. The relations can also be given both along the north-south and east-west axes (Figures 4.8, 4.9 and 4.10).

As we saw in Chapter 2, the spatial weight matrix allows to generate the spatial relations among the observations. Thus, similarly to the temporal case, the creation of a spatially lagged variable is derived from the multiplication of a vector of a given variable by the spatial weights matrix.

The quantity $\mathbf{Wy}$ forms the spatial lag variable of $\mathbf{y}$, the term $\mathbf{WX}$ forms the matrix of spatial independent lagged variables included in matrix $\mathbf{X}$ and $\mathbf{W}\epsilon$ the spatial lag error term. When the spatial weights matrix is row-standardized, the spatial lagged variables are interpreted as expressing the average value of the given variable in the neighborhood. For example, for an observation i, the spatial lag variable $\sum_{j=1}^{N} w_{ij} y_j$ represents the average of variable y for the

---

12 How can we know with certainty the optimal spatial influence radius or how can we determine the ideal form of the spatial relations?

nearby observations j. Thus, we have in matrix form the equations for the set of observations (equation [4.20]):

$$\mathbf{W}\mathbf{y} = \begin{pmatrix} \sum_{j=1}^{N} w_{1j} y_j \\ \sum_{j=1}^{N} w_{2j} y_j \\ \sum_{j=1}^{N} w_{3j} y_j \\ \vdots \\ \sum_{j=1}^{N} w_{ij} y_j \\ \vdots \\ \sum_{j=1}^{N} w_{Nj} y_j \end{pmatrix}$$ [4.20]

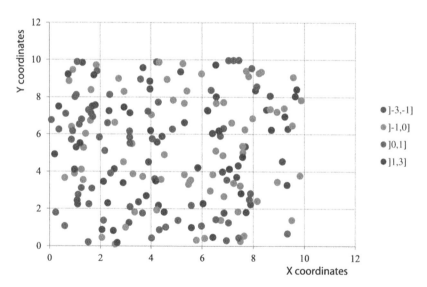

Figure 4.8. *Spatial variable mapping – positive autocorrelation Process AR(1) ($\rho = 0.1$. For a color version of the figure, see www.iste.co.uk/dube/econometrics.zip)*

The notation is similar as for the other spatial lag variables $\mathbf{W}\epsilon$ and $\mathbf{W}\mathbf{X}$.

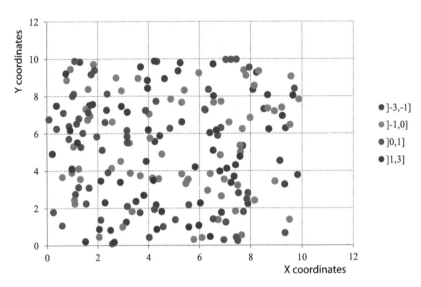

Figure 4.9. *Spatial variable mapping – positive autocorrelation Process AR(1)*
(ρ = 0.5. For a color version of the figure, see
www.iste.co.uk/dube/econometrics.zip)

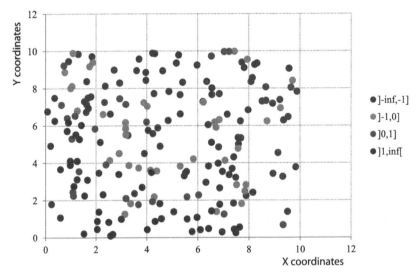

Figure 4.10. *Spatial variable mapping – positive autocorrelation Process*
AR(1) (ρ = 0.9. For a color version of the figure, see
www.iste.co.uk/dube/econometrics.zip)

As we have already mentioned, spatial autocorrelation is not itself a problem. It becomes a problem when such a pattern is detected among the residuals of the model. Exactly like in the temporal case, the spatial autoregressive process of the error terms of the model can be detected in a visual fashion. Value mapping usually allows us to distinguish two extreme cases: one case in which similar values are clustered in space (Figures 4.8, 4.9, 4.10), this is called positive spatial autocorrelation; and one case in which the values alternate from low to high values (Figures 4.11, 4.12, 4.13), and is called negative spatial autocorrelation.

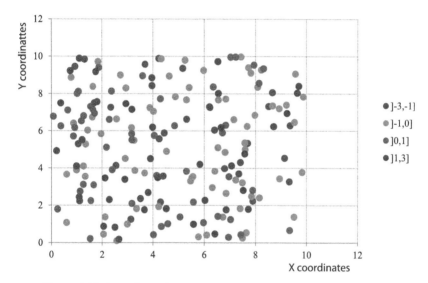

Figure 4.11. *Spatial variable mapping – negative autocorrelation Process AR(1) (ρ = −0.1. For a color version of the figure, see www.iste.co.uk/dube/econometrics.zip)*

As we saw in Chapter 3, it is also possible to measure this autocorrelation with well-known statistical methods: Moran's I statistics. As in the temporal case, omission of spatially lagged variables in the linear regression model has an impact on error term behavior and the validity of the interpretation of the results. For the results to be interpreted correctly, the error terms of the regression must meet the assumptions presented previously (Chapter 1).

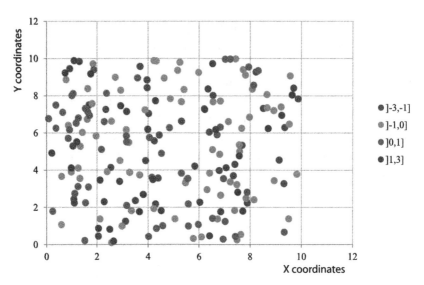

Figure 4.12. *Spatial variable mapping – negative autocorrelation Process AR(1) ($\rho = -0.5$. For a color version of the figure, see www.iste.co.uk/dube/econometrics.zip)*

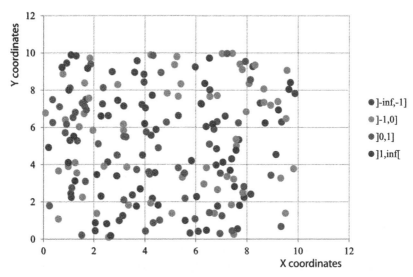

Figure 4.13. *Spatial variable mapping – negative autocorrelation Process AR(1) ($\rho = -0.9$. For a color version of the figure, see www.iste.co.uk/dube/econometrics.zip)*

The challenge in spatial analysis, like that for a time series, consists of identifying the autoregressive process that best models the data studied. The functional form of spatial autoregressive models is very similar to those related to time series. Without loss of generality, it is possible to say that there are mainly three basic spatial autoregressive specifications all of which are inspired from temporal specifications (equations [4.13], [4.14] and [4.15]). Each of the specifications has advantages and disadvantages; however, they all rely on assumptions linked to the DGP type. Of course, these specifications can also be combined to obtained more complex spatial autoregressive model.

There exist a number of statistical tests that allow us to find the preferable autoregressive form (discussed later). However, even before covering statistical tests for discriminating between the different specifications, it seems essential to understand the intuition behind choosing that model to use. Even if the spatial autoregressive specifications are similar to the temporal ones, each given DGP is based on different intuitions. It is in this spirit that section 4.4 aims to present the different spatial autoregressive models.

4.4. Spatial autocorrelation sources

The disturbance ϵ, of a linear regression model contains the information on the omissions of relations or variables (missing variable, nonlinearity in the explanatory variables, measurement errors, etc.) in the model specification. Therefore, it is possible that before anything else the detection of spatial autocorrelation among residuals comes from a poor choice (or misspecification) of the functional form selected [MCM 10]. Thus, even before proceeding to particular spatial autoregressive specifications, it is essential to check whether the relation type between the dependent variable and the independent variables cannot be modified or improved by adding variables that take into account the spatial pattern between residuals.

If the spatial autocorrelation problem among residuals persists after making the appropriate adjustments, we must then think of a strategy based on spatial pattern modeling. The spatial dependence presented between the residuals can come from various sources. LeSage and Pace [LES 09] offer a complete catalog of possible spatial relations that can generate spatial autocorrelation among residuals. Five reasons can serve as motivation for a particular spatial autoregressive model:

– presence of externalities;

– spillover effects;

– omission of important variables;

– presence of behavior spatial heterogeneity;

– mixed effects.

We propose to review each of the motivations guiding the choice of model starting from the intuition based on the DGP of each spatial model and we propose to establish parallels with temporal autoregressive models[13] to date. These five spatial autoregressive models are based on the spatial autoregressive time series models previously presented. In this sense, spatial econometrics model spatial effects based on autoregressive processes: the independent variables (spatial externalities), the dependent variable (spillover effect) and the error term (variable omission or spatial heterogeneity). The fifth case (mixed effects) proposes an autoregressive model of the dependent variable and the error term. This is similar to what is proposed by ARMA[14] models for time series.

In the five possible cases, the failure to take into account the spatial process has the effect of spatial pattern isolation in the non-observable part of the model: the error term. For this reason it is important to carry out a general detection of the spatial autocorrelation pattern among the residuals using Moran's I index.

---

13 The presentation draws largely from the one presented by LeSage and Pace [LES 09], which seems to be the most complete.

14 *Autoregressive moving average*.

4.4.1. *Spatial externalities*

An externality or external effect occurs when an individual benefits from the characterization of a given neighbor (or suffers damage) without influencing the structuration of the characteristics of its neighbor, or without incurring the costs (or receiving allowances) of the characteristics of the neighbor. It means, for example, to benefit from a pleasant view due to the beauty of a neighboring garden, or having to cope with an unpleasant smell due to living near a pig farm. Another example of a negative externality is the noise created due to the close proximity of a busy road that affects the market value of the residential houses or being located directly in front of a major subway station. In these examples, the proximity characteristics influence the situation (or welfare) of an individual. Obviously, these are only a few very specific examples; there exists a great variety of externalities that may influence a given behavior.

External effects are of real importance. Several theories, including those related to endogenous growth and new economic geography, refer to them. The researcher tries to measure their extent and impact. Since those are the characteristics of nearby observations that influence the behavior of a particular observation, the externalities refer to spatially lagged independent variables $\mathbf{WX}$. In this case, the variability of the dependent variable y_i does not solely depend on the characteristics x_{ik} specific to individual i but also the characteristics of the individuals in spatially close proximity to it x_{jk} (equation [4.21]). The nearby variables x_{jk}, define the externalities: the neighbor characteristics influence the behavior of the examined individual:

$$y_i = \alpha + \beta_1 x_{i1} + \cdots + \beta_K x_{iK} + \gamma_1 x_{j1} + \cdots + \gamma_K x_{jK} + \epsilon_i$$
$$\forall\, i = 1, \cdots, N \qquad\qquad\qquad [4.21]$$

As before, it is possible to write this equation more concisely using the matrix notation (equation [4.22]):

$$\mathbf{y} = \mathbf{X}\beta + \mathbf{WX}\gamma + \epsilon \qquad\qquad\qquad [4.22]$$

where $\mathbf{y}$ is the vector of dimension $(N \times 1)$ for N dependent variables, the matrix $\mathbf{X}$, of dimension $(N \times (K + 1))$ in which a unit vector included on the first column that represents the constant, followed by K individual characteristics. The variable matrix $\mathbf{WX}$ of dimension $(N \times K)$ measures the average behavior of the set of K characteristics stack in the vector $\mathbf{X}$ for the neighbor area[15]. Finally, ϵ is an error term vector of dimension $(N \times 1)$, and assumed of zero mean, homoscedastic variance and non- (auto) correlated (or independent). The model parameter vectors, β and γ are, respectively, of dimension $((K + 1) \times 1)$ and $(K \times 1)$ dimensions. All other things being equal, the vector β measures, the contribution of the features x_k in establishing the nature of the dependent variable, y; and the vector γ measures the average effect of the nearby observations on the behavior of y. This specification has the advantage of expressing and measuring the externality effects in a simple manner.

The main advantage of this autoregressive formulation is related to its specification. Since the variables appearing on the right-hand side are all independent (and exogenous) variables that are spatially lagged (SLX model), it is possible to estimate the model using the OLS method. For this reason, it is the spatial autoregressive model that is the easiest to implement. Its specifications are very similar to the finite lag model for a time series (equations [4.13]): independent lagged variables are used as new variables to control for spatial autocorrelation that is otherwise found in the error term.

A characteristic of this specification is that it is based on the decomposition of the marginal effects, and this requires a more complex expression. Thus, a change in the characteristics, x_{ik}, of an individual influences not only its own nature, y_i, but also the average behavior of the neighborhood, x_{jk} or $\mathbf{WX}$, which in turn influences the nature of its nearby individuals, y_j. The marginal effect calculations are more complex. The marginal effect can be divided into

---

15 The matrix product of the spatial weight matrix, $\mathbf{W}$, of $(N \times N)$ dimensions, can also be based on a subset of the matrix $\mathbf{X}$ of $(N \times L)$ dimensions providing a vector of $(N \times L)$ dimensions. It must be noted that we must have $L \leq K$ since only the certain variables are retained.

two effects: the direct effect, measured by the parameter β; and an indirect effect, measured by the parameter γ (equation [4.23]):

$$\frac{\partial \mathbf{y}}{\partial \mathbf{X}} = \mathbf{I}\beta + \mathbf{W}\gamma \qquad [4.23]$$

where $\mathbf{I}$ is the identity matrix of dimension $(N \times N)$. The spatial lag model over the exogenous (independent) variables (or SLX) model is interesting because it allows to account for spatial autocorrelation detected among the residuals of the multiple linear regression. Thus, in this type of model, statistical inference is only valid when the model residuals are not spatially correlated. For this reason, it is therefore advised to check for the presence of spatial autocorrelation among the residuals of the SLX specification using Moran's I index. If the test leads to rejection of the null hypothesis, this confirms the presence of a spatial structure between the residuals, it will them mean that different (or increased) specification of the spatial autoregressive model should be used. This can be based on an autoregressive process of the dependent variable or error term.

4.4.2. *Spillover effect*

Exactly as in the temporal case, it is possible that spatial autocorrelation is generated by a dynamic effect: the dependent variable behavior depends on the nature of the other dependent variables located in close proximity. In the spatial case, the spillover effect normally occurs rather than the dynamic effect. This means that for a particular observation the data generating process is influenced by the nature of the dependent variables related to the nearby observations. This is the case, for example, when the sales prices of neighboring houses affect the market value of a given house, or when the increase in employment growth in a region results in employment growth in the neighboring regions. This type of specification is called the spatial autoregressive (SAR) model (equation [4.24]):

$$y_i = \rho y_j + \alpha + \beta_1 x_{i1} + \cdots + \beta_K x_{iK} + \epsilon_i \quad \forall\, i = 1, \cdots, N \quad [4.24]$$

In matrix notation, the model can be written as (equation [4.25]):

$$\mathbf{y} = \mathbf{W}\mathbf{y}\rho + \mathbf{X}\beta + \epsilon \qquad [4.25]$$

where the vectors, $\mathbf{y}$ and ϵ, and the matrix, $\mathbf{X}$, are of usual dimensions, just like the parameter vector β. A set of assumptions is made about the error term: a mean of zero, a homoscedastic variance and independence (absence of correlation) among residuals spatially located. The parameter ρ is a scalar and measures the (mean) spillover effect of nearby individual behaviors on a chosen individual.

This model is largely utilized in empirical applications. It is estimated using the maxiumum likelihood (ML) method [ANS 88, LES 09, LES 99][16] or by the generalized method of moment (GMM) method [KEL 98, KEL 93]. The popularity of the SAR model is attributed to the specific way the marginal effect calculations are carried out.

Unlike in an usual linear regression model, the effect of a change in a variable x_k, all things being equal, is not equal to the coefficient, β_k. A variation in variable x_{ik} causes a change in the variable y_i which leads to a variation in the variable y_j for the observations located around i which in turn causes a change in the variable y_i and so on. The marginal effect can be separated once more into two parts: the first part is related to the direct effects and the second part measures the indirect effects that depend on the autoregressive coefficient, ρ, but are also associated with the independent variable β_k (equation [4.26])[17]:

$$\frac{\partial \mathbf{y}}{\partial \mathbf{X}} = (\mathbf{I} - \mathbf{W}\rho)^{-1}\mathbf{I}\beta \qquad [4.26]$$

---

16 The maximum likelihood of the SAR model is presented in the Appendix, section A3.3.

17 It should be noted that the marginal effect also largely relies on the structure of the weights matrix, $\mathbf{W}$.

where $\mathbf{I}$ is the identity matrix of dimension $(N \times N)$. LeSage and Pace [LES 09] propose to simplify the expression $(\mathbf{I} - \mathbf{W}\rho)^{-1}$ by using the properties of an infinite series (equation [4.27]):

$$(\mathbf{I} - \mathbf{W}\rho)^{-1} = \mathbf{I} + \mathbf{W} + \mathbf{W}^2\rho^2 + \cdots + \mathbf{W}^N\rho^N \qquad [4.27]$$

Replacing $(\mathbf{I} - \mathbf{W}\rho)^{-1}$ with its decomposed version (equation [4.27]) in the marginal effect formula [4.26], we get a more complex expression than the one using the standard linear regression model (equation [4.28]):

$$\frac{\partial \mathbf{y}}{\partial \mathbf{X}} = \mathbf{I}\beta + \rho\mathbf{W}\beta + \rho^2\mathbf{W}^2\beta + \ldots + \rho^N\mathbf{W}^N\beta \qquad [4.28]$$

LeSage and Pace [LES 09] propose a more compact way of writing this expression by simplifying the decomposition expression of an infinite series using $V(\mathbf{W})$ (equation [4.29]):

$$V(\mathbf{W}) = \mathbf{I} + \mathbf{W}\rho + \mathbf{W}^2\rho^2 + \ldots + \mathbf{W}^N\rho^N \qquad [4.29]$$

Similarly LeSage and Pace [LES 09] show that the infinite sum leads to an expression that summarizes the total marginal effects (equation [4.30]):

$$\frac{\partial \mathbf{y}}{\partial \mathbf{X}} = N^{-1}\iota'V(\mathbf{W})\beta\iota \qquad [4.30]$$

where ι is a vector of 1 of dimension $(N \times 1)$. This expression is the equivalent for the one obtained using time series for calculating long term effects: $\beta(1 - \rho)^{-1}$. There is therefore, as previously mentioned, a very strong similarities not only between time series and spatial models but also in terms of marginal effect decomposition.

The decomposition of the round of marginal effects can be divided into three components: the direct effects (equation [4.31]), the total effects (equation [4.32]) and the indirect effects (equation [4.33]):

$$\bar{M}_{direct} = N^{-1}\text{trace}(V(\mathbf{W}))\beta \qquad [4.31]$$

$$\bar{M}_{total} = N^{-1}\iota'V(\mathbf{W})\beta\iota \qquad\qquad\qquad [4.32]$$

$$\bar{M}_{indirect} = \bar{M}_{total} - \bar{M}_{direct} \qquad\qquad\qquad [4.33]$$

The direct effect corresponds to the sum of elements that appear on the main diagonal. This is the usual expression of the marginal effect; although the parameter β is different, since the weights matrix, when raised to certain levels returns non-zero elements on the main diagonal. The total effects represent the cumulative round overflow, until the round becomes zero. They mark the variation effect of variable y adjacent to the variable y which in turn influences y and its neighbors and so on. For their part, the indirect marginal effect is defined as the difference between the total and direct effects.

Steimetz [STE 10] shows that this decomposition can be created using simpler expressions. He suggests taking the parameter β for calculating the direct marginal effect and taking the product $\beta(1-\rho)^{-1}$ for calculating the total effect. The indirect effect is thus simply obtained using the difference between the two effects: $\beta(1-\rho)^{-1} - \beta = \rho(1-\rho)^{-1}\beta$. This interpretation, however, is different from that of LeSage and Pace, and more similar to the decomposition proposed by Abreu et al. [ABR 04]. The main advantage of this notation is that it is easy to interpret and direct to obtain.

The SAR model is interesting for interpretation and measuring spillover effects, as well as the decomposition of the marginal effect offered. Obviously, just as before, the model type is only appropriate, if it allows us to adequately and fully control for spatial autocorrelation among the residuals of the multiple linear regression model. However, it is possible that this specification is not the best to achieve this. It is therefore sensible to practically check for the presence of spatial autocorrelation using Moran's I test on the SAR model residuals. If the presence of spatial autocorrelation is still detected, it means that the specification fails to adequately control the spatial autocorrelations present in the residuals.

If the SAR model fails to control for the problem of residual spatial autocorrelation, several alternatives exist. The first, and simplest, consists of including an autoregressive specification of the independent variables (SLX) in the SAR specification. The second is to consider another specification based on the spatial autoregressive specification of the error term. Finally, the third alternative is to take into account a mixed specification.

4.4.3. *Omission of variables or spatial heterogeneity*

Spatial autocorrelation can be generated due to the omission of an important variable in the regression model. The omitted variable can be from two sources: (1) a spatially structured latent variable, z; or (2) the (fixed) composition effects marking a form of spatial heterogeneity. In all cases, not taking into account these effects results in a spatial association pattern located in the error term. The error terms then become spatially structured and, for this reason, it is necessary to opt for an autoregressive specification of the error term.

On the one hand, it is often difficult to identify the set of explanatory factors of a given behavior, it is also very likely that an important variable has been omitted from the equation. The variable may be absent from the analysis due to impossibility of measuring it. For example, how can an employee's motivation be measured? On the other hand, as expressed by Jayet [JAY 01], "any statistical analysis of a population assumes that the elements of this population have similarities on which to base comparisons and establish patterns. However, spatial data generally show a significant level of heterogeneity which implies that the value of the observations varies in space". It is quite possible to imagine, for example, the neighborhood effects, the effects of socioeconomic and sociodemographic composition or infrastructure. When these characteristics remain constant over time, they are similar to moving fixed effects in panel data econometrics, where the fixed effects are included in localization effects. In both cases, the relation error term takes on a different form (equation [4.34]):

$$y_i = \alpha + \beta_1 x_{i1} + \cdots + \beta_K x_{iK} + \nu_i \quad \forall\, i = 1, \ldots, N \qquad [4.34]$$

where ν_i represents an error term that can contain the omission of certain variables in the model. In the case of a spatially structured variable, the relation displays an autoregressive form of the error term (equation [4.35]):

$$\nu_i = \nu_j \lambda + \epsilon_i \quad \forall\, i = 1, \ldots, N \qquad [4.35]$$

where ϵ_i is an error term with a mean of zero, the variance is constant for all observations and independent of other error terms.

In the case where the omitted variable represents a fixed effect of shared localization for several statistical units, the relationship partly depends on the characterization of the medium. This effect is taken into consideration by the fixed effect η_i (equation [4.36]):

$$\nu_i = \eta_i \quad \forall\, i = 1, \ldots, N \qquad [4.36]$$

As previously mentioned, the characteristics are strongly independent of each other, and we can thus express this relationship as being spatially autoregressive (equation [4.37]):

$$\eta_i = \eta_j \lambda + \epsilon_i \quad \forall\, i = 1, \ldots, N \qquad [4.37]$$

Finally, the two specifications lead to a similar expression that allows to generate a model where the error term is spatially autocorrelated (equation [4.38]):

$$y_i = \alpha + \beta_1 x_{i1} + \cdots + \beta_K x_{iK} + (1 - \lambda)^{-1}\epsilon_i \quad \forall\, i = 1, \ldots, N \, [4.38]$$

Disturbance spatial autocorrelation can arise from the omission of a spatially correlated (or non-measurable) variable or the presence of a form of spatial heterogeneity. This formulation can be simplified by the matrix notation (equation [4.39]):

$$\mathbf{y} = \mathbf{X}\beta + (\mathbf{I} - \lambda\mathbf{W})^{-1}\epsilon \qquad [4.39]$$

Exactly as for the SAR model, the spatial error model (SEM) can be estimated using the ML method or using the GMM.

This leads to the generation of a model that incorporates spatially correlated disturbances. A specific characteristic of this model type is that the vector of parameters β of equation [4.39] estimated using OLS is unbiased. In contrast, the variance of parameter β estimated using OLS is not efficient. The inefficiency of the variance affects statistical tests, such as significant test based on t test. The marginal effect calculations are similar to the ones for a classic linear model and are given by the vector β (equation [4.40]):

$$\frac{\partial \mathbf{y}}{\partial \mathbf{X}} = \mathbf{I}\beta \qquad [4.40]$$

It is also possible to express the SEM model differently: using the spatial Durbin model.

4.4.3.1. *Spatial Durbin model*

Another way to express the SEM models is to use a transformation that ensures that the relationship error term in its reduced form is not spatially correlated. This transformation is called the spatial Durbin model (SDM) and proposes a rewriting of the model [4.39]. By multiplying each term by $(\mathbf{I} - \mathbf{W}\lambda)$, we can rewrite the spatial error autoregressive model (equation [4.41]):

$$(\mathbf{I} - \lambda\mathbf{W})\mathbf{y} = (\mathbf{I} - \lambda\mathbf{W})\mathbf{X}\beta + \epsilon \qquad [4.41]$$

The left side can be simplified to obtain the final form of the estimate (equation [4.42]):

$$\mathbf{y} = \mathbf{W}\mathbf{y}\lambda + \mathbf{X}\beta - \mathbf{W}\mathbf{X}\beta\lambda + \epsilon \qquad [4.42]$$

Thus, the spatially autocorrelated error model (SEM) can be rewritten in a form introducing an autoregressive process in the dependent variable (SAR) and the independent variables (SLX). In this sense, the SDM model generalizes the spatial autoregressive model (SAR) while imposing some constraints on the parameters to be estimated over the SLX process. Once more, this model can be estimated using the ML method. MatLab scripts and R packages for estimating this model type are freely available. GeoDA, meanwhile sadly does not have the procedures for estimating this model: it only includes the possibility to estimate SAR and SEM model[18].

4.4.3.2. *Correlated latent effects*

It may be possible that the omitted variables of the model represent non-measurable characteristics or locally fixed effects that also correlated with one or more of the independent variables. In this case, the estimator of parameter β obtained using OLS is no longer unbiased and its variance is no longer effective.

The expressions [4.35] and [4.37] become equal to the general expression including a relation with one or several independent variables (equation [4.43]):

$$\nu = \mathbf{W}\nu\lambda + \mathbf{X}\theta + \epsilon \qquad [4.43]$$

This situation could explain why in some cases the detection of spatial autocorrelation among the residuals of a model [4.39] still shows spatial autocorrelation: the latent term is correlated with the independent variables. The expression of the complex form of the model is given by the equation [4.44]:

$$\mathbf{y} = \mathbf{X}\beta + (\mathbf{I} - \lambda\mathbf{W})^{-1}\mathbf{X}\theta + (\mathbf{I} - \lambda\mathbf{W})^{-1}\epsilon \qquad [4.44]$$

---

18 By creating spatial lag variable of the independent variables through simple matrix calculation, both specifications can also includes the SLX specification, thus making possible to estimate mixed specification models.

After simplifying, we obtain a more complex expression for the matrix variables $\mathbf{X}$ that depends on several parameters (equation [4.45]).

$$\mathbf{y} = \mathbf{X}(\beta\theta) + \mathbf{W}\mathbf{X}(-\lambda\beta) + \epsilon \qquad [4.45]$$

It must be noted that the estimation using OLSs for the parameter vector β is biased. In addition, the estimate by OLS of the equation [4.44], produces inefficient estimators because the disturbances of this model are spatially correlated.

This possibility partly explains why, despite using an SEM model, it is possible to detect certain spatial autocorrelation between the model residuals with Moran's I test. In this case, a simple autoregressive specification of the error term is not enough: the correlation with other independent variables is not taken into account. When there is a correlation between the omitted variable and the independent (or explanatory) variables, the parameter vector β estimate is biased. In both cases (fixed effects and omission of a variable), the marginal effect calculations change: thus we cannot draw conclusions in the same way as in the classic regression analysis. In the same way as in the SLX and SAR autoregressive models, the marginal effect calculations can be separated into two effects: the direct effect, and the indirect effect, one of which is related to the dependent variable and another to the independent variables. We will review this in section 4.4.4 on mixed effects.

4.4.4. *Mixed effects*

A general specification allowing the inclusion of mixed autoregressive effects consists of a set of autoregressive patterns in the regression equation. Spatial autoregressive specification of the dependent variable is then introduced over the independent variables and the error term. This is called a generalized spatial autoregressive model (GAR – equation [4.46]):

$$y = \mathbf{W}y\rho + \mathbf{X}\beta + \mathbf{W}\mathbf{X}\gamma + \eta \qquad [4.46]$$

$$\eta = \mathbf{W}\eta\lambda + \epsilon \qquad [4.47]$$

This specification generalizes the possibilities presented previously and based on the spatial autoregressive model of the error terms (SEM), the spatial autoregressive model of the independent variables (SLX) and the spatial autoregressive model on the dependent variable (SAR). This model also allows to generalize the SDM while permitting parameter flexibility for estimating the spatial autoregressive processes. There are no parameter vectors formed by the multiplication of two parameters, as in the case of SDM ($\gamma = \beta\lambda$).

The spatial weights matrix $\mathbf{W}$ can be the same for all autoregressive processes or different, depending on the specification. On the one hand, LeGallo [LEG 02] suggests using different weights matrices for the estimation procedures in order to avoid falling into a trap associated with over-identification related to the parameter ρ. On the other hand, Anselin and Bera [ANS 98] argue that this type of model is usually the result of poor spatial weights matrix specification rather than a realistic data generating process.

In summary, this model type allows us to generalize all the specifications met so far. However, this expression complicates the likelihood calculations and takes considerable time to estimate, especially for a large sample size. In addition the expression of marginal effects is more complicated in that it incorporates both the particularity of SLX and SAR models (equation [4.48]):

$$\frac{\partial \mathbf{y}}{\partial \mathbf{X}} = (\mathbf{I} - \mathbf{W}\rho)^{-1}\mathbf{I}\beta + (\mathbf{I} - \mathbf{W}\rho)^{-1}\mathbf{W}\gamma \qquad [4.48]$$

Thus despite some possible shortcomings of this specification type related to microdata cross-sectional application, it is possible to use this model type in a spatio-temporal case. We will return to spatio-temporal autoregressive models in Chapter 5.

4.5. Statistical tests

Once we present all the spatial autoregressive models and the intuition underlying their DGP, a question arises: which model is more convenient for empirical analysis? There exists two ways to proceed. The first way is to retain the theoretical considerations that may give preference to one model rather than another. The considerations are mainly related to testable hypotheses or to the relations a researchers want to deal with. The second approach, for reasons of convenience suggests that a series of statistical tests should be carried out on the different specifications of the spatial autoregressive models to adopt the ones that better control for spatial autocorrelation among residuals. The idea is to develop an objective measures that allows us to discriminate between the possible forms.

In statistics, there are three philosophies that underline the main test types and each of them is based on different approaches; however all of them have the same goal. The three tests are based on the asymptotic properties of the ML estimate. The best known test and the first to be introduced is the likelihood ratio [BUS 82]. This test is used to compare the difference between the value of the (log)likelihood of a specification considered to be unconstrained and the value of (log)likelihood obtained for a constrained model specification (equation [4.49]). The likelihood ratio test is designed to evaluate the distance that separates the values of the two likelihoods: if the distance is small, then the constrained model is comparable to the unconstrained model. In this case, the constraint version is "acceptable" and do not reduce the performance of the model. It is thus statistically possible to not reject the null hypothesis (the postulated constraints prove to be credible). In other words, the constraints cannot be rejected and the constrained model is thus as efficient as the unconstrained model (Figure 4.14). The statistical likelihood ratio test can be written as:

$$LR = 2(\log L(\theta_0) - \log L(\theta_1)) \sim \chi_g^2 \qquad [4.49]$$

where $\log L(\theta_0)$ represents the log-likelihood value of the unconstrained model and $\log L(\theta_1)$ represents the log-likelihood value for the constrained model. The number of constraints imposed, g, may vary depending on the specification. The unconstrained and constrained log-likelihood ratio follows a Chi-2 law with g degrees of freedom.

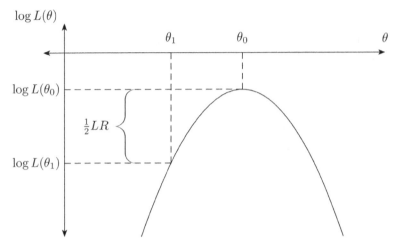

Figure 4.14. *The likelihood ratio test*

If the likelihood value of a unconstrained model strays too far from the constrained model, we cannot accept the null hypothesis: the gap is too large for the constraint to be considered realistic. This distance separating the two log-likelihood values, obtained by [4.49], is compared to the critical Chi-2 value at g degrees of freedom for a significance threshold of $1 - \alpha$, where α is traditionally fixed at 5%. It must be noted that the distance between the two log-likelihood values depends on the shape of the curve of the function. This curve is named $C(\theta)$ and can be calculated using the second derivative of the likelihood with respect to the parameter value θ (equation [4.50]).

$$C(\theta) = \frac{\partial^2 \log L}{\partial \theta^2} \qquad [4.50]$$

A second approach, based on the comparison of the distances between the estimated parameters in constrained and unconstrained form, is the Wald test. This approach suggests that, if the distance between the parameter estimates θ_1 and θ_0 is too high, the data fail to support the null hypothesis. In such circumstances, the null hypothesis cannot be accepted.

Formally, the Wald test proposes to calculate the distance between unconstrained estimators (θ_0) and the constrained estimators (θ_1). This distance can be expressed by $(\theta_0 - \theta_1)^2$ and is influenced by the shape of the likelihood curve (Figure 4.15 and equation [4.51]):

$$W = (\theta_0 - \theta_1)^2 C(\theta_0) \sim \chi_g^2 \qquad [4.51]$$

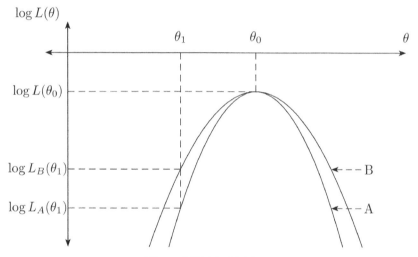

Figure 4.15. *The Wald test*

The Wald statistic is distributed asymptotically according to a Chi-2 law with g degrees of freedom, where g represents the number of constraints tested. A large value of W means that the null hypothesis should be rejected, and, conversely, a small value suggests non-rejection of the null hypothesis. More precisely the decision rule states that if the calculated statistic, W, is greater than the critical value of Chi-2 at a risk of $\alpha = 5\%$ (level of significance of $1 - \alpha = 95\%$), the null hypothesis is rejected.

In practice, the function $C(\theta_0)$ is replaced by $I(\theta_0) = E(\frac{\partial^2 \log L}{\partial \theta_0^2})$, the information matrix[19]. The Wald test commonly uses unconstrained model estimates for evaluating the statistical value of W. Thus, the researcher needs to estimate only the unconstrained model for hypothesis testing. This is different from the likelihood ratio test where both unconstrained and constrained models need to be estimated in order to compare their likelihoods.

Finally, the third approach is the Lagrange multiplier (LM) test. This approach is also based on the log-likelihood function curve, with the slope of the likelihood function being evaluated by the constraint type. The idea is that when the constraints are verified, the value of the estimated parameters (θ_0) is such that the likelihood function slope at this point is zero (equation [4.52])[20]. The goal is to compare, whether the slope evaluated using the constrained model is zero (0) or strays too far from 0. In the last case, the null hypothesis must be rejected (Figure 4.16). If the difference between the slopes is too high, then the test statistic is greater than the critical value of Chi-2 with g degrees of freedom for a fixed significance level of $1 - \alpha$:

$$LM = S(\theta_1)^2 C(\theta_1)^{-1} \sim \chi_g^2 \qquad [4.52]$$

As in the case of Wald statistics, the function $C(\theta_1)$ is replaced by $I(\theta_1)$ and the null hypothesis is rejected, if the test statistic is too great. The main advantage of the LM statistic is that it only requires the constrained model to be estimated, and it is very often less complex since it mainly lies on the OLS. This is one of the reasons that has lead to the widespread use of this approach.

In the case of a the spatial autoregressive models, the null hypothesis that we want to test is that the spatial autoregressive parameter is not

---

19 The inverse of this matrix is the parameter covariance variance matrix, where their standard deviations are on the diagonal. The more significant the log-likelihood curve function, the smaller the standard deviations.

20 Implying that the maximum is reached, so the first derivative of this function is zero.

significant (ρ and λ). Thus, the failure to reject a hypothesis, leads to the estimation using a simpler model: the standard linear regression model.

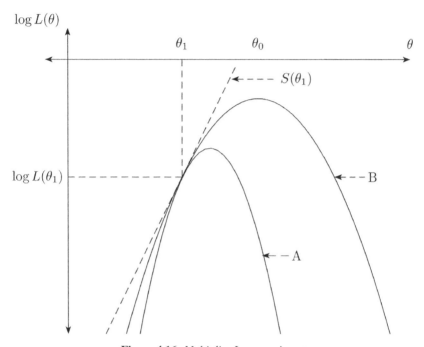

Figure 4.16. *Multiplier Lagrange's test*

The advantages of the Lagrange multiplier test make it a natural choice for building tests for discriminating between different spatial models. Anselin [ANS 88] proposes various tests for choosing the appropriate spatial autoregressive specification. These tests aim to determine which is the best spatial specification for estimating a "static" model using least squares. These tests were completed by Anselin *et al.* [ANS 96] using robust LM test methodology in the presence of nuisance parameters proposed by par Bera and Yoon [BER 93].

4.5.1. *LM tests in spatial econometrics*

In the previous sections, we have shown that spatial autocorrelation detected among residuals of the standard linear regression model can be modeled in various ways. However, the choice between different specifications requires the implementation of a series of tests, such that the alternative hypothesis would offer a more explicit spatial specification (which is not the case when using Moran's I test). These test procedures are based on the Lagrange multiplier principles because it has the advantage of only requiring the model estimation under the null hypothesis, which most often returns a standard linear regression model estimated using OLS, and thus facilitating the statistical interference.

LM statistical test construction depends on the postulated specification of the spatial autoregressive data generating process. The test statistic varies depending on the form postulated: spatial autocorrelation present in the error terms (SEM) or on the dependent variable (SAR). The usual practice is to initially use a general test for detecting residual spatial autocorrelation (Moran's I index) in order to then be able to carry out the statistical LM tests to identify the specific type of the autoregressive process. This can be done using Lagrange multiplier (LM) tests developed by Anselin *et al.* [ANS 96]. We can conclude that decisions related to choosing a particular model should be based on a combination of the results generated from the five aforementioned tests (Table 4.17).

The next few sections are devoted to the presentation of the statistical tests that are most commonly used to discriminate between the most suitable autoregressive alternatives.

4.5.1.1. *Test for the omission of error spatial autocorrelation (SEM)*

This test, proposed by Burridge [BUR 80] assumes the omission of a spatial autoregressive process of the error term η_i, where

$\eta_i = \lambda \sum w_{ij}\eta_j + \epsilon_i$ describes the standard regression model and relates to the non-significance coefficient λ:

$$\mathbf{y} = \mathbf{X}\beta + \eta$$
$$\eta = \lambda \mathbf{W}\eta + \epsilon \qquad \qquad [4.53]$$

The null hypothesis is $H_0 : \lambda = 0$. The constrained version of the SEM model can be reduced to a standard linear regression model (equation [4.54]):

$$\mathbf{y} = \mathbf{X}\beta + \epsilon \qquad \qquad [4.54]$$

The estimation of the constrained version of the SEM model using OLS allows the retrieval of residuals, called $\widehat{\epsilon}$, and the error variance $\widehat{\sigma}^2 = \frac{\widehat{\epsilon}'\widehat{\epsilon}}{N}$. By putting this into the general statistical LM test (equation [4.52]), we can obtain an expression for the LM test for a SEM specification (equation [4.55]):

$$LM_{ERR} = \frac{1}{T}\left(\frac{\widehat{\epsilon}'\mathbf{W}\widehat{\epsilon}}{\widehat{\sigma}^2}\right)^2 \qquad \qquad [4.55]$$

where $T = \text{trace}((\mathbf{W} + \mathbf{W}')\mathbf{W})$. Under the null hypothesis, this statistic converges asymptotically to a Chi-2 distribution of 1 degree of freedom[21] (χ_1^2). The null hypothesis is rejected, if the result of the statistical test LM_{ERR}, has a greater value than the critical value that can be read from the Chi-2 table for a previously established level of significance. For example, if we use a significance level of 95%, the critical value is 3,84. Thus, we reject the null hypothesis, if the value of the statistical test LM_{ERR} is greater than 3,84. We can conclude in this case that spatial autocorrelation is present in the standard linear model residuals and we must proceed to estimate the SEM specification.

---

21 A single constraint is imposed: $\lambda = 0$.

4.5.1.1.1. Test for the omission of an endogenously lagged variable (*SAR*)

The second test proposed by Anselin [ANS 88] is called LM_{LAG} and aims to check whether the detected spatial autocorrelation among the residuals of the multiple regression does not arise from the omission of spatially lagged dependent variable regressors. The unconstrained model contains spatially lagged dependent variables on the right hand side of the equation (equation [4.56]):

$$\mathbf{y} = \rho \mathbf{W} \mathbf{y} + \mathbf{X} \beta + \epsilon \qquad [4.56]$$

The null hypothesis of this test is based on the significance of the autoregressive parameter, or $H_0 : \rho = 0$. In this case the constrained model takes the form of a standard linear regression (equation [4.57]) :

$$\mathbf{y} = \mathbf{X} \beta + \epsilon \qquad [4.57]$$

If we note $T_1 = \left[(\mathbf{W} \mathbf{X} \widehat{\beta})' \mathbf{M} (\mathbf{W} \mathbf{X} \widehat{\beta}) + T \widehat{\sigma}^2 \right] / \widehat{\sigma}^2$ with $\mathbf{M} = \mathbf{I} - \mathbf{X} (\mathbf{X}' \mathbf{X})^{-1} \mathbf{X}'$ the test statistic LM is simplified in order to obtain the final expression (equation [4.58]):

$$LM_{SAR} = \frac{1}{T_1} \left(\frac{\widehat{\varepsilon}' \mathbf{W} \mathbf{y}}{\widehat{\sigma}^2} \right)^2 \qquad [4.58]$$

Under the null hypothesis, the test asymptomatically converges according to the Chi-2 distribution to 1 degree of freedom. The null hypothesis is rejected when the value of the statistic test, LM_{SAR} is greater than the tabulated value of Chi-2 at 1 degree of freedom, which means 3,84 when the significance level is fixed at 5%.

Anselin and Bera [ANS 98], however, showed that in the presence of a local autocorrelation related to the omission of a spatially lagged dependent variable (spatially autocorrelated error, respectively) the corresponding statistical test statistics are not distributed according to the Chi-2 rule at 1 degree of freedom. Two approaches are thus possible. The first involves the testing of the joined hypothesis $H_0 : \lambda = \rho = 0$ in the general spatial model; while the second approach relies on testing for the omission of disturbance spatial autocorrelation in a model that includes an endogenously lagged variable and vice versa.

4.5.1.2. *Join test for lagged variables and error spatial autocorrelation*

The approach of the joined test consists of testing the simultaneous significance for two autocorrelation parameters λ and ρ ($H_0 : \lambda = \rho = 0$) in the general autoregressive model (equation [4.59]):

$$\begin{aligned} \mathbf{y} &= \rho\mathbf{W}\mathbf{y} + \mathbf{X}\beta + \nu \\ \nu &= \lambda\mathbf{W}\nu + \epsilon \end{aligned} \qquad [4.59]$$

When the null hypothesis H_0 is accepted, the constrained model can be simplified to a standard linear regression (equation [4.60]):

$$\mathbf{y} = \mathbf{X}\beta + \epsilon \qquad [4.60]$$

The LM test statistic for joined significance is given by the equation [4.61]:

$$LM_{\lambda\rho} = \widehat{E}^{-1}\left[(\widehat{d_\lambda})^2\frac{\widehat{D}}{\widehat{\sigma}^2} + (\widehat{d_\rho})^2 T_{22} - 2\widehat{d_\lambda}\widehat{d_\rho}T_{12}\right] \qquad [4.61]$$

where $\widehat{E} = ((\frac{D}{\sigma^2})T_{22} - (T_{12})^2)$ with $T_{ij} = (\text{trace}(\mathbf{W}_i\mathbf{W}_j + \mathbf{W}_i'\mathbf{W}_j))$; $T = [(\mathbf{W}' + \mathbf{W})\mathbf{W}]$ and $\widehat{D} = ((\mathbf{W}_1 X\beta)'\mathbf{M}(\mathbf{W}_1 X\beta) + T_{11}\sigma^2)$. The values d_ρ and d_λ represent the scores based on ρ and λ, respectively. For H_0, this statistic is distributed according to the Chi-2 distribution with 2 degrees of freedom ($LM \sim \chi^2(2)$).

Rejection of the null hypothesis means that the autoregressive parameters are not equal to zero. This does not imply that the two parameters are significant, as it can be that only one of them is actually significant and not equal to 0. It then becomes interesting to try to identify which parameter is significant (assuming that one is). In this case, it is possible to use an alternative approach based on a conditional significance test.

4.5.1.3. *Conditional tests*

This approach uses the Lagrange multiplier test to verify the presence of a data spatial dependence type (lagged endogenous variable or error spatial autocorrelation) when the other form is not constrained. For example, we can test the null hypothesis for significance for the parameter λ when the parameter ρ is significantly different from zero. In this case, and for both specifications, the unconstrained model is a particular specification of the GAR model (equation [4.59]) in which the spatial autoregressive specification is based on the dependent variable (SAR) and on the error term (SEM). LeSage and Pace [LES 09] refer to this specification as the SAC model (equation [SAC]).

$$SAC : y = \rho \mathbf{W}1\mathbf{y} + \mathbf{X}\beta + \eta$$
$$\eta = \lambda \mathbf{W}2\eta + \epsilon$$

To test for the significance of the autoregressive effect on the autoregressive specification of the error term, the constrained model takes the form of a SAR model (equation [4.62]):

$$y = \rho \mathbf{W}1 + \mathbf{X}\beta + \epsilon \qquad [4.62]$$

The test is based on the residuals obtained from the SAR model and the statistics given by equation [4.63]:

$$LM_{\lambda|\rho} = \frac{\widehat{d_{\widehat{\rho}}^2}}{T_{22} - (T_{21A})^2 \widehat{V}(\widehat{\rho})} \qquad [4.63]$$

with $T_{21A} = \text{trace}\left[\mathbf{W}_2\mathbf{W}_1\mathbf{A}^{-1} + \mathbf{W}_2'\mathbf{W}_1\mathbf{A}^{-1}\right]$, $\mathbf{A} = (\mathbf{I} - \widehat{\rho}\mathbf{W}_1)$ and $\widehat{V}(\widehat{\rho})$ is the variance of the parameter ρ from the SAR model. Under the

H_0 hypothesis, the test statistic, $LM_{\lambda|\rho}$, is distributed according to the Chi-2 distribution with one degree of freedom.

Similarly, it is possible to check for the significance of the ρ parameter, which means that $H_0 : \rho = 0$, when the parameter λ is significantly different from zero. The non-constrained model type does not change and represents the SAC model (equation [SAC]). The specification of the constrained form can be expressed by the SEM model (equation [4.64]):

$$
\begin{aligned}
\mathbf{y} &= \mathbf{X}\beta + \nu \\
\nu &= \lambda\mathbf{W}2 + \epsilon
\end{aligned}
\qquad [4.64]
$$

The test statistic is based on the residuals obtained from the SEM model and is given by the equation [4.65]:

$$
LM_{\rho|\lambda} = \frac{\left(\hat{\epsilon}'\mathbf{B}'\mathbf{B}\mathbf{W}_1 y\right)^2}{H_\rho - H_{\theta\rho}\widehat{V}(\widehat{\theta})H'_{\theta\rho}}
\qquad [4.65]
$$

with $\hat{\epsilon}$ being the estimate residual vector, using MLs, of a spatially autoregressive error model, $\theta = (\beta', \lambda, \sigma^2)$ and $\mathbf{B} = (\mathbf{I} - \widehat{\lambda}\mathbf{W}_2)$ and:

$$
H_\rho = \mathrm{trace}(\mathbf{W}_1^2) + \mathrm{trace}(\mathbf{B}\mathbf{W}_1\mathbf{B}^{-1})'(\mathbf{B}\mathbf{W}_1\mathbf{B}^{-1})
$$
$$
+ \frac{(\mathbf{B}\mathbf{W}_1\mathbf{X}\beta)'(\mathbf{B}\mathbf{W}_1\mathbf{X}\beta)}{\sigma^2}
$$

$$
\mathbf{H}'_{\theta\rho} = \left(
\begin{array}{c}
\dfrac{(\mathbf{B}\mathbf{X})'\mathbf{B}\mathbf{W}_1\mathbf{X}\beta}{\sigma^2} \\
\mathrm{trace}(\mathbf{W}_2 B^{-1})'\mathbf{B}\mathbf{W}_1\mathbf{B}^{-1} + \mathrm{trace}(\mathbf{W}_2\mathbf{W}_1\mathbf{B}^{-1}) \\
0
\end{array}
\right)
$$

and finally where $\widehat{V}(\widehat{\theta})$ is the variance-covariance matrix for the estimator $\widehat{\theta}$ of parameter θ of the SEM model. Under the null hypothesis, H_0, this test follows a Chi-2 distribution with one degree of freedom.

Thus by using the different possible autoregressive specifications, it becomes possible to identify an optimal specification based purely on statistical criteria, such as the LM tests.

4.5.1.4. *In practice*

In practice, Anselin and Rey [ANS 91] propose a combination of tests for choosing the most adequate spatial model for representing the given data when the Moran' I index rejects the hypothesis of a lack of spatial autocorrelation. Using decision rules provided by Anselin and Florax [ANS 95], the use of these tests allows to discriminate between the SAR and SEM models. In general, the selection criteria for choosing an appropriate spatial autoregressive model can be summarized in the following decision rules (Figure 4.17):

– when the test LM_{LAG} value is significant and the LM_{ERR} is insignificant, the most appropriate model is the spatial autoregressive (SAR) model;

– symmetrically, when the test LM_{ERR} value is significant and the LM_{LAG} value is insignificant, the most appropriate model is the error (SEM) autocorrelation model.

However, it is possible that both statistical tests are significant. In this case, one decision rule can be as follows:

– when the test LM_{LAG} value is higher than the test LM_{ERR} value, it would be best to consider the spatial autoregressive (SAR) model;

– when the test LM_{ERR} value is higher than the test LM_{LAG} value, it would be best to consider the error (SEM) autocorrelation model.

Of course, if both statistics are significant, it could also well be appropriate to estimate a general autoregressive model (SAR or GAR). This simple approach helps to guide the choices related to spatial autoregressive models.

4.6. Conclusion

This chapter has focused on the reasons motivating the choice of a particular spatial autoregressive specification from a theoretical point of view, by presenting the data generating processes underlying each of the different possibilities. After this intuitive presentation, we have focused on some statistical tests involving the Lagrange multiplier to choose the appropriate specification. The reader interested in the application of spatial econometric models should now have at his disposal the most essential information regarding the intuition behind spatial econometric model applications in a very condensed form.

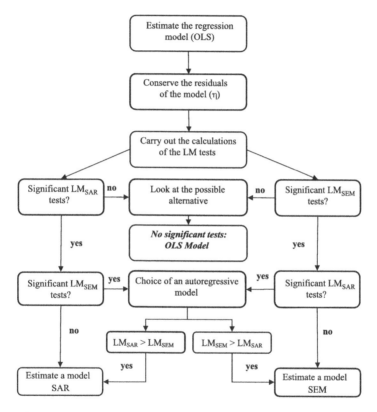

Figure 4.17. *Strategies for testing for residual spatial autocorrelation and consequences on the estimation method*

Special attention was paid to the presentation of DGP that enables the researcher to determine, *a priori*, the possible type of the spatial autoregressive process and thus propose a suitable modeling approach. If the statistical tests allow us to formally discriminate between the different specifications, the fact remains that the researcher often has his own ideas about the effects that he wants to test before starting the statistical analysis. In this sense, the use of one spatial autoregressive process rather than another can be easily inspired by the theoretical approach. The intuitive presentation of DGP should allow the reader to understand the advantages/disadvantages of each of the autoregressive specification.

The researcher may also be interested in determining the form taken by the spatial structure present in the residuals of the model, based on a purely statistical point of view. Finally, the reader should understand that the presence of spatial autocorrelation among residuals can have different consequences depending on the autoregressive process type suggested, as suggested by the DGP.

Avoiding discussing the estimation methods and the development of the estimators is a deliberate choice: there is a set of essential and good references in the field. Our goal is mainly to explain the intuition behind the choice of a given spatial autoregressive specification. This proves to be very helpful for researchers who intend to work with spatial data, while not having a full background in econometrics nor statistics. The reader wishing to have a more detailed view of the estimation methods can consult the works of LeSage and Pace [LES 09], LeSage [LES 99] and Anselin [ANS 88] or books that combine diverse authors and thus present the research advancement in certain more specialized fields [ANS 95, FIS 10].

We would like to repeat that our approach was designed mainly to ensure that the basics, which for some seem hard to grasp, be made a lot more simple, or at least intuitive. It is also important that the reader should better understand the implications and uses of spatial autoregressive models. After all, conclusion validity depends on statistical analysis.

To investigate the consequences of neglecting the fact that data are autocorrelated over space, we have developed a program in the appendix, which follows what has been discussed in Chapters 2 and 3. This program simulates spatial data and allows to estimate spatial autoregressive models. These programs, similar to a Monte Carlo experiment, allow to generate data based on the underlying DGP. The reader can calculate the test statistics presented in the actual chapter, such as the LM test, as well as the Moran I index starting with construction of a chosen spatial weight matrix. It also shows how, using Stata, the different spatial autoregressive specification, can be estimated. The estimation of the SLX model are not formally presented, but are straightforward applications based on the standard OLS models.

We believe that the application of the formulas at a small scale, will allow the reader to make better connections between the theoretical concepts covered in this chapter and the empirical applications. This program can then be modified to create your own exercises or simply to perform Monte Carlo type experiments for personal enjoyment or research.

5

Spatio-temporal Modeling

5.1. Introduction

The previous chapters have focused on demonstrating how the spatial dimension could be incorporated in the descriptive analysis of microdata in order to find out if the distribution of a variable is structured spatially (see Chapter 3) and how to include this potential spatial structure of data into modeling (see Chapter 4). The inclusion of the spatial structure of the data is based largely upon its construction based on an exogenous spatial weights matrix which synthesizes the relations linking the observations among themselves and which is then standardized (Chapter 2) in order to reflect the first law of geography. Evidently, the shape of these relations depends on the type of microdata used: cross-sectional or spatio-temporal data.

Up to this point, the focus has been based upon considering the spatial data as being only cross-sections. However, observation collection is not always performed in a strictly spatial context. Spatial cross-section data can sometimes be pooled over time. In this case, a temporal dimension is added to the spatial dimension. This temporal dimension influence during the data generating. Without the loss of generalities it is possible to identify two types of spatio-temporal data: data from spatial panels and spatial data (cross-sections) pooled over time. Although the difference between the two types of data is limited, it is nonetheless important. For spatial panel data, the same spatial units are observed at regular temporal intervals. A panel is called balanced when all the spatial units are observed exactly during the same period of time[1]. However, the application of estimation methods does not necessarily require that the panel is balanced [BAL 05, HSI 05, WOO 01].

Several analyses, notably in regional science, are based on a different consideration of the panel data. The spatial units are based upon the aggregation of individual spatial units in order to designate a geographical (or spatial) unit. This kind of panel data must be called pseudo-panel [DEA 85, HEC 85, MOF 93]: one observation represents the mean or the sum of a set of micro units which, over time, can change or move from one spatial unit to another. The possibility of migratory movement, as well as the appearance and disappearance of micro units implies that observations were not made in the same way over time. It is often called panel data in this instance but the correct term is pseudo-panel as it is not a panel in the strict sense of the word.

In summary, the difference between the panel and pseudo-panel approaches are mainly linguistic because, as it is suggested by several authors, the estimation process of such data is made in a similar manner [PAQ 04, VER 92]. For this reason, this particularity is not generally distinguished. Most of these applications are therefore based on pseudo-panel data but the methods used were based on the panel.

One of the main problems with the panel approach (and pseudo-panel) is that the individual behaviors are aggregated to produce a single observation and this aggregation diminishes the variability present in microdata. It is therefore useful to work directly with the individual spatial data observed over time even if the individual units are not repeated.

It is at this point that spatio-temporal data consist of spatial data pooled over time. The use of this kind of data has had little development. In fact, most of the empirical applications lying on this kind of data make the implicit assumption that the temporal dimension

---

1 The pace of time is identified beforehand, generally in years, trimesters, months, etc.

can be neglected in the data generating process. As a consequence, the estimation process is based on the spatial methods already covered in previous chapters [PAE 09]. However, the application of spatial methods for spatio-temporal data can introduce certain biases on the statistics and tests and thus invalidate the analyses. The spatial data pooled over time on the one hand, integrates information on the spatial variability of behaviors and on the other hand, integrates information of the evolution of behavior over time. Therefore, the difference between spatial data pooled over time and spatial panel data comes from the fact that the spatial units are not repeated over time. One specific unit is observed once over time. There are numerous examples of this type of data: housing transactions, accidents (road or otherwise), crime, the creation/closure of companies, etc. The difference with spatial panel data is therefore based on the plurality/singularity of spatial observations over time.

The literature and the methods of statistics relative to spatial panel data has been widely developed[2]. This literature finds many applications in urban and regional economics because of the large amount of information available at a regional level and over several periods of time.

However, there exists very little important work on data composed of both spatial and temporal characteristics without being structured as a panel. It is nonetheless important to integrate the spatial reality of observations in the statistical methodology, as well as that of the period of time in which these observations were collected. This double consideration is crucial because the effects are different: the spatial dimension is multidirectional whereas the temporal dimension is unidirectional. Both considerations produce a three dimensional scheme of DGP that must be accounted for.

The next few pages will focus on the presentation of the characteristics of spatial data pooled over time. They will examine the

---

2 Arbia [ARB 11] mentions that this field of research has probably been the most active of spatial econometrics during the second half of the 2000s. Readers interested in this topic should consult the book written by Elhorst [ELH 13].

collection process for this type of data and will establish the differences from the strictly spatial consideration [DUB 13a, DUB 13b]. A thorough comprehension of the DGP allows for the proposition of a new manner of building the weights matrix in order to reflect the temporal constraints on the spatial relations. This new matrix allows for the exploitation of all the potential of the methods discussed in Chapter 4, while considering the restrictions of the directionality of the temporal dimension. Particular attention is given to the representation of the reality of data collection and to the importance of considering both multidirectional spatial and unidirectional temporal relations.

Section 5.2 presents the impact of the double dimension (spatial and temporal) on the structure of the links uniting the observations (points) between themselves, all this from the examples used in the Chapter 1. Section 5.4 focuses on the study of the possible DGP of individual spatial data pooled over time. The presentation is based on the simple, yet concrete, example of the process of accumulation of spatial observation over time and shows how the schematization differs from the strictly spatial case. Section 5.5 then presents the impact of the spatial and temporal dimensions on the construction of weights matrices. Section 5.7 addresses the manner in which to construct matrices of temporal weights which allow for the consideration of unidirectional, spatial relations. In order for this to happen, it is necessary to develop a temporal weights matrix allowing for the development of a (unique) spatio-temporal weights matrix. Section 5.9 lists (in a non-exhaustive manner) studies that have focused on the exploitation of the potential of the time and space dimensions while the spatial data has been pooled over time. Finally, section 5.10 proposes a brief discussion on the principal notions raised in this chapter.

5.2. The impact of the two dimensions on the structure of the links: structuring of spatio-temporal links

As was seen in Chapter 4, the spatial relations are multidirectional, while the temporal relations are unidirectional. The particularity of the spatio-temporal data lies therefore in the direction of the relations between the observations. Through an illustration, it is possible using arrows to formalize the relations between the observations. These relations can be bilateral (multidirectional for spatial relations over the same period of time) or unilateral (unidirectional for spatially localized temporal relations). The hybrid form of the relations (schematized by arrows) thus permits the conceptualization of the temporal reality of the collection of spatial observations by varying the connectivity of the arrows (by double or single directions).

By taking the example of the Figure 1.1 and by assuming that the two first observations of the variable y, y_1 and y_2, are collected during the first period, and that the following two observations y_3 and y_4, are from the second period, the diagram of the relations changes according to the time dimension (Figure 5.1). Therefore, the realizations y_1 and y_2 are linked in a multidirectional manner (the arrow goes in both directions), in the same way as the realizations y_3 and y_4. However, the arrows become one way between the observations made at different time periods. Based on the constraints linked to the chronology of the events, the observations y_1 and y_2 can influence the behaviors of the observations y_3 and y_4, while the opposite is impossible. The arrows are unidirectional and are based on the temporal relation of the observation collection.

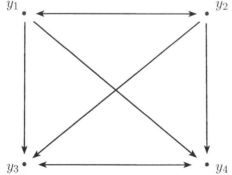

Figure 5.1. *Representation of the spatial relations between variables for four observations*

It is therefore necessary, within the framework of spatial data pooled over time[3], to develop relations of a hybrid form since the inclusion of those single spatial effects will bias the links of the spatial relations between observations [DUB 13a]. However, this bias can have many undesirable consequences especially when using strictly spatial methods to deal empirically with data of a spatio-temporal nature. The autoregressive spatial coefficient can be greatly biased, resulting in errors when calculating marginal effects [LES 09] and bringing about, *in fine*, many other problems, such as the unit roots problem [DUB 13b].

Furthermore, a bias of the autoregressive coefficient can introduce a contention with other spatially structured independent variables. This contention of effects can lead to marginalizing the effect of an independent variable whose marginal contribution we are seeking to measure [DUB 12, DUB 14a].

So how does we bypass the possible problem of bias in the autoregressive spatial effect in a spatio-temporal context? This is the question that will be answered in the following sections.

5.3. Spatial representation of spatio-temporal data

The bias of the spatial effect in a spatio-temporal context comes in great part from the representation which is laid out *a priori* on the DGP. The strictly spatial representation rests on the cartography of a collection of points distributed on east–west and north–south dimensions (Figure 5.2). This two-dimensional representation is analogous to the one previously addressed in the Chapter 2 and does not take into account the temporal dimension since all the observed points are put in relation.

Such a representation imposes a set of relatively strong assumptions on the DGP. The first assumption is that the temporal dimension has no role in the value determination process of variables. In other words,

---

3 We will refer to this as spatio-temporal data for the rest of the presentation.

only the spatial process influences the observed realizations. The two-dimensional representation thus assumes that the temporal distance between observations has no incidence, that is to say that the observations in the previous period have the same weight, on the observations being considered here, of another observation collected many time periods before. The DGP is then strictly spatial.

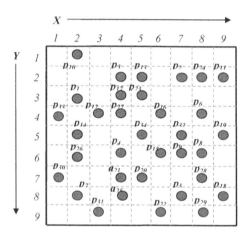

Figure 5.2. *Spatial representation of observations (all periods of time)*

A second assumption behind the two-dimensional representation is that certain future realizations affect the behavior of past realizations [DUB 13a, DUB 11]. The DGP happens in a context of perfect memory, and of perfect anticipation, thus excluding the idea of incertitude linked to future realizations. It must be admitted that these assumptions are strong and need to be verified before even assuming them to be true. For these reasons, it is important to envisage the DGP in a spatio-temporal context.

As has been previously mentioned, the spatial and temporal relations are of different natures (Chapter 4). Spatial relations are multidirectional, that is to say that the behavior of a variable for a given spatial unit, y_i is influenced by the realization of the variables of the neighboring units, y_j (equation [5.1]), of which the resultant is given by the matrix expression of the product of the matrix of the given vector of variables by the weights matrix to obtain a spatial lag variable written $\mathbf{W}\mathbf{y}$ (equation [5.2]):

$$y_i = \rho y_j + \epsilon_i \quad \forall\, i = 1, \ldots, N$$

$$y_j = \sum_{j=1}^{N} w_{ij}^{\star} y_j \qquad\qquad\qquad [5.1]$$

By using the matrix notations, we obtain:

$$\mathbf{y} = \rho \mathbf{W}\mathbf{y} + \epsilon \qquad\qquad\qquad [5.2]$$

As for the temporal equations, they are unidirectional, that is to say that the realization of a variable in the previous period, y_{t-1}, influences the realization of that variable in the present, y_t, whereas the opposite is not possible (equation [5.3]):

$$y_t = \psi y_{t-1} + \epsilon_t \quad \forall\, t = 1, \ldots, T$$

$$y_{t-1} = L.y_t \qquad\qquad\qquad [5.3]$$

As we have seen in Chapter 4, it is possible to synthesize this relation using the matrix notation. The temporal lag operator $L.$, takes the form of a weights matrix where the first elements situated directly under the principal diagonal take the value 1 whereas the other elements are fixed at 0 (equation [5.4]):

$$\mathbf{y} = \psi \mathbf{W}\mathbf{y} + \epsilon \qquad\qquad\qquad [5.4]$$

where $\mathbf{y}$ is a vector of dimension $(T \times 1)$, ϵ a vector of error terms of dimension $(T \times 1)$ and $\mathbf{W}$ a matrix of dimension $(T \times T)$.

Spatio-temporal relations must therefore take into account the multidirectionality of spatial relations, but also the unidirectionality of temporal relations. It is therefore necessary to determine a way of mixing the spatial and temporal approaches into one integrated approach which would allow taking simultaneously into account both dimensions and their respective constraints. The spatio-temporal autoregressive process is the tributary of the two separate autoregressive processes. The non-constrained form of the spatio-temporal autoregressive expression must therefore integrate two indexes in its expression, one relate to spatial dimension, i, and one relate to temporal dimension, t (equation [5.5]):

$$y_{it} = \rho y_{jt} + \psi y_{jt-1} + \epsilon_{it} \qquad [5.5]$$

where:

$$y_{jt} = \sum_{j=1}^{N} w_{ij}^{\star} y_{jt} \qquad [5.6]$$

and:

$$y_{jt-1} = L.y_{jt} \qquad [5.7]$$

In matrix notation, the spatio-temporal autoregressive (STAR) model is expressed by (equation [5.8]):

$$\mathbf{y} = \rho \underline{\mathbf{S}} \mathbf{y} + \psi \underline{\mathbf{W}} \mathbf{y} + \epsilon \qquad [5.8]$$

where $\underline{\mathbf{S}}$ is a spatial weights matrix accounting for relations among observations of the same period (multidirectional relations) and $\underline{\mathbf{W}}$ represents a spatial weights matrix linking observations from the previous time period $(t-1)$ to the actual time period t (unidirectional relations). Both matrices are of the same dimensions, here $(N_T \times N_T)$ (it will be discussed later). The parameters ρ and ψ measure, respectively, the degree of spatial dependence in the same period (spatial spillover effect) and the degree of spatial dependence for the previous period (dynamic spatial effect).

The challenge of spatio-temporal analysis thus consists of creating matrices of spatio-temporal weights with the intention of measuring correctly the effects of spatial (spillover) and temporal (dynamic) effects [DUB 14a]. It should be mentioned, at this stage, that as compared to the panel case, there is no temporal dynamic effect relate to the values of y_i in the previous period. This is because a given observation, i, is only collected once over the entire temporal dimension. Thus, there is no possibility of introducing the spatio-temporal lag value of y_i, usually written as y_{it-1}. This is a major difference that help greatly to simply the estimation process of the models.

5.4. Graphic representation of the spatial data generating processes pooled over time

The graphic representation of the accumulation of the spatial layers pooled over time allows for a better understanding of the process which originates spatio-temporal realizations. From this graphic representation (Figure 5.2), the possibility of splitting the accumulation process in various spatial layers according to the dates of realizations of the observations becomes evident. The realizations of the first spatial layer can thus be seen as the result of the traditional spatial connections among the whole observations (Figure 5.3).

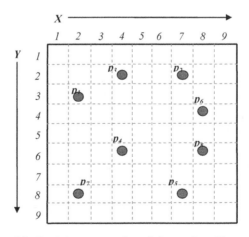

Figure 5.3. *Spatial representation of observations (first period)*

The second period can yield to the realization of other observations, different from those of the first period. The second spatial layer is thus composed of nine new observations (Figure 5.4) which can be spatially linked (as is the case for the spatial data collected in the first time period), but which can potentially be influenced by the realizations of the previous period. This second possibility formally introduces the dynamic effect of spatial data collected from the previous time period.

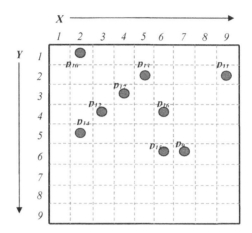

Figure 5.4. *Spatial representation of observations (second period of time)*

Similarly, a third period shows the collection of ten spatially linked realizations (Figure 5.5). These observations can be influenced by the realization of the observations of the first or second period, but cannot influence the realizations from the previous time periods. This characteristic derives from the unidirectionality of the temporal dimension.

Finally, seven realizations arise during a fourth period (Figure 5.6). Once again, these realizations can be spatially linked between them but cannot have any influence on past realizations, that is to say those observed from the last three periods.

In the end, the set of available realizations after four periods (Figure 5.2) is a cumulative process which can be split into different spatial processes which succeed one another over time, but also in accordance with past processes which shape the present and the future. The realizations are thus the result of a continuous collection of spatial data over time. The spatial structure thus lies on an accumulation of two-dimensional layers on a third dimension: time [DUB 13a]. The collection of spatial layers brings a set of constraints on the relations between observations [DUB 13b].

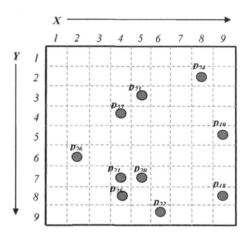

Figure 5.5. *Spatial representation of observations (third period of time)*

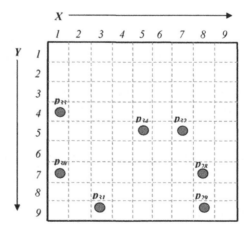

Figure 5.6. *Spatial representation of observations (fourth period of time)*

The most important is now to find a way of expressing the structure of the links between the realizations while respecting the directional constraints on the relations. The simplest approach consists of assuming that the spatial relations are multidirectional only for a given period. Thus, only the observations of a same layer are characterized by [DUB 14b] a bidirectional link (Figure 5.7). It is possible to extend this representation to the situation where the realizations of the previous period influence the realizations of the present period. In this case, these links adopt a mixed form: multidirectional relations become apparent (double direction arrows), as do unidirectional ones (one direction arrows), for the set of periods where the observations are collected (Figure 5.8).

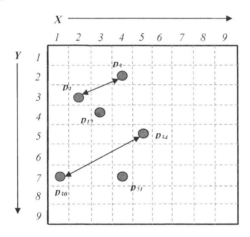

Figure 5.7. *Spatial links between observations*

In a similar manner to spatial relations, it is possible to generate a set of temporal relations of a higher order in order to link observations from previous period $(t - p)$ to the period t for $p > 1$. This construction can generate a set of diagrams linking the observations between themselves for periods of time which are not necessarily subsequent (Figure 5.9). These relations are unidirectional since they report the temporal connection between spatial observations.

It is also possible to link future observations to present observations and thus postulate a simultaneous relation or even an anticipation effect [DUB 14c]. The observations of different periods can be linked in a multidirectional manner (simultaneity); or the observations of subsequent periods can be linked in a unidirectional manner to the present periods (anticipation).

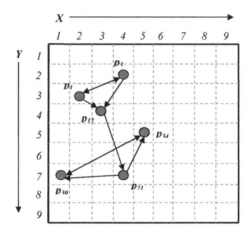

Figure 5.8. *Possible links between observations taking temporal constraints into account*

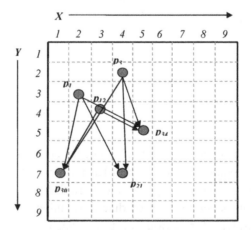

Figure 5.9. *Spatial links of a higher order between observations (including temporal constraints)*

If the multidirectional links between future and present observations are possible from the decomposition of the global weights matrix, many debates and questions remain. If the anticipation process is possible and likely, the probability of the anticipated phenomenon realizing itself exactly is low and that probability decreases as the considered period increases.

The set of these possibilities and representations have an impact on the structure of the weights matrix. A spatio-temporal weights matrix which takes into account spatial structure as well as the chronology of the realizations must then be developed.

5.5. Impacts on the shape of the weights matrix

The graphic representation of spatio-temporal relations guides the construction of the (spatio-temporal) weights matrix. The temporal constraints of unidirectionality limit the taking into account of some spatial links.

Before discussing each case, it is necessary to sort the observations chronologically. By doing so, the first line of the database represents the first unit collected (the oldest), whereas the last line represents the most recent one. This chronological order allows for an easier representation of the matrices of weight [DUB 13a, DUB 13c].

Once the observations are sorted in chronological order, it is possible to examine different scenarios in the construction of the weights matrices in the spatio-temporal case.

The first case assumes that the multidirectional, spatial relations are only possible for the same time period (equation [5.2]). In this case, only the observations over the same period of time can be linked together spatially and the temporal links (dynamic effects) are thus assumed null[4]. The resulting weights matrix is a matrix is a block

---

4 In technical terms, this assumes that the parameter ψ of equation [5.8] is set to zero.

diagonal type[5]. This representation is similar to the one used to capture the spatial effect in the models developed for spatial panel data.

The second case links the realizations of the previous period to those of the present period (equation [5.4]). Unidirectional relations therefore permit the formalization of this reality. The elements of the upper triangular part of the weights matrix are null matrix as well as the elements on the block diagonal matrix are null. Only the elements on the lower part of the block diagonal are non-null. This representation allows the capture of the effect of spatial relations accounting for the constraints on the temporal (dynamic) relations.

The creation of two distinct weights matrix (one using the element on the principal diagonal and another using the lower triangular elements) allows to measure on the one hand the force of simultaneous spatial links, and on the other hand, the force of the temporal links that occur spatially.

Of course, the realizations of several periods previous to the present period. In this case, a supplementary set of unidirectional relations is added. These new relations increase the number of non-null elements under the principal diagonal. The temporal relations can be weighted according to their (temporal) remoteness and can consider the diminutions of the effect over time. It is therefore an extension of the previous case. The representation allows for the capture of both the spatial and spatialized temporal relations weighted for their relative positioning, temporal as much as spatial. The weights matrix takes a full lower triangular form which is added to the composing block diagonal, marking the spatial relations for the observations gathered at the same period of time. Once again, this full matrix can also be split into two distinct weights matrix: one that accounts only for spatial multidirectional effects, and another one that accounts for unidirectional spatial (dynamic) effects.

---

5 Technically, this representation refers to a specification of the weights matrix which is structured around the principal diagonal (see equations [5.2] and [5.8]).

An extreme case is when the spatial weights matrix is developed as in the strictly spatial case, when the only elements of the principal diagonal are fixed at 0. This is similar to applying spatial autoregressive model (Chapter 4) to spatio-temporal data. This specific case assumes that all the realizations are linked together in a multidirectional manner. In other words, the anticipation process is assumed to be done in a perfect manner and the realizations product of several periods passed are weighted by the same weight of the realizations produced by the previous period. This representation thus captures the spatial effects between the realizations, as well as the spatialized temporal relations. It is impossible, from such a specification, to isolate the spatial effect of multidirectional relations, which explains to a certain extent the bias that can occur in the identification of the spatial effect while the spatial data is being collected over time. In such context, the weights matrix does not express this process of data construction.

It is important to mention that the development of the spatio-temporal weights matrix allows to isolate and decompose the spatial effects when the spatial realizations are being collected continuously over time. The development of a spatio-temporal weights matrix can allow to capture the dynamic effects, linked to the factor of time, in a spatial context. To resume, it is possible to consider a set of spatio-temporal weights matrices that will allow to adequately isolate the spatial spillover effect, as well as the dynamic spatial effect. The different possible representations of DGP entail that the weights matrix, before standardization, is not necessarily symmetrical. In brief, there are as many DGP as possibilities on the spatio-temporal weights matrix [DUB 14a, DUB14b].

The shapes of the weights matrix is inspired in part by the spatial weights matrix, but also by the development of a temporal weights matrix. The consideration of the two matrices allows for the acquirement of the spatio-temporal weights matrix. This will be discussed later. For the moment, let us move on to the presentation of the shape the temporal weights matrix.

5.6. The structuring of temporal links: a temporal weights matrix

The temporal relations, like the spatial relations (Chapter 2) can be synthesized by a temporal weights matrix. The structure of the latter allows for the expression of the relations that occur at the same period as well as the relations that occur before and after. The simple way of structuring such a matrix is to order the realizations chronologically.

By considering that the observations result from a discrete period of time (for example, a month in the year), it is possible to decompose the relations from a general specification which looks like the one postulated to express the spatial relations (equation [2.17]) with the main difference that the measure of distance is not symmetrical and is not based on Pythagoras theorem, for example [DUB 13b, DUB14a, DUB14b]. The measure of temporal distance must be based on a new metric allowing for the expression of temporal distance separating the periods of time.

By using the information available over a year ($yyyy$) for observations collected in a specific month (mm), the calculation of temporal distance can be measured by the number of months that have passed between the realization of i and the realization j. By assuming that the realizations are collected continuously over several years, the general shape of the function allowing for the establishment of a chronological order can be given by the equation [5.9]:

$$v_i = 12 \times (yyyy_i - yyyy_{min}) + mm_i \ \forall \ i, j \qquad [5.9]$$

where $yyyy_{min}$ represents the first year when the data is collected. This specification can be extended to other measures of time, such as quarters[6] or days[7] Afterwards, the measure of temporal distance

---

6 In such a case, the measure of temporal distance between observations can be obtained by the relation $v_i = 4 \times (yyyy_i - yyyy_{min}) + qq_i \ \forall \ i, j$, where qq represents the quarter when the observations was collected.

7 In this case, the definition can be approached by $v_i = 365 \times (yyyy_i - yyyy_{min}) + 31 \times (mm_i - 1) + dd_i$, where dd represents the day when the observation was collected. Evidently this equation is but an approximation seeing as it does not take into account the fact that months do not have the same number of days.

between the realizations can be used to generate a measure which can express the temporal relation that unites observation i to observation j (equation [5.10]):

$$v_{ij} = (v_i - v_j) \quad \text{if } v_i \neq v_j \tag{5.10}$$

As previously, the (temporal) distances can be classified in a square table in which each line i shows the temporal distancing of the observation i from the other observation j. From this general construction, can be created the general, temporal, distance matrix (equation [5.11]):

$$L = \begin{pmatrix} 0 & v_{12} & v_{13} & \cdots & v_{1N} \\ v_{21} & 0 & v_{23} & \cdots & v_{2N} \\ v_{31} & v_{32} & 0 & \cdots & v_{3N} \\ \vdots & \vdots & \vdots & \ddots & \vdots \\ v_{N1} & v_{N2} & v_{N3} & \cdots & 0 \end{pmatrix} \tag{5.11}$$

The very definition of the function of time value entails that the temporal matrix cannot be symmetrical: the weights linking the past realizations to the present realizations are positive, whereas the weight linking the future realizations to the present realizations are negative. The observations collected previously are found under the principal diagonal and take on positive value. The zero values appearing in the upper triangular block show a simultaneity of the collection of spatial units.

Generally, and with the exception of the principal diagonal, a general element of the matrix v_{ij} takes on a value of 0 when the observations are being collected at the same time. The principal diagonal of the temporal matrix contains zeroes indicating that the temporal distance separating one observation from itself is null. In the same way, the other elements expressing the temporal distance between realizations product of a same period also take on a value of 0. This information thus marks a temporal simultaneity of spatial observations.

By way of example, in considering the realizations of the first periods from the Figure 5.2, it is therefore possible to obtain the shape of the following temporal distance matrix (Table 5.1).

The chronological ordering enables the decomposition of the creation of temporal weights matrix according to the characterization of the triangular parts of the temporal distance matrix and the identification of the elements equal to 0. Given this construction, it is easy to eliminate the relations that are not needed. As such, in placing constraints on the temporal relations, the shape of the temporal distance matrix is simplified and contains a more or less important number of elements fixed at zero while the temporal constraints are not respected. The shape of this matrix largely influences the form of the spatio-temporal weights matrix.

The temporal weights matrix is constructed from information on the temporal distance separating the spatial observations. It is preferable to have a temporal weights matrix in which the weights are equal to 1 for the observations of the same period and the lesser weights underlining the temporal distancing (in a manner analogous to the spatial distance.) In order to do so, weights, t_{ij}, is constructed using the temporal distances v_{ij} obtained by the equation [5.10] and express the temporal proximity between the observations i and j (equation [5.12])[8]:

$$t_{ij} = \begin{cases} \kappa |v_{ij}|^{-\gamma} & \text{if } v_{ij} > 0 \\ 1 & \text{if } v_{ij} = 0 \\ 0 & \text{if } v_{ij} < 0 \end{cases} \qquad [5.12]$$

where κ is a scalar of which the value is inferior or equal to one ($\kappa \leq 1$), allowing for the consideration of the fact that the relations linking the observations i and j of a different period have distances time different

---

8 The case in which it is not desirable to consider the effect of anticipation can be created from this general form: the addition of a constraint to the system. This constraint provides for a general element of the temporal weights matrix being zero if the temporal distance is null, as is v_j is superior to $v_i : t_{ij} = 0$ if $v_i < v_j \, \forall \, i = j$.

from the distance time when the two observations have been collected at the same period. The parameter γ, as in the case of the spatial weights matrix, is a scalar which penalizes more or less strongly the temporal distancing[9] By considering this transformation, and from the previous example (Table 5.1), the shape of the temporal weights matrix takes on the form of Table 5.2 while κ is fixed at 0. In this instance, only the spatial links of the same period are considered.

Points	1	2	3	4	5	6	7	8	9	10	11	12	13	14	15	16	17
1	0	0	0	0	0	0	0	0	-1	-1	-1	-1	-1	-1	-1	-1	-1
2	0	0	0	0	0	0	0	0	-1	-1	-1	-1	-1	-1	-1	-1	-1
3	0	0	0	0	0	0	0	0	-1	-1	-1	-1	-1	-1	-1	-1	-1
4	0	0	0	0	0	0	0	0	-1	-1	-1	-1	-1	-1	-1	-1	-1
5	0	0	0	0	0	0	0	0	-1	-1	-1	-1	-1	-1	-1	-1	-1
6	0	0	0	0	0	0	0	0	-1	-1	-1	-1	-1	-1	-1	-1	-1
7	0	0	0	0	0	0	0	0	-1	-1	-1	-1	-1	-1	-1	-1	-1
8	0	0	0	0	0	0	0	0	-1	-1	-1	-1	-1	-1	-1	-1	-1
9	1	1	1	1	1	1	1	1	1	0	0	0	0	0	0	0	0
10	1	1	1	1	1	1	1	1	1	0	0	0	0	0	0	0	0
11	1	1	1	1	1	1	1	1	1	0	0	0	0	0	0	0	0
12	1	1	1	1	1	1	1	1	1	0	0	0	0	0	0	0	0
13	1	1	1	1	1	1	1	1	1	0	0	0	0	0	0	0	0
14	1	1	1	1	1	1	1	1	1	0	0	0	0	0	0	0	0
15	1	1	1	1	1	1	1	1	1	0	0	0	0	0	0	0	0
16	1	1	1	1	1	1	1	1	1	0	0	0	0	0	0	0	0
17	1	1	1	1	1	1	1	1	1	0	0	0	0	0	0	0	0
Time passed between observations																	

Table 5.1. *Matrix of temporal distances between the observations*

By placing the wanted constraints on the temporal relations (notably by varying the values of the parameters κ and γ), the temporal weights

---

9 As previously seen, the parameter γ can take on the values 0 (no penalization), 1 (inverse temporal distance) or 2 (square of the inverse temporal distance).

matrix is simplified and contains null elements. The shape of the matrix is determined by the construction of the spatio-temporal weights matrix.

Points	1	2	3	4	5	6	7	8	9	10	11	12	13	14	15	16	17
1	0	1	1	1	1	1	1	1	0	0	0	0	0	0	0	0	0
2	1	0	1	1	1	1	1	1	0	0	0	0	0	0	0	0	0
3	1	1	0	1	1	1	1	1	0	0	0	0	0	0	0	0	0
4	1	1	1	0	1	1	1	1	0	0	0	0	0	0	0	0	0
5	1	1	1	1	0	1	1	1	0	0	0	0	0	0	0	0	0
6	1	1	1	1	1	0	1	1	0	0	0	0	0	0	0	0	0
7	1	1	1	1	1	1	0	1	0	0	0	0	0	0	0	0	0
8	1	1	1	1	1	1	1	0	0	0	0	0	0	0	0	0	0
9	0	0	0	0	0	0	0	0	0	1	1	1	1	1	1	1	1
10	0	0	0	0	0	0	0	0	1	0	1	1	1	1	1	1	1
11	0	0	0	0	0	0	0	0	1	1	0	1	1	1	1	1	1
12	0	0	0	0	0	0	0	0	1	1	1	0	1	1	1	1	1
13	0	0	0	0	0	0	0	0	1	1	1	1	0	1	1	1	1
14	0	0	0	0	0	0	0	0	1	1	1	1	1	0	1	1	1
15	0	0	0	0	0	0	0	0	1	1	1	1	1	1	0	1	1
16	0	0	0	0	0	0	0	0	1	1	1	1	1	1	1	0	1
17	0	0	0	0	0	0	0	0	1	1	1	1	1	1	1	1	0
Identification of the observations at the same period																	

Table 5.2. *Temporal weights matrix for the same time period*

The constraints can also be seen as coming from the construction of a matrix of connectivity using the temporal weights matrix. In both cases, the term by term product of the temporal weights matrix (or of connectivity) and the spatial weights matrix allows the acquirement of a spatio-temporal weights matrix which takes into account the DGP. This point will be presented in the next section.

The constraints can also come from the construction of matrix of connectivity from the temporal weights matrix. In each case, the term by term matrix helps to produce a unique spatio-temporal weights matrix [DUB14b, DUB 14c].

5.7. Creation of spatio-temporal weights matrices

The directionality of the effects can be introduced with the help of a single matrix of (spatio-temporal) weights which enables the consideration of the respective particularity of the relations. The structure of the matrix can be done by developing two matrices: a spatial weights matrix (multidirectionality of effects) and a temporal weights matrix (unidirectionality of effects). This approach is generally retained in empirical literature [DUB 13a, DUB 13b, DUB 11, HUA 10, NAP 11, SMI 09].

Formally, the structure of the general spatio-temporal weights matrix is defined by combining the elements of the spatial weights, s_{ij}, to the corresponding temporal weights, t_{ij}, and this the whole set of observations[10] (equation [5.13]):

$$\mathbf{W} = \mathbf{S} \odot \mathbf{T} = \begin{pmatrix} 0 & s_{12} \times t_{12} & s_{13} \times t_{13} & \cdots & s_{1N} \times t_{1N} \\ s_{21} \times t_{21} & 0 & s_{23} \times t_{23} & \cdots & s_{2N} \times t_{2N} \\ s_{31} \times t_{31} & s_{32} \times t_{32} & & \cdots & s_{3N} \times t_{3N} \\ \vdots & \vdots & \vdots & \ddots & \vdots \\ s_{N1} \times t_{N1} & s_{N2} \times t_{N2} & s_{N3} \times t_{N3} & \cdots & s_{NN} \times t_{NN} \end{pmatrix}$$

$$[5.13]$$

The final structure of the matrix is adaptable and can be adjusted to a set of specific situations. The first case is when the spatio-temporal weights matrix is equal to the spatial weights matrix ($\mathbf{W} = \mathbf{S}$). In this case, the set of elements of the temporal weights matrix is equal to one and the relations are assumed to be all simultaneous.

The second case is when only the realizations collected at the same period maintain multidirectional relations while the rest of the temporal relations are fixed at 0. In this case, the non-null elements of the spatio-temporal weights matrix are concentrated around the principal diagonal.

---

10 This matrix allows us to isolate spatial multidirectional effects and estimate the spatial spillover effect (rho) suach as in equations [5.2] and [5.8].$w_{ij} = s_{ij} \times t_{ij}$.

This structure is known as block diagonal, which is constituted of a set of matrices of squared spatial weight for each period. (equation [5.14]):

$$\underline{\mathbf{S}} = \begin{pmatrix} \mathbf{S}_{11} & 0 & 0 & \cdots & 0 \\ 0 & \mathbf{S}_{22} & 0 & \cdots & 0 \\ 0 & 0 & \mathbf{S}_{33} & \cdots & 0 \\ \vdots & \vdots & \vdots & \ddots & \vdots \\ 0 & 0 & 0 & \cdots & \mathbf{S}_{TT} \end{pmatrix} \tag{5.14}$$

where $\mathbf{S}_{tt}$ is the spatial weights matrix spatially linking each observation i and j collected during the period t.

This matrix allows to isolate spatial multidirectional effects and estimate the spatial spillover effect (rho) such as in equations [5.2] and [5.8].

The third case is when there exist relations between past and present observations. In this case, certain elements of the inferior, triangular part are no longer null. As such, the general form of the matrix is a mixture of the spatial matrices from the previous time period and the multiplication of the spatial relations between the observations of different periods weighted for their spatial distancing. The reader will be able to show that the general shape of the spatio-temporal weights matrix has the following shape (equation [5.15]):

$$\underline{\mathbf{W}} = \begin{pmatrix} 0 & 0 & 0 & \cdots & 0 \\ \mathbf{W}_{21} & 0 & 0 & \cdots & 0 \\ \mathbf{W}_{31} & \mathbf{W}_{32} & 0 & \cdots & 0 \\ \vdots & \vdots & \vdots & \ddots & \vdots \\ \mathbf{W}_{T1} & \mathbf{W}_{T2} & \mathbf{W}_{T3} & \cdots & 0 \end{pmatrix} \tag{5.15}$$

when the general matrix, $\mathbf{W}_{qp}$, links the spatial realizations i of the period q to the realizations j of the previous period p. The link postulated considers on the one hand, their temporal and spatial distancing. This possibility does not consider in any way the possibility of anticipation: it is assumed to be null.

This representation allows to isolate the dynamic effects (psi) such as in equations [5.4] and [5.8]. The consideration of the anticipation can turn out, at least in the short term, realistic. The relations of anticipation appear on the superior triangular part of the temporal weights matrix (equation [5.16]).

$$\overline{\mathbf{W}} = \begin{pmatrix} 0 & \mathbf{W}_{12} & \mathbf{W}_{13} & \cdots & \mathbf{W}_{1T} \\ 0 & 0 & \mathbf{W}_{23} & \cdots & \mathbf{W}_{2T} \\ 0 & 0 & 0 & \cdots & \mathbf{W}_{3T} \\ \vdots & \vdots & \vdots & \ddots & \vdots \\ 0 & 0 & 0 & \cdots & 0 \end{pmatrix} \qquad [5.16]$$

where the general matrix $\mathbf{W}_{pq}$ allows for the linking of the realizations i of the period q to the realizations j to the subsequent period p. This anticipation can be weighted to take into account both the spatial and temporal distancing.

It is possible to limit the temporal influence of the ulterior or subsequent period or to decompose the effect so that it may to proper to each period [DUB 13a]. It is also possible to construct a spatio-temporal weights matrix considering the set of spatial relations, while weighting the temporal distancing of observations. This shape, which is a variant of the matrix of strictly spatial weight takes the general shape given by [5.17]:

$$\mathbf{W} = \begin{pmatrix} \mathbf{S}_{11} & \mathbf{W}_{12} & \mathbf{W}_{13} & \cdots & \mathbf{W}_{1T} \\ \mathbf{W}_{21} & \mathbf{S}_{22} & \mathbf{W}_{23} & \cdots & \mathbf{W}_{2T} \\ \mathbf{W}_{31} & \mathbf{W}_{32} & \mathbf{S}_{33} & \cdots & \mathbf{W}_{3T} \\ \vdots & \vdots & \vdots & \ddots & \vdots \\ \mathbf{W}_{T1} & \mathbf{W}_{T2} & \mathbf{W}_{T3} & \cdots & \mathbf{S}_{TT} \end{pmatrix} \qquad [5.17]$$

In matrix form, we obtain a complete decomposition such as:

$$\mathbf{W} = \underline{\mathbf{S}} + \underline{\mathbf{W}} + \overline{\mathbf{W}} \qquad [5.18]$$

Different shapes of matrices of spatio-temporal weights can be considered according to the constraints the researcher has placed and according to the assumptions that are placed on the DGP. In the end, the standardization of the spatio-temporal weights matrix enables the performance of analyses discussed in Chapter 3 and the modeling examined in Chapter 4 by substituting the definitions of the matrices of weight. The new matrices also consider the spatio-temporal structure on the magnitude of statistics and the estimated coefficients. It is therefore possible to use the existing estimation methods in spatial cases and to transpose them to spatio-temporal cases.

5.8. Applications of autocorrelation tests and of autoregressive models

The development of the matrices of spatio-temporal weight enables the development of tests and of models that are adapted to the spatial data pooled over time. The simplest way is to use the set of tests and existing, econometric models (Chapters 3 and 4), but to replace to the definition of the weights matrix so that it respects the pooled structure of spatial data. This idea is presented for the detection test based on the statistic I de Moran [DUB 13a].

As mentioned before (Chapter 4), the spatio-temporal weights matrices can be used to propose a model adapted to the context [DUB 14c]. As such, in simply resuming the expression of the spatial, autoregressive model, (SAR equation [5.19]) or the model with spatially lagged errors (SEM equation [5.20]), a spatio-temporal model can be proposed, allowing for the capture of the effects of spatial spillover effect when the spatial data is pooled over time (equations [5.19] and [5.20]):

$$\mathbf{y} = \underline{\mathbf{S}}\mathbf{y}\rho + \mathbf{X}\beta + \epsilon \qquad [5.19]$$

$$\mathbf{y} = \mathbf{X}\beta + \epsilon$$
$$\epsilon = \underline{\mathbf{S}}\epsilon\lambda + \eta \qquad [5.20]$$

where $\underline{S}$ is the spatial weights matrix, developed in a spatio-temporal context which can synthesize the spatial relations between the observations collected at the same period (equation [5.14])[11].

These equations can be modified to include the dynamic, temporal effects, as in the influence of past realizations of the variable depending on present realizations (equations [5.21] and [5.22]):

$$y = \underline{\mathbf{W}}\mathbf{y}\psi + \underline{\mathbf{S}}\mathbf{y}\rho + \mathbf{X}\beta + \mathbf{n} \qquad [5.21]$$

$$y = \underline{\mathbf{W}}\mathbf{y}\psi + \mathbf{X}\beta + \epsilon$$
$$\mathbf{n} = \underline{\mathbf{S}}\epsilon\lambda + \epsilon \qquad [5.22]$$

where $\underline{\mathbf{W}}$ is a spatio-temporal weights matrix which allows the consideration of the spatial proximity of the observations that have been recorded over one or several previous periods $(t - s)$, (equation [5.15]). The most used case is certainly when $s = 1$. In that way, the dynamic effect, measured by the coefficient ψ, enables taking into account the effect of dynamic persistence which would otherwise be falsely attributed the spatial dimension which does not consider the time dimension. This is a major contribution for modeling: to isolate and decompose the spatial effect according to the temporal dimension.

This type of model can be called STAR model seeing as it incorporates on the one hand, the idea of spatial autocorrelation linked to either the dependent variable or the error term, and on the other hand the idea of temporal autocorrelation (spatially located) linked to the dependent variable. The STAR model can thus capture the effects linked to both spatial and temporal dimensions, but in an individual way. The spatial dimension operates in a period of time defined beforehand (present period), while the temporal dimension operates in an equally established spatial demarcation (influence radius).

---

11 The reader will find in the Appendix, a program which can simulate this type of data. The exercise can easily be extended to other cases: but that will be left up to the reader.

The same logic is applied to models using spatial panel data, with the notable exception for instances where spatial data is pooled over time, the spatial observations are not repeated over time, which complexify the shape of the spatio-temporal weights matrix. At the moment, the spatio-temporal applications dedicated to spatial data pooled over time are rare. Nevertheless, it is possible to identify certain works that have had an interest in these types of models, particularly in the applications related to real estate.

5.9. Some spatio-temporal applications

The first works in regards to this potential adaption of the models where the spatial data is collected over time by Pace *et al.* [PAC 00, PAC 98] who develops a STAR model based on the decomposition of the weights matrix into various elements: a spatial weights matrix, a temporal weights matrix and a crossed product of the two matrices. The developed model searched to capture the spatial, temporal and spatial temporal effects of the process which determines the market value of real estate.

The same STAR model is reused by Tu *et al.* [TU 04] and Sun *et al.* [SUN 05] who propose to decompose the spatial effect of the value determination process of the condominiums into two components: one building component and one neighboring component. It is therefore no longer the case of only one spatial weights matrix being used, but two matrices. The first matrix enables the identification of transactions taking place in the same building, the second enables the identification the common components of the neighborhood for the set of buildings. The temporal weights matrix takes on the same form as in the works of Pace *et al.* [PAC 98] and the decomposition of the autoregressive effect thus takes on a more complex structure, considering the addition of the spatial weights matrix. The STAR approach is also held by Nappi-Choulet and Maury [NAP 11] and applied to real estate transactions in Paris.

However, one question remains with this type of application: can the decomposition of spatio-temporal effects really take place with a set of matrices without taking into account the directionality of the effects? This approach, although promising, does carry some assumptions which can be rejected. Smith and Wu [SMI 09] were the first to identify the restrictive hypotheses of the decomposition of spatial, temporal and spatio-temporal effects which can only indirectly capture spatio-temporal relations. The authors suggest that the development of a single spatio-temporal weights matrix could capture spatial effects in a temporal context. They propose an autoregressive temporal form of the error term to capture the effects of dynamic temporal overflows. The same type of matrix development is also suggested by Huang *et al.* [HUA 10] who propose a geographically weighted regression (GWR) using a spatio-temporal weights matrix (GTWR).

Finally, recent developments headed by Dubé and Legros [DUB 13a, DUB 13b, DUB 13c, DUB 11] show how the creation of several matrices of spatio-temporal weight can capture the effects of spatial overflows on the process of determination of real estate value, but mainly how the matrices of weight can also be used to generate new variables capable of isolating the localized temporal dynamic effects. The development of a set of spatio-temporal weights matrices can also take into account the spatial effects regarding temporal constraints of transaction realizations, as well as the temporal effects regarding the geographical localization of the observations.

5.10. Conclusion

In conclusion, the reader will notice that it can be easy to use the existing approaches and spatial statistics models and transpose them to a spatio-temporal case where the individual spatial data is collected over time while not being repeated. This modification can be made by developing a weights matrix which takes into account for both the spatial and the temporal dimensions of the collection of data. The construction of the spatio-temporal weights matrix rests on the development of two independent weights matrices: a spatial weights matrix (see Chapter 2) and a temporal weights matrix. The spatial weights matrix spatially links the observations between them, whereas the temporal weights matrix helps take into account the chronological order of the collection of observation, thus imposing certain constraints to the form of spatial relations.

The combination of the two matrices produces a unique weights matrix which takes into account the temporal reality of the unique collection of spatial data. Empirical examples show that neglecting the temporal dimension in the analysis of spatial data collected over time usually biases the effects of spatial correlation. The extent of this angle depends largely on the importance of the time dimension[12].

The properties of the statistical tests of spatial autocorrelation detection between variables (Chapter 3) and those of the spatial statistical models (Chapter 4) remain the same in a spatio-temporal context where individual spatial data are pooled over time, while not being repeated. Only one modification of the shape of the weights matrix is necessary to make the magnitude of the statistics and that of the coefficients reflect the reality associated with the collection of data. As we have seen before, the weights matrix remains a key factor in spatial econometrics (Chapter 2) and its construction must reflect as realisticly as possible the reality analyzed to make sure that the measured effects are as close as possible to that which is suggested by the DGP.

Adjusting the weights matrix turns out to be essential in order to avoid the trap of a useless correction of the spatial autocorrelation phenomenon and thus open the way to what is described by some as the new paradigm of spatial autocorrelation [LEG 93]. More generally, in order to better take into account the spatial and temporal dimensions, the adjustment of the weights matrix approaches the first law of geography [TOB 70] with respect to the constraints fixed by the possible realization in space time [HÄG 70].

It is important to note that the development of multiple matrices of spatio-temporal weight has other consequences, such as the creation of new variables allowing for the capture of various effects. This

---

12 The extent of the angle depends partly on the size of T.

approach namely allows for the introduction of the notion of comparables in the determination of sales prices [DES 10] in terms of certain parameters such as the delimitation of the radius of influence [DUB 14a] and the possibility of dividing this radius in various areas of influence [DUB 13c]. The creation of new variables namely allows for the estimation of dynamic effects despite the fact that the data is not structured in a typical panel framework.

Finally, the reader will notice that the construction of spatio-temporal weights matrices from the Hadamar product of two different matrices can be transposed to several other specific cases. The temporal weights matrix T can be used as a matrix of connectivity. The same general formula can obtain a shape of matrix adapted to another specific situation. This general approach can be applied in multiple contexts.

Conclusion

C.1. A brief review

This work aims to be an introduction to applied spatial econometrics using microdata. We do not claim to be revolutionizing the academic world with this work, but we do wish to provide a work of reference for those who are interested in quantitative spatial approaches without being econometricians. Different software and routines exist now and their use has become increasingly widespread in empirical applications. However, just because a tool exists does not mean it is necessarily used properly. In this sense, this book is meant to be a piece of work that links practice to theory. Our main objective was to present, in an intuitive way, the existing techniques and models. The researchers will now be able to use existing toolboxes and softwares without feeling as if they are dealing with black box that returns results without knowing what it means. Given the recent interest in spatial econometrics and the advantage for researchers outside of economics to use such models that consider spatial dimension, it seems important to present to idea behind the spatial econometrics approach.

Ignoring the spatial dimensions linked to geolocated data will likely result in problems in the usual models of linear regression. The consequences have been presented:

– the non-efficiency of the estimated variance and the non-validity of the usual tests of significance;

– depending on the form of the data generating process (DGP), a bias in the estimated coefficients for models based on spatial autoregressive specification over independent variables (SLX), over dependent variable (SAR), and over the error term (SEM) when the omitted variable is correlated with the independent variables.

For these reasons, it is important to know and to use the right data generating process (DGP) if the researcher wishes to make the most precise conclusions possible. Obviously, the consideration of the spatial dimensions does not make other possible problems disappear, such as:

– the right choice of the functional form;

– possible presence of nonlinear effects;

– the omission of important, measurable and significant variables in the analysis.

This book is meant to be progressive in its description of the characteristics of geolocalized microdata. The first chapter of the book presents a brief review of the models of linear regression, the assumptions underlying the validity of the usual approach, the types of data most used in empirical analyses and a brief (historical) introduction to spatial econometrics. This part clearly presents the advantage of spatial econometrics and its specificities. Readers wondering about the relevance of this approach can find answers on why it is relevant to consider spatial models when working with spatial data.

The second chapter of the book then deals with the way in which it possible to structure spatial relations from the distance separating the observations. These structures are usually synthesized through (spatial) weights matrix that make up the cornerstone of spatial econometrics as much for the tests of detection as for the statistical models. Particular attention is also given to the different forms of spatial relations that can exist: those founded on the transformation of the distance separating the observations (continuous relations) and those based on dichotomy (nearest neighbors).

The structuring of data and spatial links between variables is formally presented and supported with the help of simple schematic representations. These visual representations make up an interesting support for novices that wish to better understand the DGP of spatial data. In our opinion, it is also vital, for any researcher, to first focus on the possible process that leads to the generation of the values that are observed. Moreover, this is the basis of the chapter on databases containing both information on the spatial dimension and the temporal dimension (Chapter 5). The row-standardization of the spatial weights matrix proves to be a routine operation in spatial econometrics so as to obtain the comparable coefficients between them as well as simplifying the interpretation of the autoregressive coefficients[1]. Some simple examples allow the reader to follow the row-standardization operations (Chapter 2) and thus carry out a better follow-up of the operations to carry out. This approach is the same when it comes to standardizing the spatio-temporal weights matrix. A brief discussion on the "optimal" structure of such matrices is covered. However, in practice, there is no consensus on such an optimal structure: this discussion comes back in Chapter 3.

The third chapter proposes a review of the main statistics that allows us to verify if, for a given variable, there exists a certain pattern of spatial (auto)correlation between the observations. The calculation of Moran's I index allows us to measure the direction and the intensity of the global relation of spatial autocorrelation. This index remains the most used to test the presence of spatial autocorrelation among the residuals of the classical linear statistical model. Moreover, some authors recommend that this statistic is one of the most robust in detecting the spatial autocorrelation among residuals [ANS 95].

In addition to the calculation of the index of global spatial autocorrelation, the third chapter presents the calculation of the local indices of spatial association (or autocorrelation) (LISA) (I_i). These statistics allow the decomposition of the global Moran's I index as a function of the contribution of each of the pairs of observations in the calculation: the value of a given variable, y_i, and the associated value of the variable in its neighborhood, y_j. It also allows a complete

---

1 It is also of some interest when decomposing the marginal effect, as seen in Chapter 4.

exploratory spatial descriptive analysis (ESDA) and the identification of certain zones of observations for which the values are significantly opposed to the values taken in the neighborhood (*diamonds in the rough* or *black sheep*). This analysis can enable the identification of certain spatial patterns that can correspond to certain spatial variables likely to have been omitted from the analysis and, thus, benefiting the starting empirical analysis. Obviously, the calculation of Moran's I index as much as the local I_i indices, rely on the construction, of a spatial weights matrix. Once again, we can see the central role of the weights matrix in spatial econometrics, in general, and in exploratory spatial data analysis, in particular.

The fourth chapter presents the essence of processes likely to generate spatial autocorrelation in the residuals of the classical linear regression model or in any other variables. Actually, the detection of the pattern of spatial autocorrelation among residuals is only a step aiming to correct the problem so as to ensure that the results from the analysis can be interpreted properly, ensuring that conclusions based from these analyses are correct. However, it is possible that certain phenomena, described in detail in the DGP, create the measured spatial pattern detected among residuals of the linear regression model. The DGP is implicit to all statistical analyses since the researcher, whether he/she wants to or not, is making a hypothesis on the way the dependent variable is linked to the independent variables when they specify the regression model. Expressed differently, the researcher postulates a functional form without being sure of the real relation. Thus, the theoretical reflection on the possible omissions of spatial relations between the observations has an influence on the choice of the autoregressive process that the researcher postulates. Therefore, the relations and the reasons that guide the choice of one model over another are presented at the start of the Chapter 4.

Next, the spatial models are exposed from another angle: the angle of statistical tests. The development of *Lagrange multiplier (LM)* tests that allow us to discriminate, statistically speaking, between certain autoregressive specifications allows us to complement Moran's I test. Moran's I index is only useful in detecting the presence/absence of spatial pattern among the residuals of a classical model of linear regression. The LM tests allow us to determine, for the functional form postulated, the form of the spatial DGP from statistical criteria. Nevertheless, a difficulty in the application of these tests is that, most of the time, the two usual specifications, SAR and SEM, prove to be significant. While the empirical approach recommends the use of the model whose statistics are highest, or most significant, both forms are still possible simultaneously. The use of generalized spatial autoregressive models (GAR or SAC – see Chapter 4)[2], despite the criticisms that they receive, can therefore prove to be an interesting option, as is pairing the SAR and SLX models, or even exploiting the SEM processes in the spatial Durbin model (SDM) form.

Chapter 5 proposes an introduction for dealing with spatial microdata pooled in time. In fact, most of the models covered in Chapter 4 can be easily applied to the spatio-temporal case by previously transforming the weights matrix to take into account both the spatial and the temporal dimensions of the DGP. It must be noted that this particular approach is different from the case where the spatial data are gathered at each available time period (the spatial panel case). Nevertheless, a simple modification of the weights matrix allows us to use all of the tests and models covered in the previous chapters (Chapters 3 and 4). Once again, particular emphasis is placed on the structure of the DGP in a spatio-temporal context. Thus, the DGP allows the determination of the form of the weights matrix that must be applied in such a context.

Therefore, the spatio-temporal weights matrix is developed from two matrices: a spatial weights matrix (Chapter 2) and a temporal weights matrix (Chapter 5). The latter is obtained by chronologically ordering the observations and proceeding with a triangular decomposition allowing the decomposition of the effect of passed observations on actual observations (lower triangle), the effect of actual observations on actual observations, and the effect of future

---

2 Or the generalized spatial autoregressive model (GSM), as designed by Elhorst [ELH 14].

observations on actual observation (higher triangle). From some selection operators that penalize more highly for a greater temporal distance, the development of the temporal weights matrix also allows the generation of the new explicative variables that take into account the passed characteristics as well as possible dynamic effects.

A short opening allows us to appreciate the possible generalization of the spatial econometric approach to the spatio-temporal context. While recently, some applications are underlined and presented quickly. This short opening allows us to make the link between the theoretical foundations covered and the applications that call upon data that contain both spatial and temporal dimensions.

C.2. Opening

Evidently, all the approaches presented in the latter chapters of the work (Chapters 3, 4 and 5) rely on an exogenous structure of the weights matrix, a central and crucial element in spatial econometrics. Therefore, it is possible to consider the application of spatial econometrics in various domains by changing the form of the weights matrix. As an example, we could think of applying the techniques of spatial econometrics to social, cultural, organizational or institutional proximity [DUB 14e]. The general presentation of the techniques multiplies the possibilities for application in spatial econometrics.

The greatest challenge is to ensure the precision of the form of the relation between the observations from the weights matrix. Another alternative, for individual microdata, would be to take into account the real distances (accessibility) rather than physical distances. It is not because a location is two kilometers away that it is necessarily closer to an observation than to another located five kilometers away, but quicker to access. For this reason, it is important to mention that one of the challenges of spatial econometric approaches still remains the structuring of the weights matrix.

However, it is this that makes all the potential and the attractivity of spatial econometrics: the development possibilities of such matrices are great and important. We hope that this work will allow several, non-econometrician researchers to make the most of the methods presented, while using different notions of distance and varied research objects.

Glossary

Autocorrelation: measurement of the correlation of a given variable with the same variable for a defined neighborhood (spatially or temporally).

Autoregressive model: model of regression where the value of a variable is linked to the value of the same variable for a defined neighborhood (temporal or spatial).

Black sheep: observation that possesses a low value for a given variable, while the value taken for the neighborhood is high.

Data generating process (DGP): this is the mathematical process postulated on the way in which a (dependent) variable is generated. This involves evaluating, from external information (independent variables), the value taken by the variable of interest. The DGP is the very essence of the statistical model.

Diamonds in the rough: observation that possesses a high value of a given variable, while the value taken by the neighborhood is low.

Distance as a crow flies: distance to cover in a straight line to go from one point to another. The shortest line connecting two points.

Econometric model: an equation that links the behavior of a dependent variable as a function of a set of independent (explicative) variables and an error term, in which the unknown parameters serve to determine, all other things being equal, the effect of each of the independent variables on the dependent variable.

Econometrics: statistical branch of economics. It allows the evaluation of economic relations, the testing of economical theories and hypotheses, the evaluations of policies and to make predictions.

External effects: see *externalities*.

Externalities: refer to the gains or the losses that result from external events or realities, but also gains or losses that affect third parties. They can be positive or negative.

First law of geography: general law that states that all of the observations are linked between themselves, but that the observations that are closer together are more strongly linked than observations that are far apart.

Geographic information system (GIS): system allowing the generation of information that is organized in space and spatially structured (georeferenced). It allows us, through localization, to link a set of information layers between themselves.

Geostatic approach: statistical modeling applied to geolocated data and exploiting the relative positioning of the observations over space instead of building a weights matrix. The geostatic approach is mainly based on methods of smoothing or extrapolation of values continuously over a given space.

Global spatial autocorrelation: measurement of average spatial autocorrelation, for all of the observations.

Linear regression: statistical model that allows the linking, linearly in the parameters, of a set of explicative variables to a variable of interest (or dependent variable).

Local indicators of spatial autocorrelation (LISA): see *local spatial autocorrelation*.

Local spatial autocorrelation or association: measurement of the linear association between the value of a variable for a given observation and the value of the same variable in the neighborhood. Measurement for a pair of observations.

Model: a relation derived from a given theory or a particular reasoning.

Methods of exploratory analysis of spatial data (ESDA): descriptive analysis of statistics of linear association for a given variable among the different observations.

Multidirectionality: describes relations that go both ways: the influence is reciprocal.

Multiple linear regression: linear regression in which several independent variables are considered.

Nearest neighbor: criterion of spatial proximity based on a fixed number of spatial relations or connections.

p-value: probability associated with a particular value of a given distribution. It is the probability that the value obtained be lower than other possible values.

Permutational p-value: p-value obtained from a distribution determined by permutation.

Simple linear regression: linear regression in which only one independent variable is considered.

Spatial autocorrelation: measurement of the linear associated between a variable for a given observation and the average of the values taken by the same variable for the neighboring observations, defined from a spatial weights matrix.

Spatial distance: general measurement enabling the judgment of the relative proximity between all of the available spatial observations.

Spatial distancing: synonym of spatial distance. See *spatial distance*.

Spatial econometrics: branch of econometrics that looks at spatialized or geolocated data.

Spatial proximity: the is the relative measurement separating the observations in space.

Spatial weights matrix: matrix allowing the synthesis of spatial relations between connecting a given observation to the observations located in their neighborhood. The matrix allows the expression of these relations for all of the available observations. It enables the attribution of greater weights to closer observations and lower weights to observations that are further apart.

Spatially lagged variable: variable that defines the (average) value taken by a set of neighboring values of a given observation i. Usually denoted by y_j.

Statistic model: see *econometric model*.

Temporal autocorrelation: measurement of linear association between a given variable at period t and the value taken by the same variable at the previous period $(t-1)$.

Temporal lag: operator that allows the identification of the value taken by a variable at a previous period.

Temporally lagged variable: variable that defines the value taken by the variable at a previous period.

Variogram: two-dimensional representation that allows the expression of the value taken by Moran's I index, on the y axis, as a function of the threshold distance considered, on the x axis.

Appendix

A.1. Chapter 2 appendix

A.1.1. *Calculations of the distances and creation of a spatial weights matrix*

Starting with the example based on the nine fictive points (Table 2.1), it is possible to build a program that uses the two vectors of geographical coordinates, calculates the distances between the points and constructs the spatial weights matrix; all this using a matrix language. The example is conducted using the Stata software, and notations precisely from the Mata platform, allowing programming in a matrix language.

Obviously, there are certain commands that allow for the creation of spatial weights matrices directly from geographical coordinates. However, these modules usually rely on one single spatial relation specification: the inverse of the distance. Moreover, this command is based on a loop function, which is time and memory consuming. For these reasons, here we propose a complete program that will allow the researcher to create the matrix that they want. They can thereafter export the resulting matrix in Stata and use it in the calculation of indices of spatial autocorrelation or the estimation of the spatial and spatio-temporal autoregressive models. In fact, having the possibility of generating its own weights matrix appears to be especially useful in the case of spatio-temporal modeling.

The creation of a weights matrix relies on geographical coordinates. The first logical step is therefore to import them in Mata and then carry out the necessary and required transformations.

1) Start Mata. Once Stata is open, type:

```
mata
```

2) Create the geographical coordinates vectors:

```
XC = (4, 8, 7, 8, 6, 3, 3, 2, 2)'
YC = (1, 7, 2, 5, 4, 3, 6, 5, 2)'
```

3) Create a vector of 1, ι of dimension $(N \times 1)$ as well as the general matrices that will be used a bit later (identity matrix $\mathbf{I}$, and a matrix of elements all equal to 1, $\mathbf{J}$, both of dimension $(N \times N)$):

```
N    = length(XC)
iota   = J(N,1,1)
I = I(N)
J = J(N,N,1)
```

4) Calculate the distances between the coordinates X and Y (equations [2.5] and [2.4]) for all of the observations:

```
XX = (XC*iota') - (iota*XC')
YY = (YC*iota') - (iota*YC')
```

5) From the distances between the coordinates, establish the calculation of the distances between each of the observations and construct the Euclidian distance matrix $\mathbf{D}$ (equation [2.6]):

```
D   = sqrt((XX:*XX) + (YY:*YY))
```

6) Create the spatial weights matrix, $\mathbf{W}$ from the desired transssformation on the distance separating the observations (points). In the present case, we use the inverse of the distance:

```
W = (D+I):^(-1) -I
```

7) Generate the vector allowing the standardization of the weights matrix, i.e. sum the elements on each rows.

```
Wi   = colsum(W)'
```

8) Next, we extend this vector to make it the same dimension of the distance matrix and the spatial weights matrix:

```
Wis = Wi*iota'
```

9) By conducting a division term by term, or dividing each of the elements of the lines by total of the elements of the line, we get the row-standardized spatial weights matrix, $\mathbf{W}^{\star}$:

```
WS = W:/Wis
```

10) It is then possible to show all of the matrices used in the program simply by writting the name of the matrix we desire to see:

```
XC
YC
D
W
WS
```

The reader can reuse the code and change the form of the spatial relation to consider, for example, the negative exponential of the distance:

```
W = exp(-D)-I
```

The reader can also consider a relation of contiguity from a previously identified threshold distance (here 3 km):

```
W = (D:<=3)-I
```

The reader can also repeat the exercise using the Manhattan distance ($D^{\star}$ - equation [2.7]) rather than the Euclidian distance:

```
DS = abs(XX) + abs(YY)
```

A.2. Chapter 3 appendix

A.2.1. *Geary's c index*

Geary's c coefficient [GEA 54] is constructed with the squares of the difference from the arithmetic average between the values taken by the variable y in the neighboring regions. Geary's c index is formally defined by the equation [A.1]:

$$c = \frac{(N-1)\sum_{i=1}^{N}\sum_{j=1}^{N} w_{ij}(y_i - y_j)^2}{2S_0 \sum_i (y_i - \bar{y})^2} \qquad [\text{A.1}]$$

where N is the number of points or observations in the considered space, w_{ij} is the element of the spatial weights matrix, $\mathbf{W}$, located at the intersection of line i and column j and represents the spatial relation linking observation i to observation[1] j. Variable y_i is the value of variable y recorded for observation i, y_j is the value of variable y taken from the neighborhood of observation i and and $\bar{y}$ is arithmetic average of variable y. Finally, the expression $S_0 = \sum_{i=1}^{N}\sum_{j=1}^{N} w_{ij}$ represents the sum of elements w_{ij} over all of the lines i. This sum is equal to N when the spatial weights matrix is row-standardized[2].

Geary's c index is based on a ratio of estimations of the spatial and a-spatial variance[3]. Under the null hypothesis, H_0, i.e. in the absence of spatial autocorrelation, the value expected of the index is 1 [CLI 81, GEA 54].

Thus, when the c index takes a value located in the interval $[0, 1[$, the spatial autocorrelation is positive. In opposition, when the c index is located in the interval $]1, +\infty[$, the spatial autocorrelation is then negative.

Geary's c coefficient does not have an upper limit for the value of the index. However, the index has a lower limit of 0, which corresponds to a situation where the spatial autocorrelation is maximal. In such a case, the values of y_i et y_j are identical.

---

1 The weights matrix is usually expressed in its row-standardized form.

2 By definition, the sum of the elements of a line is necessarily equal to one when the spatial weights matrix is row-standardized, see Chapter 2.

3 Let us note that the total variance that appears in the calculation of Geary's c index is the estimated variance (calculated with $(N-1)$) while the variance that appears in the calculation of Moran's I is the descriptive variance (calculated with N).

Out of commodity, Nijkamp and Paelinck [NIJ 75] propose the calculation of the "spatial influence coefficient" that is represented by the γ index (equation [A.2]), which is not linked to the definition seen previously in [3.38]:

$$\gamma = 1 - c \qquad\qquad \text{[A.2]}$$

This index presents similar behavior to that of a regular correlation coefficient, with one exception. In the absence of spatial correlation, the value of the index is zero ($\gamma = 0$), while in the present of positive spatial autocorrelation, the value of the index is positive ($\gamma > 0$) and reach a maximum value of one ($\gamma = 1$). In the presence of negative spatial autocorrelation, the value of the index is negative without necessary having a lower limit. This is the main difference between the γ index and the classical correlation coefficient, or even with Moran's I index.

The expectation and the variation of Geary's c statistic are traditionally calculated using two distinct hypotheses [CLI 81]. The first one assumes that the values y_i taken by the random variable y on the different observations come from N independent draws in a normal population. The second hypothesis, presumes that the values y_i are realization of a random variable y whose distribution is unknown. In this case, we must consider all of the $N!$ possible permutations of the values of the random variable y on the territory considered, as each of the permutations is just as likely to appear.

Under the hypothesis of normality of the random variable y, the expectation and the variance of Geary's c statistic are respectively provided by the equations [A.3] and [A.4]:

$$E(c) = 1 \qquad\qquad \text{[A.3]}$$

$$Var(c) = \frac{(2S_1 + S_2)(N - 1) - 4S_0^2}{2(N + 1)S_0^2} \qquad\qquad \text{[A.4]}$$

Under the hypothesis of random distribution of the variable y, the variance of Geary's c statistic is given by a different expression (equation [A.5]):

$$Var(c) = \frac{A - B}{N(N-2)(N-3)S_0^2} + \frac{\left[S_0^2\left(N^2 - 3 - (N-1)^2 b_2\right)\right]}{N(N-2)(N-3)S_0^2}[A.5]$$

where $A = (N-1)S_1(N^2 - 3N + 3 - (N-1)b_2)$, $B = -\left[\frac{1}{4}\left((N-1)S_2(N^2 + 3N - 6 - (N^2 - N + 2)b_2)\right)\right]$, N is the total number of observations considered and where the expression S_0, S_1 and S_2 are respectively defined by the identities [3.12], [3.13] and [3.14] and where the terms $w_{i.}$, $w_{.i}$ and b_2 are respectively defined by the quantities [3.15], [3.16] and [3.26].

A.2.2. Comparison: Geary's c and Moran's I

Starting with the previous theoretical presentations on the calculations of Geary's c and Moran's I statistics, it is possible to highlight some commonalities between them. We summarize, in Table A.1, the values that can be taken by statistics of autocorrelation, Geary's c and Moran's I, covered previously.

		Geary (c)	Moran (I)
Positive spatial autocorrelation	concentrated, grouped	$0 < c < 1$	$I > 0$
Negative spatial autocorrelation	dispersed, contrasted	$c > 1$	$I < 0$

Table A.1. *Summary*

There is therefore quite a strong link between the two statistics of detection of spatial autocorrelation of a given variable, y. The results nevertheless suggest that the detection test based on Moran's I statistic is more robust and powerful than when it is based on the Geary's c statistic. Moreover, some authors have also shown that Moran's I statistic is more robust against the form of the spatial weights matrix used [ANS 95].

These two reasons explain in large part why most empirical applications rely on Moran's I statistic.

A.2.3. *Calculation of the I and I_i indices for fictitious values*

From the program allowing the generation of the distance matrix and the row-standardized spatial weights matrix (section A.1), it is possible to calculate the degree of spatial autocorrelation (global and local) for a given variable y whose values are provided in Table 3.1. For this, we must create the data vector y and demean it, that is, expressing its deviation from the mean (or average). Next, the usual calculations for the creation of the weights matrix must be carried out to then perform the calculations of the indices of spatial autocorrelation.

It is possible to proceed with the calculations of the different statistics and tests. For this the formulae presented in Chapter 3 are applied, as much for the I as for the I_i. The following program demonstrates the calculations and can easily be transposed to any other variable, by replacing the vectors of the geographical coordinates and the vector of the variable of interest, y by any other variable:

```
mata

XC = (4, 8, 7, 8, 6, 3, 3, 2, 2)' /* Coordinates vector  X*/
YC = (1, 7, 2, 5, 4, 3, 6, 5, 2)' /* Coordinates vector Y*/
y  = (7, 15, 11, 13, 12, 8, 10, 9, 7)' /* Defining the variables vector y*/

N    = length(y)                /* Size of the vector  - number of observations*/
iota = J(N,1,1)                 /* Vector of one of size N x 1*/
I = I(N)                        /* Identified matrix of size N x N*/
J = J(N,N,1)                    /* Identified matrix of one N x N*/

yt   = sum(y)                   /* Sum of the elements of vector y*/
ym   = yt/N                     /* Calculation of the average of y*/
ys   = (y-(ym*iota))            /* Variable y demeaning*/

XX = (XC*iota') - (iota*XC')    /* Distances between the X */
YY = (YC*iota') - (iota*YC')    /* Distances between the Y */

D  = sqrt((XX:*XX) + (YY:*YY))  /* Euclidian distance between the points */
DS = abs(XX) + abs(YY)          /* Manhattan distance between the points */

W = (D+I):^(-1) -I              /* Spatial weights matrix */
                                    /* with inverse distance */
Wi  = colsum(W)'                /* Total of the lines (N x 1)*/
Wis = Wi*iota'                  /* Total of the lines (N x N)*/
WS = W:/Wis                     /* Row-standardized spatial weights matrix */

IM   = (ys'*WS*ys)/(ys'ys)      /* Moran's (I) index*/
Ii   = ys:*(WS*ys)              /* Local Moran's (I) indices*/
```

```
EI   = -1/(N-1)                    /* Expectation of the I*/
S0   = iota'*WS*iota                  /* Calculation of S0 (S0 = N)*/
S1   = (1/2)*(iota'*((WS+WS):^2)*iota) /* Calculation of S1*/
wio  = WS*iota                     /* Sum of the elements in lines*/
woj  = (iota'*WS)'                 /* Sum of the elements in columns*/
S2   = iota'*((wio+woj):^2)        /* Calculation of S2*/
VarI = (N^2*S1 - N*S2 + 3*S0^2)/(S0^2*(N^2-1)) - (EI)^2
                                   /*Calculation of the variance of I*/
StatI = (IM-EI)/sqrt(VarI)         /* t statistic of the I*/
pvalueI = normalden(StatI)         /* Calculation of the associated probabilities*/


EIi  = -(WS*iota)/(N-1)            /* Expectation of the local I*/
wi2  = (WS:^2)*iota               /* Sum of the elements squared on the lines*/
m4   = iota'*(ys:^4)/N            /* Calculation of m4*/
m2   = iota'*(ys:^2)/N            /* Calculation of m2*/
b2   = m4/(m2^2)                  /* Calculation of b2*/
wikh = ((WS*iota:*WS*iota)-wi2)   /* Calculation of wikh*/
VarIi = ((wi2*(N-b2)/(N-1)) + wikh*(2*b2-N)/((N-1)*(N-2))) - (EIi):^2
                                   /*Calculation of the variance of the local I*/
StatIi = (Ii-EIi):/sqrt(VarIi)    /* t statistics for each index*/
pvalueIi = normalden(StatIi)      /* Calculation of the associated probabilities*/

StatDesI = (IM, EI, VarI, StatI, pvalueI)
                                   /* Synthesis of the statistics - I Moran*/
StatDesIi = (Ii, EIi, VarIi, StatIi, pvalueIi)
                                   /* Synthesis of the statistics - local I*/


StatDesI                          /* Results show  - I Moran*/
StatDesIi                         /* Results show - local I*/

end
```

A.3. Chapter 4 appendix

A.3.1. *Estimation by the ordinary least squares (OLS)*

The estimator of the ordinary least squares of the vector of the parameters (OLS) $\beta = (\alpha, \beta_1, \ldots, \beta_K)$, written $\widehat{\beta} = (\widehat{\alpha}, \widehat{\beta}_1, \ldots, \widehat{\beta}_K)$, is obtained by resolving the following minimization program:

$$\widehat{\beta} = \underset{\beta}{\arg\min} \sum_{i=1}^{N} \epsilon_i^2 = \underset{\beta}{\arg\min} \sum_{i=1}^{N} (y_i - \alpha - \beta_1 x_{i1} - \beta_2 x_{i2} - \cdots$$
$$-\beta_K x_{iK})^2 \qquad \text{[A.6]}$$

in condensed form:

$$\widehat{\beta} = \arg\min_{\beta} \sum_{i=1}^{N} (y_i - X_i\beta)^2 y_i - \alpha - sumk = 1Kbeta_k X_{ik}$$

By writing $S(\beta) = \sum_{i=1}^{N}(y_i - X_i\beta)^2$, the minimization function becomes:

$$\widehat{\beta} = \arg\min_{\beta} S(\beta)$$

The problem lies therefore in the minimization of a scalar function with $(K + 1)$ parameters. We must therefore resolve the system formed by the $(K + 1)$ first order conditions (FOC) calculated for the solutions $\widehat{\alpha}, \widehat{\beta}_1, \ldots, \widehat{\beta}_K$, *i.e.* the value of the vector β allowing to equal each first order condition at zero:

$$\left.\frac{\partial S(\alpha, \beta_1, \ldots, \beta_K)}{\partial \alpha}\right|_{\beta=\widehat{\beta}} = 0 \qquad\qquad\qquad \text{[A.7]}$$

$$\left.\frac{\partial S(\alpha, \beta_1, \ldots, \beta_K)}{\partial \beta_1}\right|_{\beta=\widehat{\beta}} = 0 \qquad\qquad\qquad \text{[A.8]}$$

$$\left.\frac{\partial S(\alpha, \beta_1, \ldots, \beta_K)}{\partial \beta_K}\right|_{\beta=\widehat{\beta}} = 0 \qquad\qquad\qquad \text{[A.9]}$$

A.3.2. *Matrix expression of the estimator of the OLS*

The estimator of the OLS can be written in matrix form. Going back to the expression of the model of linear regression:

$$\mathbf{y} = \mathbf{X}\beta + \epsilon$$

the minimization function becomes:

$$\widehat{\beta} = \arg\min_{\beta} S(\beta) = \arg\min_{\beta} (\epsilon'\epsilon) = \arg\min_{\beta} (\mathbf{y} - \mathbf{X}\beta)'(\mathbf{y} - \mathbf{X}\beta)$$

By developing the expression to minimize, we get:

$$S(\beta) = (\mathbf{y} - \mathbf{X}\beta)'(\mathbf{y} - \mathbf{X}\beta) = (\mathbf{y}' - \beta'\mathbf{X}')(\mathbf{y} - \mathbf{X}\beta)$$
$$= \mathbf{y}'\mathbf{y} - \mathbf{y}'\mathbf{X}\beta - \beta'\mathbf{X}'\mathbf{y} + \beta'\mathbf{X}'\mathbf{X}\beta$$

The quantities $\mathbf{y}'\mathbf{X}\beta$ and $\beta'\mathbf{X}'\mathbf{y}$ are scalar and are the transpositions of each other, meaning that they are equal to each other. The minimization criterion then becomes:

$$S(\beta) = \mathbf{y}'\mathbf{y} - 2\mathbf{y}'\mathbf{X}\beta + \beta'\mathbf{X}'\mathbf{X}\beta$$

This criterion is derived to obtain the first order conditions. Function $S(\beta)$ is minimal at $\widehat{\beta}$ if:

$$\frac{\partial^2 S(\beta)}{\partial\beta^2}\bigg|_{\beta=\widehat{\beta}} > 0$$

By applying the rules of the derivation of matrices, we get the following expression:

$$\frac{\partial S(\beta)}{\partial\beta} = -2\mathbf{X}'\mathbf{y} + 2\mathbf{X}'\mathbf{X}\widehat{\beta} = 0$$

By re-writing the expression, this results in:

$$\mathbf{X}'\mathbf{X}\widehat{\beta} = \mathbf{X}'\mathbf{y}$$

This system of equations is called normal equations system and has a single solution of the matrix $\mathbf{X}'\mathbf{X}$ is invertible, *i.e.* if it is of full rank, which is equal to $(K+1)$. The matrix expression of the estimator of the OLS of β as part of multiple linear regression is therefore:

$$\widehat{\beta} = (\mathbf{X}'\mathbf{X})^{-1}\mathbf{X}'\mathbf{y} \qquad\qquad [\text{A.10}]$$

The expression of the second order derivative, $\frac{\partial^2 S(\beta)}{\partial\beta\partial\beta'}\Big|_{\beta=\widehat{\beta}} = 2\mathbf{X}'\mathbf{X}$ is a positive-defined matrix. The expression of the estimator $\widehat{\beta}$ is indeed the optimal solution.

A.3.3. *Estimation by maximum likelihood (ML)*

The use of the principle of maximum likelihood (ML) as method of estimation of the spatial models was first outlined by the work by Cliff and Ord [CLI 73] and Ord [ORD 75] who applied it to the spatial autoregressive model (SAR) and to the spatially autocorrelated error model (SEM). When it is applied to spatial models, the method of maximum likelihood requires that certain conditions be met, ensuring the convergence, the efficiency and the asymptotic normality of the estimators[4].

---

4 These conditions of regularity were defined by Heijmans and Magnus [HEI 86a, HEI 86b, HEI 86c] and Magnus [MAG 78] and rely mainly on the existence of the function of log-likelihood, continuity and the differentiability of the elements of score and the associated Hessian matrix. For the most common spatial models, these conditions relate to restrictions on the spatial weights and to the space of the parameters associated with the spatial autoregressive coefficients [ANS 88].

A.3.3.1. *Estimation of the SAR by maximum likelihood*

The structural form of the spatial autoregressive model (SAR) is written:

$$y = \rho Wy + X\beta + \epsilon \qquad [A.11]$$

The SAR model can also be presented in its reduced form:

$$y = (I - \rho W)^{-1}X\beta + (I - \rho W)^{-1}\epsilon \qquad [A.12]$$

The disturbances ϵ are assumed to be independent and normally distributed:

$$\epsilon \sim \mathcal{N}(0, \sigma^2 I) \qquad [A.13]$$

By expressing ϵ in function of the other quantities, this results in:

$$\epsilon = (I - \rho W)y - X\beta \qquad [A.14]$$

Let us now calculate the Jacobian of ϵ, this is:

$$J = \left| \frac{\partial \epsilon}{\partial y} \right| = |I - \rho W| \qquad [A.15]$$

The likelihood function of the SAR model is written:

$$\ln L(\beta, \rho, \sigma^2 | y, X) = -\frac{N}{2}\ln(2\pi) - \frac{N}{2}\ln(\sigma^2)$$
$$+ \ln|I - \rho W| - \frac{1}{2\sigma^2}\epsilon'\epsilon \qquad [A.16]$$

By replacing the vector of the disturbances ϵ by its expression of the equation [A.14], the log-likelihood function becomes:

$$\ln L(\beta, \rho, \sigma^2 | \mathbf{y}, \mathbf{X}) = -\frac{N}{2} \ln(2\pi) - \frac{N}{2} \ln(\sigma^2) + \ln |\mathbf{I} - \rho\mathbf{W}|$$
$$-\frac{1}{2\sigma^2} (\mathbf{y} - \rho\mathbf{W}\mathbf{y} - \mathbf{X}\beta)'(\mathbf{y} - \rho\mathbf{W}\mathbf{y} - \mathbf{X}\beta)$$

[A.17]

If some conditions of regularity are satisfied ([HEI 86a, HEI 86b, HEI 86c] and [MAG 78]), the asymptotic properties of maximum likelihood estimators are too. For this, we need that the Jacobian, $|\mathbf{I} - \rho\mathbf{W}|$ is positive so the parameter ρ has to be in the interval $[-1, 1]$.

To get the estimators of the maximum likelihood of parameters β, σ^2 and ρ, the log-likelihood function is maximized with respect to these parameters. The first order condition implies that the partial derivatives of the log-likelihood with respect to each of the parameters of interest β, σ^2 and ρ are equal to zero:

$$\frac{\partial \ln L(\beta, \rho, \sigma^2 | y, X)}{\partial \beta} = \frac{\mathbf{X}'(\mathbf{y} - \rho\mathbf{W}\mathbf{y} - \mathbf{X}\beta)}{\sigma^2} = 0 \qquad [A.18]$$

$$\frac{\partial \ln L(\beta, \rho, \sigma^2 | y, X)}{\partial \sigma^2} = -\frac{N}{2\sigma^2} + \frac{\epsilon'\epsilon}{2\sigma^4} \qquad [A.19]$$

$$\frac{\partial \ln L(\beta, \rho, \sigma^2 | y, X)}{\partial \rho} = \frac{(\mathbf{W}\mathbf{y})'}{\sigma^2} - \mathrm{trace}\left(\mathbf{W}(\mathbf{I} - \rho\mathbf{W})^{-1}\right) \qquad [A.20]$$

The condition [A.18] allows us to express β as a function of $\mathbf{y}$, $\mathbf{W}$ and of ρ. The estimator of the maximum likelihood of parameter β, written $\widehat{\beta}_{ML}$ is:

$$\widehat{\beta}_{ML} = (\mathbf{X}'\mathbf{X})^{-1}\mathbf{X}'(\mathbf{I} - \rho\mathbf{W})\mathbf{y} \qquad [A.21]$$

In the same manner, we get the estimator of the maximum likelihood of σ^2, $\widehat{\sigma}^2_{ML}$, to be:

$$\widehat{\sigma}^2_{ML} = \frac{\widehat{\epsilon}'_{ML}\widehat{\epsilon}_{ML}}{N} \qquad [A.22]$$

with $\widehat{\epsilon}_{ML} = (\mathbf{y} - \rho\mathbf{W}\mathbf{y} - \mathbf{X}\widehat{\beta}_{ML})$ the residuals obtained by replacing the parameter β by its estimator of the maximum likelihood $\widehat{\beta}_{ML}$. We remark that these estimators are those obtained by the method of the least squares applied to the filtered model $\mathbf{y}^\star = \mathbf{X}\beta + \epsilon$ with $\mathbf{y}^\star = (\mathbf{I} - \rho\mathbf{W})\mathbf{y}$. By writing $\beta_0 = (\mathbf{X}'\mathbf{X})^{-1}\mathbf{X}'\mathbf{y}$, the estimator coming from the regression of $\mathbf{y}$ on $\mathbf{X}$ with $\epsilon_0 = \mathbf{y} - \mathbf{X}\beta_0$, β_1 the estimator of the ordinary least squares coming from the regression of $\mathbf{W}\mathbf{y}$ on $\mathbf{X}$ with $\epsilon_1 = \mathbf{y} - \mathbf{X}\beta_1$, the estimators of the maximum likelihood of β and of σ^2 respectively written $\widehat{\beta}_{ML}$ and $\widehat{\sigma}^2_{ML}$ are given by:

$$\widehat{\beta}_{ML} = \widehat{\beta}_0 - \rho\widehat{\beta}_1 \qquad [A.23]$$

The vector of the residuals obtained by the method of maximum likelihood, written $\widehat{\epsilon}_{ML}$ can be decomposed into two parts:

$$\widehat{\epsilon}_{ML} = \mathbf{y} - \rho\mathbf{W}\mathbf{y} - \mathbf{X}\widehat{\beta}_{ML}$$
$$\widehat{\epsilon}_{ML} = \widehat{\epsilon}_0 - \rho\widehat{\epsilon}_1$$

with $\widehat{\epsilon}_0 = \mathbf{y} - \mathbf{X}\widehat{\beta}_0$ and $\widehat{\epsilon}_1 = \mathbf{W}\mathbf{y} - \mathbf{X}\widehat{\beta}_1$. Thus, according to the equation (A.22), the variance of the disturbances, σ^2, can be written:

$$\widehat{\sigma}^2_{ML} = \frac{(\widehat{\epsilon}_0 - \rho\widehat{\epsilon}_1)'(\widehat{\epsilon}_0 - \rho\widehat{\epsilon}_1)}{N} \qquad [A.24]$$

By substituting β and σ^2 by their estimators given in equations [A.23] and [A.24] in the likelihood function [A.16], we obtain the concentrated likelihood function with respect to parameters β and σ^2

which is a function of the parameter ρ only:

$$\ln L_c(\rho) = -\frac{N}{2}\ln(2\pi) - \frac{N}{2}\ln\left(\frac{(\hat{\epsilon}_0 - \rho\hat{\epsilon}_1)'(\hat{\epsilon}_0 - \rho\hat{\epsilon}_1)}{N}\right)$$
$$+ \ln|\mathbf{I} - \rho\mathbf{W}| \qquad\qquad [A.25]$$

In the end, the estimation process can be synthesized and decomposed into four steps:

– regression of $\mathbf{y}$ on $\mathbf{X}$ to obtain an estimation of $\widehat{\beta}_0 = (\mathbf{X}'\mathbf{X})^{-1}\mathbf{X}'\mathbf{y}$ to calculate the residuals $\widehat{\epsilon}_0 = \mathbf{y} - \mathbf{X}\widehat{\beta}_0$;

– regression of $\mathbf{W}\mathbf{y}$ on $\mathbf{X}$ to obtain an estimation of $\widehat{\beta}_1 = (\mathbf{X}'\mathbf{X})^{-1}\mathbf{X}'\mathbf{W}\mathbf{y}$ to calculate the residuals $\widehat{\epsilon}_1 = \mathbf{W}\mathbf{y} - \mathbf{X}\widehat{\beta}_L$;

– maximization[5] of the concentrated log-likelihood function with respect parameters β and σ^2 $L_C(\rho)$ given $\widehat{\epsilon}_0$ and $\widehat{\epsilon}_1$ to obtain an estimator of the maximum likelihood, written $\widehat{\sigma}_{ML}$, for the parameter σ:

– estimation by maximum likelihood of the parameters β and σ^2 :

$$\widehat{\beta}_{ML} = \widehat{\beta}_0 - \widehat{\rho}\widehat{\beta}_L \qquad\qquad [A.26]$$

$$\widehat{\sigma}^2_{ML} = \frac{1}{N}\left(\widehat{\epsilon}_0 - \widehat{\rho}_{ML}\widehat{\epsilon}_L\right)'\left(\widehat{\epsilon}_0 - \widehat{\rho}_{ML}\widehat{\epsilon}_L\right) \qquad\qquad [A.27]$$

A.3.3.2. *First order conditions for the estimation of the SEM by maximum likelihood*

The spatial error model (SEM) is given by the following equations system:

$$\mathbf{y} = \mathbf{X}\beta + \eta \qquad\qquad [A.28]$$

$$\eta = \lambda\mathbf{W}\eta + \epsilon \qquad\qquad [A.29]$$

---

5 Because the concentrated likelihood is nonlinear in the parameter ρ we have to use numerical optimization procedures to obtain an estimation of the parameter ρ.

The disturbances ϵ are assumed to be independent and normally distributed:

$$\epsilon \sim \mathcal{N}\left(0, \sigma^2 \mathbf{I}\right) \tag{A.30}$$

The reduced form of the SEM model is:

$$\mathbf{y} = \mathbf{X}\beta + \left(\mathbf{I} - \lambda\mathbf{W}\right)^{-1}\epsilon \tag{A.31}$$

From equation [A.31], we obtain the expression of ϵ:

$$\epsilon = \left(\mathbf{I} - \lambda\mathbf{W}\right)\left(\mathbf{y} - \mathbf{X}\beta\right) \tag{A.32}$$

Let us now calculate the Jacobian of ϵ, this is:

$$J = \left|\frac{\partial\epsilon}{\partial\mathbf{y}}\right| = |\mathbf{I} - \lambda\mathbf{W}| \tag{A.33}$$

The log-likelihood function is written:

$$\ln L\left(\beta, \lambda, \sigma^2 | \mathbf{y}, \mathbf{X}\right) = -\frac{N}{2}\ln(2\pi) - \frac{N}{2}\ln\sigma^2 + \ln|\mathbf{I} - \lambda\mathbf{W}|$$
$$-\frac{1}{2\sigma^2}\epsilon'\epsilon \tag{A.34}$$

By replacing the vector of the disturbances ϵ by its expression of equation [A.32], the log-likelihood function is written:

$$\ln L\left(\beta, \lambda, \sigma^2 | \mathbf{y}, \mathbf{X}\right) = -\frac{N}{2}\ln(2\pi) - \frac{N}{2}\ln\sigma^2 + \ln|\mathbf{I} - \lambda\mathbf{W}|$$
$$-\frac{1}{2\sigma^2}\left(\left(\mathbf{I} - \lambda\mathbf{W}\right)\left(\mathbf{y} - \mathbf{X}\beta\right)\right)'$$
$$\times\left(\mathbf{I} - \lambda\mathbf{W}\right)\left(\mathbf{y} - \mathbf{X}\beta\right) \tag{A.35}$$

The introduction in the likelihood function of the term $\ln|\mathbf{I} - \lambda\mathbf{W}|$ implies that the maximum likelihood estimator for the parameter β is not equal to the estimator of the ordinary least squares. These two estimators are equal when λ tends towards zero.

Like in the SAR model, asymptotic properties are verified if some regularity conditions are met such as the positivity of the Jacobian:

$$\mathbf{J} = |\mathbf{I} - \lambda\mathbf{W}| > 0 \qquad\qquad [A.36]$$

For a row-standardized weights matrix, $\mathbf{W}$, this requires that the autoregressive parameter be in the interval $[-1, 1]$.

The first-order condition to obtain the maximum likelihood estimator of parameters β, λ and σ^2 is that the first-order derivative with respect to each parameter be zero, canceling each of the partial derivatives of the log-likelihood:

$$\frac{\partial L\left(\beta, \lambda, \sigma^2\right)}{\partial \beta} = 0 \qquad\qquad [A.37]$$

$$\frac{\partial L\left(\beta, \lambda, \sigma^2\right)}{\partial \sigma^2} = 0 \qquad\qquad [A.38]$$

$$\frac{\partial L\left(\beta, \lambda, \sigma^2\right)}{\partial \lambda} = 0 \qquad\qquad [A.39]$$

Since the parameter β only appears in the term $\epsilon'\epsilon = \left((\mathbf{I} - \lambda\mathbf{W})(\mathbf{y} - \mathbf{X}\beta)\right)'(\mathbf{I} - \lambda\mathbf{W})(\mathbf{y} - \mathbf{X}\beta)$, the partial derivative of the log-likelihood function with respect to the parameter β, $\frac{\partial L\left(\beta, \lambda, \sigma^2\right)}{\partial \beta}$ is equal to the derivative of the quantity $\epsilon'\epsilon$ with respect to the parameter β. The quantity $\epsilon'\epsilon$ can be written as follows:

$$\epsilon'\epsilon = \mathbf{y}'(\mathbf{I} - \lambda\mathbf{W})'(\mathbf{I} - \lambda\mathbf{W})\mathbf{y} - 2\mathbf{y}'(\mathbf{I} - \lambda\mathbf{W})'(\mathbf{I} - \lambda\mathbf{W})\mathbf{X}\beta$$
$$+ \beta'\mathbf{X}'(\mathbf{I} - \lambda\mathbf{W})'(\mathbf{I} - \lambda\mathbf{W})\mathbf{X}\beta$$

The first order condition for the parameter β is:

$$\frac{\partial L(\beta, \lambda, \sigma^2)}{\partial \beta} = \mathbf{X}'(\mathbf{I} - \lambda\mathbf{W})'(\mathbf{I} - \lambda\mathbf{W})\mathbf{y}$$

$$-\mathbf{X}'(\mathbf{I} - \lambda\mathbf{W})'(\mathbf{I} - \lambda\mathbf{W})\mathbf{X}\beta = 0 \qquad [A.40]$$

The first order condition [A.37] implies:

$$\mathbf{X}'(\mathbf{I} - \lambda\mathbf{W})'(\mathbf{I} - \lambda\mathbf{W})\mathbf{X}\beta = \mathbf{X}'(\mathbf{I} - \lambda\mathbf{W})'(\mathbf{I} - \lambda\mathbf{W})\mathbf{y} \qquad [A.41]$$

By resolving the equation [A.41], we obtain the estimator of the maximum likelihood:

$$\widehat{\beta}_{ML} = \left(\mathbf{X}'(\mathbf{I} - \lambda\mathbf{W})'(\mathbf{I} - \lambda\mathbf{W})\mathbf{X}\right)^{-1} X'(\mathbf{I}-\lambda\mathbf{W})'(\mathbf{I}-\lambda\mathbf{W})\mathbf{y} \qquad [A.42]$$

which is equivalent to the estimator of the generalized least squares $(\widehat{\beta}_{ML} = \widehat{\beta}_{MCG})$. We can see this as an estimator of the least squares coming from a regression of $\mathbf{y}^\star$ on $\mathbf{X}^\star$ where:

$$\mathbf{y}^\star = (\mathbf{I} - \lambda\mathbf{W})\mathbf{y} \qquad [A.43]$$

and:

$$\mathbf{X}^\star = (\mathbf{I} - \lambda\mathbf{W})\mathbf{X} \qquad [A.44]$$

The estimator of the maximum likelihood $\widehat{\beta}_{ML}$ can be obtained by carrying out a regression by ordinary least squares after having transformed the variables according to equations [A.43] and [A.44]. The partial derivative of the log-likelihood function with respect to the parameter σ^2 is written:

$$\frac{\partial L(\beta, \lambda, \sigma^2)}{\partial \sigma^2} = -\frac{N}{2\sigma^2} + \frac{1}{2\sigma^4}\epsilon'\epsilon \qquad [A.45]$$

This derivative has to be equal to zero to determine the the maximum likelihood estimator for the parameter σ^2:

$$-\frac{N}{2\sigma^2} + \frac{1}{2\sigma^4}\epsilon'\epsilon = 0 \qquad [A.46]$$

By simplifying equation [A.46], we have:

$$\sigma^2 = \frac{1}{N}\epsilon'\epsilon$$

By using the expression of ϵ of equation [A.32], the estimator of the maximum likelihood of σ^2 can be calculated by using the estimator of the maximum likelihood, $\widehat{\beta}_{ML}$ of β of equation [A.42]:

$$\widehat{\sigma}^2_{ML} = \frac{1}{\epsilon}\left(\mathbf{y} - \mathbf{X}\widehat{\beta}_{ML}\right)'(\mathbf{I} - \lambda\mathbf{W})'(\mathbf{I} - \lambda\mathbf{W})\left(\mathbf{y} - \mathbf{X}\widehat{\beta}_{ML}\right) \qquad [A.47]$$

where the vector of the residuals is defined by:

$$\widehat{\epsilon} = \mathbf{y} - \mathbf{X}\widehat{\beta}_{ML} \qquad [A.48]$$

$$\widehat{\sigma}^2_{ML} = \frac{1}{N}\widehat{\epsilon}'(\mathbf{I} - \lambda\mathbf{W})'(\mathbf{I} - \lambda\mathbf{W})\widehat{\epsilon} \qquad [A.49]$$

Let us note that the two maximum likelihood estimators, $\widehat{\beta}_{ML}$ and $\widehat{\sigma}^2_{ML}$ depend on the parameter λ. A maximum likelihood estimator for the parameter λ can be obtained by maximizing, with respect to λ, the concentrated log-likelihood function, which is obtained by inserting the maximum likelihood estimators $\widehat{\beta}_{ML}$ and $\widehat{\sigma}^2_{ML}$ in the likelihood function:

$$\ln L_c(\lambda) = -\frac{N}{2} - \frac{N}{2}\ln\left(\frac{1}{N}\epsilon'(\mathbf{I} - \lambda\mathbf{W})'(\mathbf{I} - \lambda\mathbf{W})\epsilon\right)$$
$$+ \ln|\mathbf{I} - \lambda\mathbf{W}| \qquad [A.50]$$

The concentrated log-likelihood function, is a nonlinear function of λ for which there is no analytical solution. Thus an estimator of the maximum likelihood for the parameter λ is obtained by using algorithms of numerical optimization. However, the vector of the residuals in the function of concentrated log-likelihood function also indirectly depends on λ since the calculation of $\widehat{\beta}_{ML}$ requires a value of λ (equation [A.42]). As a result, the iteration procedure must allow an update of the parameters λ and β conditionally one to the other.

A.3.4. *Program for the creation of spatially correlated data*

We present a program that allows the simulation of data based on the creation of fictitious spatial microdata, based on a fixed geographical area. This program can be modified by the reader to incorporate the other steps of the modeling and test different assumptions regarding the performance of the spatial autoregressive models according to some changes. This is basically the idea underlying the Monte Carlo experiment. Before doing so, here are some details to understand certain steps and lines of code:

– in the present case, the uniform law is used to produce the geographical coordinates in a square area of 10×10. This unit can be kilometers, for example. We could have chosen another configuration that would have brought a different distribution of the points. For example, to obtain the classical case of a town developed around a center[6], the command "uniform()" would be replaced by the command "invnorm(uniform())", while the size of the geographical area can also change

– the vectors and matrices of 1 as well as the identified matrix are necessary to carry out the operation in matrix terms;

– it is also necessary to transform the variables of interest into vectors and matrices. The matrix operations are then carried out on the declaration of these vectors and matrices under the Mata platform;

– several matrix operations rely on the Hadamard product which allows us to conduct operation terms by term rather than standard matrix

---

6 Which is usually referred to as the CBD (Central Business District) in economic geography.

operations. These operators imply the use of the double commas (:) before the usual operators;

– in the present case, the spatial weights matrix is constructed by using the inverse of the exponential of the distance. This case could be changed to consider the inverse of the distance, or even a relation of contiguity.

By going back to all of the operation carried out in the previous chapters, we propose a simple program which allows the generation of autocorrelated spatial data based on the different DGP assumed.

```
set more off
clear
clear mata
drop _all

set more off
clear
clear mata
drop _all

set obs 150                    /* Desired number of observations */
set seed 123457

quietly generate id=_n         /* Generate a unique ID */

quietly generate double coordX = 10*uniform()    /* Coordinates X*/
quietly generate double coordY = 10*uniform()    /* Coordinates Y*/
quietly generate double x = 3*invnorm(uniform())
                                  /* Vector of explicative variables x*/
quietly generate double e = invnorm(uniform())   /* Vector of the error terms*/

quietly generate xlag  = .  /* Preparation of the storage vector - x spatial*/
quietly generate yols  = .  /* Preparation of the storage vector - ols*/
quietly generate yslx  = .  /* Preparation of the storage vector - slx*/
quietly generate ysem  = .  /* Preparation of the storage vector - sem*/
quietly generate ysar  = .  /* Preparation of the storage vector - sar*/
quietly generate ysac  = .  /* Preparation of the storage vector - sac*/

mata

beta  = 1                   /* Parameter beta fixed*/
rho   = .5                  /* Parameter rho fixed*/
gama  = .5                  /* Parameter gamma fixed*/
N  = st_nobs()              /* Generate a scalar N (number observations)*/

XC = st_data(.,"coordX")    /* Export the coordinates X in Mata*/
YC = st_data(.,"coordY")    /* Export the coordinates Y in Mata*/
```

```
x  = st_data(.,"x")        /* Export the x in Mata*/
e  = st_data(.,"e")        /* Export the epsilon in Mata*/

I = I(N)                   /* Identified matrix of size N x N*/
J = J(N,N,1)               /* Matrix of 1 of size N x N*/
iota = J(N,1,1)            /* Vector of 1 of size N x 1*/

XX = (XC*iota') - (iota*XC')  /* Distances between the X */
YY = (YC*iota') - (iota*YC')  /* Distances between the Y */
D  = abs(XX) + abs(YY)        /* Distances (Manhattan) between the points */

W  = exp(-D)-I      /* Spatial weights matrix - negative exponential */
Wi = colsum(W)'     /* Total of the lines (N x 1)*/
Wis= Wi*iota'       /* Total of the lines (N x N)*/
WS = W:/Wis         /* Standardized spatial weights matrix */

EV = eigenvalues(WS)   /* Vector of the eigenvalues of matrix WS*/

xlag = WS*x              /* Creation of the variable x spatially shifter */
yols = x*beta + e        /* Creation of the variable y by ols*/
yslx = x*beta + (WS*x)*gama + e   /* Creation of the variable y by SLX*/
ysem = x*beta + invsym(I - rho*WS)*e /* Creation of the variable y by SEM*/
ysar = invsym(I-rho*WS)*(x*beta + e)  /* Creation of the variable y by SAR*/
ysac = invsym(I-(rho*WS))*(x*beta + invsym(I - rho*WS)*e)
                         /*Creation of the variable y by SAC*/

st_store(.,("yols","yslx","ysem","ysar","ysac"),(yols,yslx,ysem,ysar,ysac))
st_store(.,("xlag"),(xlag))

st_matrix("W",W)             /* Storage of matrix W for use in Stata*/

end

**Export the matrices created for the use of programs
spmat putmatrix WMata W, normalize(row) eig(EV) id(id) replace
spmat note WMata : "Standardized spatial weights matrix"

**Autoregressive model (SLX) estimated by OLS
reg yslx x xlag, noconst

**Autoregressive model (SAR) estimated by ML
spreg ml ysar x, noconst id(id) dlmat(WMata)

**Autoregressive model (SEM) estimated by ML
spreg ml ysem x, noconst id(id) elmat(WMata)

**Autoregressive model (SAC) estimated by ML
spreg ml ysac x, noconst id(id) dlmat(WMata) elmat(WMata)
```

The program therefore generates five dependent variables, y depending on the DGP assumed: OLS (y_{ols}), SLX (y_{slx}), SEM (y_{sem}), SAR (y_{sar}) et SAC (y_{sac}).

The reader will then be able to carry out the classical linear regressions for the variables created.

```
regress yols x, noconst
regress yslx x, noconst
regress ysem x, noconst
regress ysar x, noconst
regress ysac x, noconst
```

The reader is also invited to estimate a given dependent variable for a fixed DGP (say the SAR process), but using alternative spatial autoregressive DGP (say SEM and SLX) to explore the consequence of postulating a DGP that is different from the true process. The reader can also explore the differences between the ML and the OLS estimation process of the SAR DGP by building a variable **Wy** in Mata. This simple exercise allows us to understand that such approaches introduce bias on spatial autoregressive coefficients.

In short, this simple program can be exploited to test many consequences of wrong specification of the DGP in empirical applications. Readers can easily made their own experiments.

A.4. Chapter 5 appendix

A.4.1. *Program for the creation of spatio-temporally correlated data*

```
set more off
clear all
clear mata
set more off
clear all
clear mata
drop _all

set obs 500          /* Desired number of observations */
set seed 123457
```

```
quietly generate id=_n    /*Generate an unique ID */
quietly generate double coordX = 10*uniform()  /* Coordinates X*/
quietly generate double coordY = 10*uniform()  /* Coordinates Y*/
quietly generate double date  = 10*uniform()  /* Temporal dimension t*/
#delimit ;
quietly generate double period = 1*(date<1)+2*(date>=1&date<2)+3*(date>=2&date<3)+
4*(date>=3&date<4)+5*(date>=4&date<5)+6*(date>=5&date<6)+7*(date>=6&date<7)+
8*(date>=7&date<8)+9*(date>=8&date<9)+10*(date>=9);
#delimit cr
quietly generate double x = 3*invnorm(uniform()) /* Vector of the explicative
                                                    variables x*/
quietly generate double e = invnorm(uniform())   /* Vector of the error terms*/

quietly generate yols  = .  /* Preparation of the storage vector - ols*/
quietly generate ystar = .  /* Preparation of the storage vector - star*/
quietly generate ystem = .  /* Preparation of the storage vector - stem*/
sort date                   /* Sort the observations by period t*/

mata

beta   = 1               /* Parameter beta fixed*/
rho    = .5              /* Parameter rho fixed*/
lambda = .5              /* Parameter lambda fixed*/

N  = st_nobs()           /* Generate a scalar N (number of observations)*/

XC = st_data(.,"coordX") /* Export the coordinates X in Mata*/
YC = st_data(.,"coordY") /* Export the coordinates Y in Mata*/
ZC = st_data(.,"period") /* Export the periods t in Mata*/
x  = st_data(.,"x")      /* Export the x in Mata*/
e  = st_data(.,"e")      /* Export the epsilon in Mata*/

I = I(N)                 /* Identified matrix of size N x N*/
J = J(N,N,1)             /* Matrix of 1 of size N x N*/
iota = J(N,1,1)          /* Vector of 1 of size N x 1*/

XX = (XC*iota') - (iota*XC')  /* Distances between the X */
YY = (YC*iota') - (iota*YC')  /* Distances between the Y */
ZZ = (ZC*iota') - (iota*ZC')  /* Temporal distance between the observations*/
D  = sqrt((XX:*XX) + (YY:*YY)) /* Euclidian distances between the points */

S  = exp(-D)-I           /* Spatial weights matrix (negative exponential)*/
T0 = (ZZ:==0)-I          /* Matrix identifying the observations at the same period*/
W0 = S:*T0               /* Spatio-temporal weights matrix (same period)*/

Si = colsum(S)'          /* Total of the lines (N x 1)*/
Sis= Si*iota'            /* Total of the lines (N x N)*/
SS = S:/Sis              /* Standardized spatial weights matrix */

Wi = colsum(W0)'         /* Total of the lines (N x 1)*/
Wis= Wi*iota'            /* Total of the lines (N x N)*/
```

```
WS = WO:/Wis              /* Standardized spatial weights matrix */

ES = eigenvalues(SS)    /* Vectors of the eigenvalues of SS*/
EW = eigenvalues(WS)    /* Vectors of the eigenvalues of WS*/

yols  = x*beta + e      /* Creation of the variable y by ols*/
ystar = invsym(I-(rho*WS))*(x*beta + e)  /* Creation of the variable y - star*/
ystem = x*beta + invsym(I - lambda*WS)*e /* Creation of the variable y - stem*/

st_store(.,("yols","ystar","ystem"),(yols,ystar,ystem))

st_matrix("S",S)
st_matrix("WO",WO)

end

**Export the weights matrices and the eigenvalues
spmat putmatrix WMata1 S, normalize(row) eig(ES) id(id) replace
spmat note WMata1 : "Standardized spatial weights matrix"
spmat putmatrix WMata2 WO, normalize(row) eig(EW) id(id) replace
spmat note WMata2 : "Standardized spatio-temporal weights matrix"

**Spatio-temporal autoregressive (STAR) model estimated by ML
spreg ml ystar x, noconst id(id) dlmat(WMata2)

**Spatio-temporal autoregressive model (STEM) estimated by ML
spreg ml ystem x, noconst id(id) elmat(WMata2)
```

We can use the spatio-temporal DGP to verify the impact of not taking into account the temporal dimension on the amplitude of the estimated parameters. In this case, this involves estimating the usual spatial model using the spatial weights matrix rather than the spatio-temporal weights matrix.

```
**Spatio-temporal autoregressive model (STAR) estimated by ML
spreg ml ystar x, noconst id(id) dlmat(WMata1)

**Spatio-temporal autoregressive model (STEM) estimated by ML
spreg ml ystem x, noconst id(id) dlmat(WMata1)
```

Bibliography

[ABR 04] ABREU M., DE GROOT H., FLORAX R., Space and growth: a survey of empirical evidence and methods, Report, Tinbergen Institute, no. TI 04-129/03, 2004.

[ANS 88] ANSELIN L., *Spatial Econometrics: Methods and Models*, Kluwer, Dordrecht, Netherlands, 1988.

[ANS 91] ANSELIN L., REY S., "Properties of tests for spatial dependence in linear regression models", *Geographical Analysis*, vol. 23, no. 2, pp. 112–131, 1991.

[ANS 92] ANSELIN L., "Space and applied econometrics: introduction", *Regional Science and Urban Economics*, vol. 22, no. 3, pp. 307–316, September 1992.

[ANS 95a] ANSELIN L., "Local indicators of spatial association – LISA", *Geographical Analysis*, vol. 27, no. 2, pp. 93–115, 1995.

[ANS 95b] ANSELIN L., FLORAX R.J., "New directions in spatial econometrics: introduction", ANSELIN L., FLORAX R.J. (eds.), *New Directions in Spatial Econometrics*, Advances in Spatial Science, Springer, pp. 3–18, 1995.

[ANS 96a] ANSELIN L., "The Moran scatterplot as an ESDA tool to assess local instability in spatial association", FISHER M., SCHOLTEN H.K., UNWIN D. (eds.), *Spatial Analytical Perspectives on GIS*, Taylor & Francis, London, pp. 111–125, 1996.

[ANS 96b] ANSELIN L., BERA A.K., FLORAX R., *et al.*, "Simple diagnostic tests for spatial dependence", *Regional Science and Urban Economics*, vol. 26, no. 1, pp. 77–104, February 1996.

[ANS 98] ANSELIN L., BERA A.K., "Spatial dependence in linear regression models with an introduction to spatial econometrics", ULLAH A., GILES D. (eds.), *Handbook of Applied Economic Statistics*, vol. 155, New York, pp. 237–289, 1998.

[ANS 00] ANSELIN L., FLORAX R., *Advances in Spatial Econometrics*, Marcel Dekker Inc., Springer Verlag, Heidelberg, 2000.

[ANS 04] ANSELIN L., KIM Y.W., SYABRI I., "Web-based analytical tools for the exploration of spatial data", *Journal of Geographical Systems*, vol. 6, no. 2, pp. 197–218, 2004.

[ANS 06] ANSELIN L., SYABRI I., KHO Y., "GeoDa: an introduction to spatial data analysis", *Geographical Analysis*, vol. 38, pp. 5–22, 2006.

[ANS 07] ANSELIN L., "Spatial econometrics in RSUE: retrospect and prospect", *Regional Science and Urban Economics*, vol. 37, no. 4, pp. 450–456, July 2007.

[ANS 10] ANSELIN L., "Thirty years of spatial econometrics", *Papers in Regional Science*, vol. 89, pp. 3–25, 2010.

[ARB 01] ARBIA G., "The role of spatial effects in the empirical analysis of regional concentration", *Journal of Geographical Systems*, vol. 3, pp. 271–281, 2001.

[ARB 08] ARBIA G., FINGLETON B., "New spatial econometric techniques and applications in regional science", *Papers in Regional Science*, vol. 87, no. 3, pp. 311–317, 2008.

[ARB 10] ARBIA G., KELEJIAN H., "Advances in spatial econometrics", *Regional Science and Urban Economics*, vol. 40, no. 5, pp. 253–254, 2010.

[ARB 11] ARBIA G., "A lustrum of SEA: recent research trends following the creation of the spatial econometrics association (2007–2011)", *Spatial Economic Analysis*, vol. 6, no. 4, pp. 376–395, 2011.

[BAL 05] BALTAGI B., *Econometric Analysis of Panel Data*, 3 edition, Wiley, Chichester, England, 2005.

[BEH 09] BEHRENS K., NICOUD F.R., "Krugman's papers in regional science: the 100 dollar bill on the sidewalk is gone and the 2008 Nobel Prize well-deserved", *Papers in Regional Science*, vol. 88, no. 2, pp. 467–489, 2009.

[BER 93] BERA A.K., YOON M., "Specification testing with locally misspecified alternatives", *Econometric*, vol. 9, pp. 649–658, 1993.

[BHA 11] BHATTACHARJEE A., HOLLY S., "Structural interactions in spatial panels", *Empirical Economics*, vol. 40, no. 1, pp. 69–94, February 2011.

[BIV 80] BIVAND R., "A Monte-Carlo study of correlation coefficient estimation with spatially autocorrelated observations", *Quaestiones Geographicae*, vol. 6, pp. 5–10, 1980.

[BIV 06] BIVAND R.S., "Implementing spatial data analysis software tool in R", *Geographical Analysis*, vol. 38, pp. 23–40, 2006.

[BOO 94] BOOTS B.N., DUFOURNAUD C., "A programming approach to minimizing and maximizing spatial autocorrelation statistics", *Geographical Analysis*, vol. 26, pp. 54–66, 1994.

[BOO 00] BOOTS B., TIEFELSDORF M., "Global and local spatial autocorrelation in bounded regular tessellations", *Journal of Geographical Systems*, vol. 2, no. 4, pp. 319–348, 2000.

[BOX 64] BOX G.E.P., COX D.R., "An analysis of transformations", *Journal of the Royal Statistical Society. Series B (Methodological)*, vol. 26, no. 2, pp. 211–252, 1964.

[BRE 79] BREUSCH T., PAGAN A., "Simple test for heteroscedasticity and random coefficient variation", *Econometrica*, vol. 47, no. 5, pp. 1287–1294, 1979.

[BUR 80] BURRIDGE P., "On the Cliff-Ord test for spatial correlation", *Journal of the Royal Statist*, vol. 42, no. 1, pp. 107–108, 1980.

[BUS 82] BUSE A., "The likelihood ratio, Wald, and Lagrange multiplier tests: an expository note", *The American Statistician*, vol. 36, no. 3, pp. 153–157, 1982.

[CAS 72] CASETTI E., "Generating models by the expansion method: applications to geographical research", *Geographical Analysis*, vol. 4, no. 1, pp. 81–91, 1972.

[CAS 97] CASETTI E., "The expansion method, mathematical modeling and spatial econometrics", *International Regional Science Review*, vol. 20, no. 1–2, pp. 9–33, 1997.

[CHA 08] CHASCO C.Y., LOPEZ F.A.H., "Is spatial dependence an instantaneous effect? Some evidence in economic series of Spanish provinces", *Estadistica Espanola*, vol. 50, no. 167, pp. 101–118, 2008.

[CLE 88] CLEVELAND W.S., DEVLIN S.J., "Locally-weighted regression: an approach to regression analysis by local fitting", *Journal of the American Statistical Association*, vol. 83, no. 403, pp. 596–610, 1988.

[CLI 69] CLIFF A.D., ORD J.K., "The problem of spatial autocorrelation", SCOTT A. (ed.), *London Papers in Regional Science*, Pion, London, pp. 25–55, 1969.

[CLI 73] CLIFF A.D., ORD J.K., *Spatial Autocorrelation*, Pion, London, 1973.

[CLI 81] CLIFF A.D., ORD J.K., *Spatial Processes. Models and Applications*, Pion, 1981.

[CON 99] CONLEY T.G., "GMM estimation with cross sectional dependence", *Journal of Econometrics*, vol. 92, no. 1, pp. 1–45, September 1999.

[CON 03] CONLEY T.G., TOPA G., "Identification of local interaction models with imperfect location data", *Journal of Applied Econometrics*, vol. 18, no. 5, pp. 605–618, 2003.

[COR 12] CORRADO L., FINGLETON B., "Where is the economics in spatial econometrics?", *Journal of Regional Science*, vol. 52, no. 2, pp. 210–239, 2012.

[CRE 93] CRESSIE N., *Statistics for Spatial Data*, Wiley, New York, 1993.

[DEA 85] DEATON A., "Panel data from time series of cross-sections", *Journal of Econometrics*, vol. 30, no. 1–2, pp. 109–126, 1985.

[DES 10] DES ROSIERS F., DUBÉ J., THERIAULT M., "Do peer effects shape residential values? Reconciling the sales comparison approach with hedonic price modelling", *7th Annual ERES Conference*, Milan, Italy, 2010.

[DUB 11a] DUBÉ J., DES ROSIERS F., THERIAULT M., "Impact de la segmentation spatiale sur le choix de la forme fonctionnelle pour la modélisation hédonique", *Revue d'Economie Régionale et Urbaine*, vol. 1, pp. 9–37, 2011.

[DUB 11b] DUBÉ J., DES ROSIERS F., THERIAULT M., *et al.*, "Economic impact of a supply change in mass transit in urban areas: a Canadian example", *Transportation Research Part A*, vol. 45, no. 1, pp. 46–62, 2011.

[DUB 11c] DUBÉ J., LEGROS D., Development of a spatio-temporal autoregressive (STAR) model using spatio-temporal weight matrices, Working paper of the Laboratoire d'conomie et de Gestion, Report Laboratory of Economics and Management, University of Burgundy, no. e2011-05, 2011.

[DUB 12] DUBÉ J., THERIAULT M., DES ROSIERS F., "Using a Fourier polynomial expansion to generate a spatial predictor", *International Journal of Housing Market and Analysis*, vol. 5, no. 2, pp. 177–195, 2012.

[DUB 13a] DUBÉ J., BAUMONT C., LEGROS D., "Matrices de pondérations et contexte spatio-temporel en économétrie spatiale", *Revue Canadienne de Science Régionale*, 2013.

[DUB 13b] DUBÉ J., LEGROS D., "Dealing with spatial data pooled over time in statistical models", *Letters in Spatial and Resource Sciences*, vol. 6, no. 1, pp. 1–18, 2013.

[DUB 13c] DUBÉ J., LEGROS D., "Spatial econometrics and spatial data pooled over time: towards an adapted modelling approach", *Journal of Real Estate Literature*, 2013.

[DUB 13d] DUBÉ J., LEGROS D., "A spatio-temporal measure of spatial dependence: an example using real estate data", *Papers in Regional Science*, vol. 92, no. 1, pp. 19–30, 2013.

[DUB 14a] DUBÉ J., LEGROS D., "Spatial econometrics and spatial data pooled over time: towards an adapted modeling approach", *Journal of Real Estate Literature*, vol. 22, no. 1, pp. 101–125, 2014.

[DUB 14b] DUBÉ J., LEGROS D., "Spatial econometrics and the hedonic pricing model: what about the temporal dimension?", *Journal of Property Research*, dx.doi.org/10.1080/09599916.2014.913655, 2014.

[DUB 14c] DUBÉ J., LEGROS D., THÉRIAULT M., *et al.*, "A spatial difference-in-differences estimator to evaluate the effect of change in public mass transit systems on house prices", *Transportation Researach Part B*, vol. 64, pp. 24–40, 2014.

[DUB 14d] DUBÉ J., LEGROS D., THANOS S., "Putting time into space: expectations and causality issues in the price determination process", *Proceedings of the Conference of the International Association for Applied Econometrics*, London, p. 48. 2014.

[DUB 14e] DUBÉ J., DEVAUX N., "L'économétrie spatiale au service de l'analyse territoriale: une approche mixte pour un système complexe", ROBITAILLE, M., PROULX, M.-U. (eds.), *Science du territoire – tome II: Défis méthodologiques*, Presses de l'Université du Québec PUQ, Québec, pp. 77–104, 2014.

[DUR 50] DURBIN J., WATSON G.S., "Testing for serial correlation in least squares regression, I", *Biometrika*, vol. 37, nos. 3–4, pp. 409–428, 1950.

[DUR 51] DURBIN J., WATSON G.S., "Testing for serial correlation in least squares regression, II", *Biometrika*, vol. 38, nos. 1–2, pp. 159–179, 1951.

[EDG 87] EDGINGTON E., *Randomization Tests*, Marcel Dekker, New York, 1987.

[ELH 10] ELHORST J.P., "Applied spatial econometrics: raising the bar", *Spatial Economic Analysis*, vol. 5, no. 1, pp. 9–28, 2010.

[ELH 14] ELHORST J.P., *Spatial Econometrics: From Cross-Sectional Data to Spatial Panels*, Springer, 2014.

[FIS 10] FISCHER M.M., GETIS A., *Handbook of Applied Spatial Analysis: Software Tools, Methods and Applications*, Springer, 2010.

[FOT 98] FOTHERINGHAM A.S., BRUNSDON C., CHARLTON M., "Geographical weighted regression: a natural evolution of the expansion method for spatial data analysis", *Environment and Planning A*, vol. 30, no. 11, pp. 1905–1927, 1998.

[FOT 02] FOTHERINGHAM A.S., BRUNSDON C., CHARLTON M., *Geographically Weighted Regression: The Analysis of Spatially Varying Relationships*, Wiley, 2002.

[FUJ 04] FUJITA M., KRUGMAN P., "The new economic geography: past, present and the future", *Papers in Regional Science*, vol. 83, no. 1, pp. 139–164, 2004.

[GEA 54] GEARY R.C., "The contiguity ratio and statistical mapping", *The Incorporated Statistician*, vol. 5, no. 3, pp. 115–145, 1954.

[GET 91] GETIS A., "Spatial interaction and spatial autocorrelation: a cross-product approach", *Environment and Planning A*, vol. 23, pp. 1269–1277, 1991.

[GET 92] GETIS A., ORD K.J., "The analysis of spatial association by use of distance statistics", *Geographical Analysis*, vol. 24, no. 3, pp. 189–206, 1992.

[GET 04] GETIS A., ALDSTADT J., "Constructing the spatial weights matrix using a local statistic", *Geographical Analysis*, vol. 36, pp. 90–104, 2004.

[GET 09] GETIS A., "Spatial weights matrices", *Geographical Analysis*, vol. 41, pp. 404–410, 2009.

[GET 10] GETIS A., ALDSTADT J., "Constructing the spatial weights matrix using a local statistics", ANSELIN L., REY S. (eds.), *Perspectives on Spatial Data Analysis*, Springer, pp. 147–163, 2010.

[GRI 81] GRIFFITH D.A., "Modelling urban population density in a multi-centered city", *Journal of Urban Economics*, vol. 9, no. 3, pp. 298–310, 1981.

[GRI 96] GRIFFITH D.A., "Some guidelines for specifying the geographic weights matrix contained in spatial statistical models", ARLINGHAUS S.L., GRIFFITH D.A., DRAKE W.D., *et al.* (eds.), *Practical Handbook of Spatial Statistics*, CRC Press, Boca Raton, FL, pp. 65–82, 1996.

[GRI 13] GRIFFITH D.A., "Selected challenges from spatial statistics for spatial econometricians", *Comparative Economic Research*, vol. 15, no. 4, pp. 71–85, 2013.

[HÄG 70] HÄGERSTRAND T., "What about people in regional science?", *Papers of the Regional Science Association*, vol. 24, no. 1, pp. 7–21, 1970.

[HAI 09] HAINING R., "The special nature of spatial data", FOTHERINGHAM S.R.P., ed., *The Sage Handbook of Spatial Analysis*, Sage, Thousand Oaks, CA, pp. 5–24, 2009.

[HAL 81] HALVORSEN R., POLLAKOWSKI H., " Choice of functional form for hedonic price equations", *Journal of Urban Economics*, vol. 10, no. 1, pp. 37–49, 1981.

[HEC 85] HECKMAN J.J., ROBB R.J., "Alternative methods for evaluating the impact of interventions: an overview", *Journal of Econometrics*, vol. 30, no. 1–2, pp. 239–267, 1985.

[HEI 86a] HEIJMANS R., MAGNUS J., "Asymptotic normality of maximum likelihood estimators obtained from normally distributed but dependent observations", *Econometric Theory*, vol. 2, pp. 374–412, 1986.

[HEI 86b] HEIJMANS R., MAGNUS J., "Consistent maximum-likelihood estimation with dependent observations: the general (non-normal) case and the normal case", *Journal of Econometrics*, vol. 32, pp. 253–285, 1986.

[HEI 86c] HEIJMANS R., MAGNUS J., "On the first-order efficiency and asymptotic normality of maximum likelihood estimators obtained from dependent observations", *Statistica Neerlandica*, vol. 40, no. 3, pp. 169–188, 1986.

[HEP 00] HEPPEL L., GREGORY D., JOHNSTON D.G., *et al.*, "Spatial autocorrelation", JOHNSTON D.G., PRATT G., WATTS M. (eds.), *The Dictionary of Human Geography*, 4 edition, Blackwell, Oxford, England, 2000.

[HSI 03] HSIAO C., *Analysis of Panel Data*, Cambridge University Press, Cambridge, England, 2003.

[HUA 10] HUANG B., HUANG W., BARRY M., "Geographically and temporally weighted regression for modeling spatio-temporal variation in house prices", *International Journal of Geographical Information Science*, vol. 24, no. 3, pp. 383–401, 2010.

[HUB 76] HUBERT L.J., "Seriation using asymmetric proximity measures", *British Journal of Mathematical and Statistical Psychology*, vol. 29, no. 1, pp. 32–52, 1976.

[HUB 81] HUBERT L.J., GOLLEDGE R.G., COSTANZO C.M., "Generalized procedures for evaluating spatial autocorrelation", *Geographical Analysis*, vol. 13, no. 3, pp. 224–233, 1981.

[JAY 01] JAYET H., "Économétrie et données spatiales: une introduction à la pratique", *Cahiers d'Economie et de Sociologie Rurales*, vol. 58–59, pp. 106–129, 2001.

[JET 05] JETZ W., RAHBEK C., LICHSTEIN J.W., "Local and global approaches to spatial data analysis in ecology", *Global Ecology and Biogeography*, vol. 14, no. 1, pp. 97–98, 2005.

[KEL 93] KELEJIAN H.H., ROBINSON D., "A suggested method of estimation for spatial interdependent models with autocorrelated errors, and an application to a county expenditure model", *Papers in Regional Science*, vol. 72, pp. 297–312, 1993.

[KEL 98] KELEJIAN H.H., ROBINSON D.P., "A suggested test for spatial autocorrelation and/or heteroskedasticity and corresponding Monte Carlo results", *Regional Science and Urban Economics*, vol. 28, no. 4, pp. 389–417, 1998.

[KRI 66] KRIGE D.G., "Two-dimensional weighted moving average trend surfaces for ore valuation", *Journal of the South African Institute of Mining and Metallurgy*, vol. 67, pp. 13–38, 1966.

[KRU 91a] KRUGMAN P., "Increasing returns and economic geography", *The Journal of Political Economy*, vol. 99, no. 3, pp. 483–499, 1991.

[KRU 91b] KRUGMAN P., *Geography and Trade*, Gaston Eyskens lecture series, MIT Press, Cambridge, USA, 1991.

[LEG 93] LEGENDRE P., "Spatial autocorrelation: trouble or new paradigm?", *Ecology*, vol. 74, pp. 1659–1673, 1993.

[LEG 02] LE GALLO J., "Économétrie spatiale: L'autocorrélation spatiale dans les modèles de régression linéaire", *Economie et Prévision*, no. 155, pp. 139–157, 2002.

[LES 99] LESAGE J.P., *Spatial Econometrics, The Web Book of Regional Science*, Regional Research Institute, West Virginia University, Morgantown, WV, 1999.

[LES 09] LESAGE J.P., PACE K.R., *Introduction to Spatial Econometrics*, CRC Press, New York, 2009.

[LON 01] LONGLEY P., GOODCHILD M.F., MAGUIRE D.J., *et al.*, *Geographic Information Systems and Science*, Wiley & Sons, New York, 2001.

[MAG 78] MAGNUS J., "Maximum likelihood estimation of the GLS model with unknown parameters in the disturbance covariance matrix", *Journal of Econometrics*, vol. 7, pp. 281–312, 1978.

[MAN 67] MANTEL N., "The detection of disease clustering and a generalized regression approach", *Cancer Research*, vol. 27, pp. 209–220, 1967.

[MCM 96] MCMILLEN D.P., "One hundred fifty years of land values in Chicago: a nonparametric approach", *Journal of Urban Economics*, vol. 40, no. 1, pp. 100–124, 1996.

[MCM 04] MCMILLEN D.P., MCDONALD J.F., "Locally weighted regression and time-varying distance gradients. spatial econometrics and spatial statistics", GETIS A., MUR J., ZOLLER H.G. (eds.), *Spatial Econometrics and Spatial Statistics*, Palgrave Macmillan, pp. 232–249, 2004.

[MCM 10] MCMILLEN D.P., "Issues in spatial data analysis", *Journal of Regional Science*, vol. 50, no. 1, pp. 119–141, 2010.

[MOF 93] MOFFITT R., "Identification and estimation of dynamic models with a time series of repeated cross-sections.", *Journal of Econometrics*, vol. 59, no. 1–2, pp. 99–123, 1993.

[MOR 48] MORAN P.A.P., "The interpretation of statistical maps", *Journal of the Royal Statistical Society. Series B*, vol. 10, pp. 243–251, 1948.

[MOR 50] MORAN P.A.P., "A test for the serial independence of residuals", *Biometrika*, vol. 37, no. 1/2, pp. 178–181, 1950.

[NAP 11] NAPPI-CHOULET I., MAURY T.-P., "A spatial and temporal autoregressive local estimation for the paris housing market", *Journal of Regional Science*, vol. 51, no. 4, pp. 732–750, October 2011.

[OPE 79] OPENSHAW S., TAYLOR P., "A million or so correlation coefficients: three experiments on the modifiable area unit problem", WRIGLEY N. ed., *Applications in the Spatial Sciences*, Pion, London, pp. 127–144, 1979.

[ORD 75] ORD K., "Estimation methods for models of spatial interaction.", *Journal of the American Statistical Association*, vol. 70, no. 349, pp. 120–126, 1975.

[ORD 95] ORD J.K., GETIS A., "Local spatial autocorrelation statistics: distributional issues and an application", *Geographical Analysis*, vol. 27, no. 4, pp. 286–306, 1995.

[PAC 98] PACE R.K., BARRY R., SIRMANS C.F., "Spatial statistics and real estate", *The Journal of Real Estate Finance and Economics*, vol. 17, no. 1, pp. 5–13, July 1998.

[PAC 00] PACE R.K., BARRY R., GILLEY W.O., *et al.*, "A method for spatial-temporal forecasting with an application to real estate prices", *International Journal of Forecasting*, vol. 16, pp. 229–246, 2000.

[PAE 79] PAELINCK J.H.P., KLAASSEN L.H., *Spatial Econometrics*, Gower, Westmead, Farnborough, England, 1979.

[PAE 09] PAEZ A., LE GALLO J., BULIUNG R.N., *et al.*, "Progress in spatial analysis: introduction", *Progress in Spatial Analysis: Methods and Applications*, Springer, Heidelberg, pp. 1–13, 2009.

[PIN 10] PINKSE J., SLADE M.E., "The future of spatial econometrics", *Journal of Regional Science*, vol. 50, no. 1, pp. 103–117, 2010.

[ROB 50] ROBINSON W.S., "Ecological correlations and the behavior of individuals", *American Sociological Review*, vol. 15, no. 3, pp. 351–357, 1950.

[SEN 76] SEN A., "Large sample-size distribution of statistics used in testing for spatial correlation", *Geographical Analysis*, vol. 9, pp. 175–184, 1976.

[SMI 09a] SMITH T., "Estimation bias in spatial models with strongly connected weight matrices", *Geographical Analysis*, vol. 41, pp. 307–332, 2009.

[SMI 09b] SMITH T., WU P., "A spatio-temporal model of housing prices based on individual sales transactions over time", *Journal of Geographical Systems*, vol. 11, pp. 333–355, 2009.

[STE 10] STEIMETZ S., "Spatial multipliers in hedonic analysis: a comment on 'spatial hedonic models of airport noise, proximity, and housing prices'", *Journal of Regional Science*, vol. 50, no. 5, pp. 995–998, 2010.

[SUN 05] SUN H., TU Y., "A spatio-temporal autoregressive model for multi-unit residential market analyis", *The Journal of Real Estate Finance and Economics*, vol. 31, no. 2, pp. 155–187, 2005.

[TOB 70] TOBLER W., "A computer movie simulating urban growth in the Detroit region", *Economic Geography*, vol. 46, pp. 234–240, 1970.

[TRI 67] TRIGG D.W., LEACH A.G., "Exponential smoothing with an adaptive response rate", *Operational Research Quarterly*, vol. 18, no. 1, pp. 53–59, 1967.

[TU 04] TU Y., YU S.-M., SUN H., "Transaction-based office price indexes: a spatiotemporal modeling approach.", *Real Estate Economics*, vol. 32, no. 2, pp. 297–328, 2004.

[WHE 05] WHEELER D., TIEFELSDORF M., "Multicollinearity and correlation among local regression coefficients in geographically weighted regression", *Journal of Geographical Systems*, vol. 7, no. 2, pp. 161–187, 2005.

[WHI 80] WHITE H., "A heteroskedasticity-consistent covariance matrix estimator and a direct test for heteroskedasticity", *Econometrica*, vol. 48, no. 4, pp. 817–838, May 1980.

[WID 60] WIDROW B., HOFF M.E., "Adaptive switching circuits", *1960 IRE WESCON Convention Record, Part 4*, IRE, New York, pp. 96–104, 1960.

[WOO 00] WOOLDRIDGE J., *Introductory Econometrics: A Modern Approach*, South-Western College Publishing, Cincinnati, OH, 2000.

[WOO 01] WOOLDRIDGE J., *Econometric Analysis of Cross Section and Panel Data*, The MIT Press, 2001.

Index

Other titles from

in

Geographical Information Systems

2014

HÉNO Raphaële, CHANDELIER Laure
3D Modeling of Buildings: Outstanding Sites

PLANTIN Jean-Christophe
Participatory Mapping

2013

SALLABERRY Christian
Geographical Information Retrieval in Textual Corpora:

2012

BUCHER Bénédicte, LE BER Florence
Innovative Software Development in GIS

2011

BANOS Arnaud, THÉVENIN Thomas
Geographical Information and Urban Transport Systems

DAUPHINÉ André
Fractal Geography

2010

BRUNET Roger
Sustainable Geography

CARREGA Pierre
Geographical Information and Climatology

CAUVIN Colette, ESCOBAR Francisco, SERRADJ Aziz
Thematic Cartography – 3-volume series
Thematic Cartography and Transformations – volume 1
Cartography and the Impact of the Quantitative Revolution – volume 2
New Approaches in Thematic Cartography – volume 3

LANGLOIS Patrice
Simulation of Complex Systems in GIS

MATHIS Philippe
Graphs and Networks – 2nd edition

THERIAULT Marius, DES ROSIERS François
Modeling Urban Dynamics

2009

ROCHE Stéphane, CARON Claude
Organizational Facets of GIS

2008

BRUGNOT Gérard
Spatial Management of Risks

FINKE Gerd
Operations Research and Networks

GUERMOND Yves
Modeling Process in Geography

KANEVSKI Michael
Advanced Mapping of Environmental Data

2007

DOBESCH Hartwig, DUMOLARD Pierre, DYRAS Izabela
Spatial Interpolation for Climate Data

SANDERS Lena
Models in Spatial Analysis

2006

CLIQUET Gérard
Geomarketing

DEVILLERS Rodolphe, JEANSOULIN Robert
Fundamentals of Spatial Data Quality

Printed and bound by CPI Group (UK) Ltd, Croydon, CR0 4YY

27/10/2024

14580724-0002